The Hidden Wiring

Peter Hennessy is Professor of Contemporary History at Queen Mary and Westfield College, University of London, Gresham Professor of Rhetoric at Gresham College, London, and Chairman of the Kennedy Memorial Trust. His books include *Cabinet*, *Whitehall* and *Never Again: Britain 1945–51*, for which he was awarded both the Duff Cooper Prize and the NCR Prize in 1993.

For many years he was a journalist, with spells on *The Times*, the *Financial Times* and *The Economist*. He has written columns for the *Independent*, the *New Statesman*, and *Director* magazine, was a regular presenter of the BBC Radio 4 *Analysis* programme 1986–92, and in 1994 wrote and presented the Wide Vision Productions/Channel Four Television series *What Has Become of Us?*

Peter Hennessy was educated at Marling School, Stroud; St John's College, Cambridge; the London School of Economics and Harvard (where he was a Kennedy Memorial Scholar 1971–2). He lives in north-east London with his wife and two daughters and has taught History at QMW since 1992.

D1148149

By the same author

STATES OF EMERGENCY
(with Keith Jeffery)

SOURCES CLOSE TO THE PRIME MINISTER
(with Michael Cockerell and David Walker)

WHAT THE PAPERS NEVER SAID

CABINET

RULING PERFORMANCE
(co-editor with Anthony Seldon)

WHITEHALL

NEVER AGAIN

MUDDLING THROUGH

PETER HENNESSY

The Hidden Wiring

Unearthing the British Constitution

INDIGO

First published in Great Britain 1995
by Victor Gollancz

This Indigo edition published 1996
Indigo is an imprint of the Cassell Group
Wellington House, 125 Strand, London WC2R 0BB

© Peter Hennessy 1995, 1996

Crown Copyright material in the Public Record Office
is reproduced by permission of the Controller of
Her Majesty's Stationery Office.

The right of Peter Hennessy to be identified as author
of this work has been asserted by him in accordance with
the Copyright, Designs and Patents Act, 1988.

A catalogue record for this book is
available from the British Library.

ISBN 0 575 40058 7

Typeset by Rowland Phototypesetting Ltd
Bury St Edmunds, Suffolk
Printed and bound in Great Britain by
Guernsey Press Co. Ltd, Guernsey, Channel Isles

96 97 98 99   10 9 8 7 6 5 4 3 2 1

In memory of Louis Heren,
1919–1995,
friend and mentor

CONTENTS

Illustrations   ix

Preface: A Back-of-the-Envelope Nation   1

Prologue: The Constitutionality of Putting Up or
    Shutting Up   9

Introduction: The Hardware and Software of State   21

1   The Great Ghost: Constitution, Procedure and
    the Legacy of Walter Bagehot   27

2   Monarchy: The Gilded Sponge   43

3   Premiership: Shadow and Substance   73

4   Cabinet: The Necessary Shambles   93

5   Whitehall: Gyroscope of State   119

6   Parliament: The Little Room   139

7   Overload: Stress and the Opposition of Events   161

8   Standards of Conduct in Public Life: The Nolan
    Inquiry as Ethical Workshop   179

9   A Very Discreditable Chapter? Government,
    Parliament and the Scott Inquiry   201

Conclusion: Reforming with the Grain: Thoughts on
    Walking Down Constitution Hill   217

Notes   225

Appendices: Ministerial Committees of the Cabinet
    and their Chairmen
    Cabinet Office/Office of Public Service   267

Index   270

ILLUSTRATIONS

Following page 86

The King in the garden of Buckingham Palace with Herbert Morrison, Clement Attlee, Arthur Greenwood, Ernest Bevin and A. V. Alexander (*Times Newspapers*)

The Queen in No. 10 with premiers James Callaghan, Alec Douglas-Home, Margaret Thatcher, Harold Macmillan, Harold Wilson and Edward Heath (*Press Association*)

Sir Robert Peel (*Hulton-Deutsch*)

W. E. Gladstone (*Hulton-Deutsch*)

The 1894 notebook of the future King George V (*Her Majesty Queen Elizabeth II*)

H. H. Asquith paying off a taxi (*Hulton-Deutsch*)

Peter Brookes's view of the Scott Report (*The Times*)

Clement Attlee in the Cabinet Room with Francis Williams (*Hulton-Deutsch*)

Sir Alan ('Tommy') Lascelles (*Hulton-Deutsch*)

Sir Derek Mitchell watches Harold Wilson briefing the press, Heathrow, 1964 (*Times Newspapers*)

Derek Mitchell's back-of-the-envelope drill for the 1964 election (*Controller of Her Majesty's Stationery Office*)

Sir Norman Brook and Harold Macmillan, September 1962 (*Press Association*)

Ted Heath briefing the press as Prime Minister, flanked by Sir Donald Maitland and Sir William Armstrong (*Times Newspapers*)

Following page 182

Sir Kenneth Stowe (*Times Newspapers*)

Lord Charteris in conversation with the author (*Wide Vision Productions*)

Sir John Hunt (*Times Newspapers*)

Tony Benn (*Fred Jarvis*)

Edmund Dell

Cabinet in session, Chequers, June 1977 (*The Benn Archives*)

Harold Wilson: an audience with the Queen, June 1969 (*Hulton-Deutsch*)

The author in discussion with Enoch Powell and Tony Benn (*BBC Radio 4*)

Lord Bancroft (*Brian Henson*)

Michael Heseltine, with colleagues Gummer, Shephard, Major and Portillo, after his first Cabinet meeting as First Secretary (*Press Association*)

Walter Bagehot triptych by Riddell of *The Economist* (*The Economist*)

Sir Robin Butler, students' question time, Old Treasury Board Room (*QMW Media Services*)

Nicholas Garland's view of Lord Nolan as a Frankenstein's monster (*Daily Telegraph*)

John Major at the Cabinet Table (*Daily Telegraph*)

PREFACE

A Back-of-the-Envelope Nation

Well, it works, doesn't it? So I think that's the answer, even if it is on the back of an envelope and doesn't have a written constitution with every comma and every semi-colon in place. Because sometimes they can make for difficulties that common sense can overcome.

Lord Callaghan, 1991[1]

In the transition to political democracy this country . . . underwent . . . no inner conversion. She accepted it as a convenience, like an improved system of telephones; she did not dedicate herself to it as the expression of a moral ideal of comradeship and equality, the avowal of which could leave nothing the same. She changed her political garments, but not her heart. She carried into the democratic era, not only the institutions, but the social habits and mentality of the oldest and toughest plutocracy in the world . . . she went to the ballot-box touching her hat.

R. H. Tawney, undated[2]

The Constitution is what happens.

John Griffith, 1986[3]

For all their fabled devotion to fair play, the British, at least since the franchise question was finally closed with votes-for-all-women in 1928, have been profoundly uncurious about the rules under which the hugely important 'national game' of politics and government are played. A powerful combination of smugness, insularity and sheer incomprehension have been at work here. The purpose of this book is to tackle the incomprehension problem in the hope that the smugness and the insularity might thereby be dissipated to some degree.

For nearly thirty years, ever since I first read Walter Bagehot's *The English Constitution* as an undergraduate at St John's College, Cambridge,[4] I have been increasingly drawn into a search for this mercurial yet crucial phenomenon. Whenever I try to transmit my passion to an audience or to stress the importance of grasping the centrality of this curious compound of custom and precedent, law and convention, rigidity and malleability concealed beneath layers of opacity and mystery, I am, as often as not, greeted by nervous bemusement. It's as if lecturegoers know it matters but are made profoundly uneasy by the lack of signposts and handholds, like innumerates confronted by mathematics. This entirely understandable reaction tends to trigger in me a response which is a mixture of evangelism and didacticism, or mission and enthusiasm, as if I were a fusion of Billy Graham and David Bellamy – something along the lines of: 'This may look like a murky, marginal swamp to you, but there's life in here; life that matters to you, your family, your fellow citizens as it affects the way you are required to live as electors and subjects of the Crown as well as the decencies of the system that is meant to operate in your name.'

I cannot offer certainty or all-encompassing patterns. That is not possible even for nations which, unlike the United Kingdom, have written constitutions and courts to interpret them. What I can provide are a few maps based on the topology of our constitutional landscape plus passages of history from those who have trodden its pathways as guides to their own generations since the mid-nineteenth century.

The story impinges upon political science as well as history, constitutional law, parliamentary practice – statecraft in the round. It also
has to do with the essence, the quiddity of Britain, as the constitution
is bound up with our national identity, our place in the world. John
Young, rightly, has emphasized the specialness of our constitutional
arrangements as one of the factors that contribute to the United
Kingdom's continuing difficulties with the European Union. 'The
reasons why Britain has been so reluctant to commit itself to inte-
gration with Europe', he argues,

> are not difficult to understand, considering the country's histori-
> cal development. To an extent of course Britain is 'different' from
> Europe simply because she is an island: this basic geographical
> fact has had a profound effect on national outlook. Whereas
> Continental countries have been forced over centuries to deal
> with each other every day to settle border disputes, reach
> common solutions to problems like river navigation and border
> controls, and have suffered frequent invasions during wars,
> Britain has been able to adopt an insular policy, has avoided
> *permanent* involvement in Continental affairs and has escaped
> successful invasion for nearly a thousand years.
>
> British national identity is arguably stronger because of this
> and the country has been able gradually to develop its unique,
> unwritten constitution. Both this strong national identity and
> the unwritten constitution make participation in supranational
> institutions difficult: Continental states are more used to perma-
> nent involvements and to ornate, written constitutions.[5]

In mid-twentieth-century Britain, Leo Amery, public servant, politician and defender of the imperial idea, sought to link the constitution not just to the notion of national identity, but to the very
sanguinary mixtures that made up its formative period in medieval
England. 'Our national character,' he declared somewhat enig-
matically,

> like the English language, is the result of the impact, adjustment
> and blending, under the political and social conditions created
> by the Conquest, of two entirely different elements: a compro-
> mise and balance between two antithetical temperaments. The

ever initiating, constructive, domineering Norman had to come to terms with the slower Saxon, yielding in much, but tenacious of his rights and usages.[6]

On a less vivid and more understated plane, Professor Young's insight, if not Leo Amery's, is central to both the European question and the constitutional question in late twentieth-century Britain. As Philip Ziegler expressed it, 'as a nation we do seem to be empiricists, extremely cautious about principles, strong on pragmatism, and we just *are* a sort of back-of-envelope type race.'[7] Developing the Young–Ziegler theme, we can see the Constitution as a kind of National Trust embracing a wide variety of landscapes and buildings, some of great antiquity, others surprisingly modern.

To adapt Noel Coward, the British as a people are 'the products of those homes serene and stately that only lately seem to have run to seed'.[8] It is high time that this particular 'stately home of England' was flung open fully for public inspection. I offer what follows as a guidebook to this elusive artefact of the national heritage.

In compiling it I have accumulated a great debt to many people and several institutions. Pride of place must go to that shining, ancient City institution, Gresham College. If its Council, led by Mr Brian Wilson, had not appointed me Gresham Professor of Rhetoric for 1994–6, I would not have stepped out from their base in High Holborn to retrace the path trodden by Walter Bagehot when he took his walk round the Constitution in the mid-nineteenth century. The Gresham Council was persuaded of the value of a late twentieth-century health-check upon that curiously neglected pentangle (monarchy, premiership, Cabinet, Parliament and Civil Service) at the heart of what Andrew Marr calls the 'Old Constitution'[9] – neglected in the sense that a kind of Pontius Pilatery has so afflicted many domestic British political observers as power and influence have been siphoned away by the European Union, the money markets and the myriad phenomena bundled up in the notion of 'globalization' that our homespun constitutional knitting goes relatively unexamined.

Gresham College, as befits its venerable antiquity and current vitality, is in the business of the old rubbing up against the new. And its small but immensely stimulating staff, led by Professor Peter

Nailor and Ms Maggie Butcher, have been terrific companions on my own walk round the Constitution. My fellow Gresham Professors have added to the pleasure of my attachment to the College. Brian Henson and Christine Capsalis have been both courteous and understanding when lack of forethought on my part has lumbered them with unexpected administrative burdens.

I have long been a practitioner of scholarly bigamy. I like to have at least two intellectual families on the go at any one time. My colleagues in the Department of History at Queen Mary and Westfield College, University of London, have brought me immense pleasure and stimulus since I arrived down the Mile End Road in the autumn of 1992. I have been fortunate, too, in my students. Three years' worth of 'Cabinet and Premiership' classes supplemented by one year of my 'Hidden Wiring' seminar as part of our new MA in Contemporary British History have enabled me to develop my thinking with them.

The Twentieth Century British History Seminar at the Institute of Historical Research has been a thought-booster almost since the day I began writing books. So since 1986 has been that extraordinary network of people associated with the Institute of Contemporary British History.

Professor George Jones, who spans several of my scholarly homes, has taught me a huge amount over the past twenty years. But he did me an immense service during my first week at Queen Mary and Westfield. As an afterthought to a routine piece of business conducted through the University of London's intercollegiate mailing system, he told me that as I was now a full-time academic I would never produce another book. I was furious, even though I recognize a class wind-up when I see one. George's shade is on every page. I am very grateful to him.

My production line has been blessed by Carol Toms and Liz Lynch (both of QMW) at the wordspinning end and by Gillian Bromley at the quality control stage. To say it is a treat to be working once more with my editor, Sean Magee, is an understatement of Olympian proportions.

I am grateful as always, to the staff of the Public Record Office and in several departmental records sections for their generous and interested assistance. And I am indebted to the ultimate 'boss' of all of them (as crown servants), Her Majesty the Queen, for permission to quote from material in the Royal Archives (which are themselves blessed by a superb staff).

My thanks, also, to two friends who are dab hands with the camera, Fred Jarvis and Tony Benn. Photographers, such as they, as Tony likes to put it, believe that, 'Unlike other things in life, photography is a moment of embarrassment followed by a lifetime's pleasure.'[10]

I must end, as is my custom, with a discreet thank you to my anonymous army of well placed and superbly well-primed helpers who practise open government by stealth. They know who they are and their identities are safe with me. Secrecy sharpens gratitude.

The book is dedicated to Louis Heren, my boss on *The Times*. He encouraged all my forays down the byways of British administration. Louis was a natural open government man who was vexed by the inadequacies he found in Whitehall and the Cabinet Room. He wanted the absolute best for the country he loved. Nothing else would do. I have never launched a book before without Louis' big presence at the party. I shall miss him until I join him again, when, no doubt, he will greet me with a litany of where I have gone wrong in his absence – and I shall enjoy every minute of it!

Peter Hennessy
Walthamstow, Holborn and Mile End
July 1995

Preface to the Indigo Edition

As always with a book of this kind, thanks must go to those who pointed out inaccuracies or suggested embellishments. Special gratitude is due, however, to Sir Richard Scott and his inquiry team into arms for Iraq for illuminating some of the most secret places and processes of Whitehall and for furnishing me with the material for chapter 9, which appears for the first time in this edition. Sadly,

Peter Nailor did not live to see my attempt at an assessment of an inquiry in which he had taken a close interest. Finally, a debt that should have been acknowledged in the first edition to Simon Irvine, General Secretary of the Fabian Society, for allowing me to call the book *The Hidden Wiring* – the title of a paper I delivered to the Society's New Year conference at Ruskin College, Oxford, in January 1990.[11]

Peter Hennessy
Walthamstow, Holborn and Mile End
June 1996

PROLOGUE

The Constitutionality of Putting Up or Shutting Up

There is no coup like a British coup. It comes out of a clear blue sky. It defies constitutional reason.

> Simon Jenkins, on the 'neutron bomb' exploded by
> John Major's resignation of the Tory leadership,
> June 1995[1]

I wonder why nobody has yet . . . reacted to the constitutional aspects of John Major's self-immolation? He says to the Sovereign: 'I no longer am leader of the majority party in the House of Commons; but I am carrying on as your Prime Minister.' Now, I don't think anyone can say that – at least not without inflicting damage on the constitution.

> Enoch Powell, June 1995[2]

The PM's resignation of the party leadership has presented no constitutional difficulties at all.

> Very senior Whitehall figure, June 1995[3]

The action of the Prime Minister in seeking to end the civil war in his party between the English nationalists and the 'Christian Democrats' by calling an internal party leadership election is constitutionally questionable and without precedent.

> Robert Maclennan, MP, June 1995[4]

While it lasted, the summer storm occasioned by John Major's invitation to his Tory party critics on 22 June 1995 'to put up or shut up'[5] had everything – personal drama, unexpected developments, a dash of constitutional controversy and a fluidity of potential outcomes until the very moment when the Chairman of the 1922 Committee, Sir Marcus Fox, announced the following result inside Committee Room 14 in the House of Commons at 5.20 p.m. on 4 July:[6]

John Major	218
John Redwood	89
abstentions	8
spoilt papers	12

But was the whole event, as Enoch Powell put it, tantamount to an act of 'violence which we have, without audible protest, allowed to be done to one of our most important constitutional principles', namely that 'under our constitution, the Queen governs only on the advice of a person who, in tendering it, is able to assure her that he believed it at least to have the support of a majority in the House of Commons'?[7]

In short, it was not. The unnamed very senior Whitehall figure quoted in the epigraph to this prologue was one of a small circle engaged upon checking the niceties of the procedures involved before Mr Major detonated his 'neutron bomb' in the Rose Garden of No. 10. (Some of the niceties had to be checked after the event; for example, could David Hunt become acting Secretary of State for Wales when John Redwood resigned, given that Hunt's existing job, Chancellor of the Duchy of Lancaster, did not carry the status of a Secretaryship of State? The Parliamentary Counsel advised that he could.[8]) On the procedure adopted by Mr Major – 'If I win, I shall continue as Prime Minister ... should I be defeated ... I shall resign as Prime Minister'[9] – there were 'no problems' because it was fully in line with past precedent.

For, under our unwritten Constitution, that inner circle of constitutional guardians did what they always do under such circumstances – they reaped the old files, 'a gathering of the harvest over long years of experience', as a former Cabinet Office private secretary once put it, and the primary, overarching and venerable principle in this instance was that 'the Queen's Government must be carried on.'[10] But in this instance it was a mere nineteen years' worth of experience that guided them, dating back to another surprise resignation announcement – Harold Wilson's in March 1976. On that occasion there was no precedent for a serving Premier who was head of a party with a formal voting procedure for choosing its leaders announcing his intention to resign first his party leadership, then the office of Prime Minister. In early 1976 the guardians of this particular patch of the Constitution had, in effect, to reinvent it to suit the needs of this novel contingency. The trio most concerned were Sir John Hunt, Secretary of the Cabinet; Sir Martin Charteris, Private Secretary to Her Majesty the Queen; and Sir Kenneth Stowe, Principal Private Secretary to the Prime Minister. They pondered, going back to the first principles of English and, later, British government under which the legislature (Parliament) and the executive (government) are fused.

The outcome was what have become known in the trade as 'Stowe's interlocking circles' (see figure 1). As Sir Kenneth explained it to me many years later, 'where they intersect; *that* is the Prime Minister's power and that is the key to how you make No. 10 Downing Street work.'[11] In effect, 'Stowe's interlocking circles' are two triggers and an outcome. Command of the largest single political party in terms of seats in the Commons gives you command of a majority (usually) in the House itself, which in turn propels the party leader into command of the executive, which he or she holds until command of circle 1 or circle 2 is lost either willingly or under protest. So in 1976 Harold Wilson announced his intention to vacate the premiership but remained Prime Minister until Jim Callaghan took command first of circle 1, then of circle 2. At that point, as Sir Kenneth put it, 'Mr Wilson advised Her Majesty the Queen that Mr Callaghan had been elected Leader of the Labour Party and that Mr Callaghan could, therefore, command a majority in the House

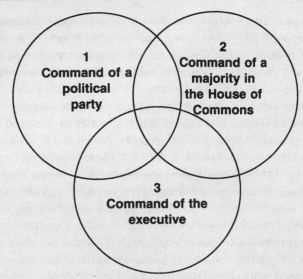

Fig 1 'Stowe's interlocking circles'
Source: Sir Kenneth Stowe

of Commons.'[12] Thereupon Mr Wilson resigned and the Queen, via Sir Martin Charteris, 'sent' for Mr Callaghan who 'kissed hands' and became Prime Minister.

The Stowe solution came into play once more in November 1990 when Mrs Thatcher relinquished her command of circle 1. It was ready for deployment again in June 1995. So far from being an example of disrespect to the monarch and a denial of 'the very principle on which our parliamentary democracy is founded', as Mr Powell put it, the events of 22 June–4 July 1995 were entirely consistent with the warp and woof of British constitutional practice since March 1976. In short, Mr Major followed a procedure hallowed by usage. Nothing could illustrate better the theme of this book, exemplifying the blend of custom and practice, improvisation and expediency which makes up so much of Britain's constitutional system (if 'system' is not too solid a word for it), especially at moments of political drama, uncertainty and crisis. As Simon Jenkins put it in the occasionally frenzied days between Mr Major's 'self-immolation'[13] and his smiling emergence from the flames: 'Britain's political institutions are so introverted that they show not the slightest strain, until one day they heave, vomit and die. One minute all is certainty, the next all is chaos. Gibbon would detect rottenness in such an empire.'[14] In the event Britain's political institutions survived intact.

An eye-catching element in the aftermath of the episode was the re-emergence, in the person of the loyal and consequently promoted Michael Heseltine, of the job of 'First Secretary of State and Deputy Prime Minister'.[15] In this instance Mr Powell was exactly right to ask: 'There is no such office, is there?'[16] There were, however, precedents for Mr Heseltine's new incarnation. R. A. Butler held exactly the same combination of posts between July 1962 and October 1963. Other more recent Deputy Prime Ministers include Sir Geoffrey Howe in 1989–90;[17] and Lord Whitelaw was de facto Deputy Prime Minister between 1979 and 1988, although he did not sport the title. The job is, in the old phrase, 'unknown to the Constitution', being mentioned in no statute; but the same impermanence applied to the job of Prime Minister itself until 1917,[18] something which seems not to have deterred or diverted most of the forty-two holders of the office[19] up to and including the passing of the Chequers Estate Act when, at last, the British Prime Minister was mentioned in an Act of Parliament.

The evanescence of the deputy premiership most certainly bothered King George VI, so much so that Anthony Eden was denied the title when the Conservatives returned to power in October 1951. As Sir John Wheeler-Bennett, the King's official biographer, described Mr Churchill's Cabinet-making, that autumn, the

> process was somewhat complicated by the tendency on the part of the Prime Minister to appoint Ministers to constitutionally non-existent offices. His first list of submissions, for example, contained the name of Mr Eden as Secretary of State for Foreign Affairs and 'Deputy Prime Minister' – an office which does not exist in the British constitutional hierarchy. The King at once noticed this irregularity and on his instructions the latter title was deleted for Mr Eden's appointment.
>
> The term 'Deputy Prime Minister' had, in fact, had an unofficial existence for some time previous to this date. Mr Chur-

chill had initiated the custom in the Coalition Government during the war when he wished to mark the special position of Mr Attlee as Leader of the Labour Party. Mr Herbert Morrison had also had this additional title, as a matter of usage, from the first appointment of the Labour Government in 1945, and, when the Government was reconstituted in 1947, the official announcement from 10 Downing Street said that he would continue as 'Deputy Prime Minister'.[20]

It was, therefore, 'not surprising', Wheeler-Bennett continued, that Churchill should commit his 'constitutional solecism'[21] in October 1951. It may seem strange that the King should object then, when he had not done so in the cases of Attlee and Morrison, but Wheeler-Bennett indicated the reason – that appointing Eden to this phantom post 'would certainly imply the establishment of a line of succession and would thereby impose a certain restriction upon one of the unquestioned prerogatives of the Sovereign'[22] (i.e. the power to send for a successor in the event of the death or resignation of a Prime Minister[23]).

Recently declassified files at the Public Record Office have shed more light on how this 'solecism' entered the British constitutional vocabulary. When Churchill replaced Neville Chamberlain as Prime Minister in May 1940, his predecessor kept a seat in the War Cabinet as Lord President of the Council and chaired the Cabinet in Churchill's absence. By the autumn of that year his worsening cancer was increasingly keeping Chamberlain away from the Cabinet Room. On 2 October 1940 the Secretary of the War Cabinet, Sir Edward Bridges, minuted Churchill about the 'order of precedence' in the War Cabinet which placed Chamberlain ahead of Attlee who was Lord Privy Seal. 'By tradition and long practice,' Bridges told the Prime Minister,

> there is an order of precedence among offices of Cabinet rank. But it is clearly established that the Prime Minister can settle the order of Cabinet Ministers *for Cabinet purposes* as he pleases . . .
>
> The main question is who you want to preside over the War Cabinet when you are away. Since Mr Chamberlain's illness Mr Attlee has presided in your absence.[24]

The following day Churchill indicated that he wished Attlee to preside when he was away.

Bridges' reply marks the moment when, de facto (to borrow his words), the deputy premiership was created in reality, though another seventeen months elapsed before any kind of formal title appeared. 'I imagine', Bridges minuted Churchill on 3 October 1940, 'you will probably not feel that you would want to disturb the Lord Privy Seal [Attlee] from the position which he has de facto occupied during the illness of Mr Chamberlain as your immediate Deputy.'[25] Not until a new order of precedence for the War Cabinet was published on 4 March 1942, however, did the title appear in full, after Churchill moved Attlee to the Dominions Office. In its first public incarnation it read: 'Secretary of State for Dominion Affairs and Deputy Prime Minister, Rt. Hon. C. R. Attlee, MP.'[26] Oddly enough, when the King initialled the minute approving Attlee's transfer on 19 February 1942, the title 'Deputy Prime Minister' was *not* appended to the Dominions portfolio.[27] Churchill, however, had written it in in red ink next to Attlee's name on one of a clutch of sheets of No. 10 notepaper dated simply 'February 1942', on which were inscribed his new ministerial dispositions:

WAR CABINET

Churchill

Attlee   Deputy PM[28]

Thus did patronage-at-the-top change in a manner that resonated fifty-three and a half years later when Michael Heseltine swept into the Cabinet Office, appropriating a grand Cabinet committee room as his base for expanded operations.[29]

To adapt Asquith's famous one-liner about the premiership,[30] the deputy prime ministership is very much what its holder chooses and is enabled or allowed by the Prime Minister (and, to some extent, his Cabinet colleagues) to make of it. Within days it was plain that Mr Heseltine was determined to make a very great deal of it indeed. This certainly did not surprise me, as I had kept a close eye on him and his career since he drove me round Toxteth in 1982 on one of his regular visits to Liverpool as Minister for Merseyside.[31]

Two days after his elevation, Mr Heseltine briefed the political correspondents of the Sunday press about the size and scope of his new domain in a manner that took away the breath of veteran observers such as Tony Bevins of the *Observer*,[32] who saw it as nothing less than 'an empire of political and executive power . . . that will stun Cabinet Ministers and Whitehall mandarins'.[33] In his briefing, Mr Heseltine disclosed the following job description he had agreed in outline with the Prime Minister and in detail with the Cabinet Secretary, Sir Robin Butler, on Tuesday 4 July as the votes of MPs were being cast in the leadership ballot across Parliament Square in Commons Committee Room 12:[34]

1 Chairing nine Cabinet committees.
2 Taking overall control of the Office of Public Service within the Cabinet Office, with his Cabinet colleague, Roger Freeman, Chancellor of the Duchy of Lancaster, as his deputy.
3 Acting as a conduit for conveying the thinking of Conservative backbenchers to the Prime Minister and the Cabinet.
4 Co-ordinating the presentation of government policy.
5 Leading various trans-Whitehall policy drives, for example on information technology.

Aware of the niceties of the constitutional balance between ministers (as he was long before he walked out of the Cabinet over Westland in 1986;[35] he was very concerned at the possibility of Mrs Thatcher's creating a Prime Minister's Department after winning the 1983 general election[36]), Mr Heseltine told the lobby journalists: 'My judgement as to whether that [the job of Deputy Prime Minister] was something I could do, or should, is based entirely on whether I think my relationship with the Prime Minister can make that relationship possible. Because without his support it isn't a job. With his support it's a wonderful job.'[37]

Mr Heseltine showed a similar sensitivity to both political reality (a resentful Cabinet could stymie him at almost every turn) and constitutional propriety (many government functions are allocated

to specific named ministers by Acts of Parliament) when he acknowledged that his capacity to do the job 'does rest on one's ability to
work with one's colleagues. It cannot be a confrontational job . . .
It is a job which at the heart is designed to help me support the
Prime Minister in any way that he thinks appropriate.'[38] Thereupon
Mr Heseltine, a great one for managerial efficiency,[39] produced an
'organogram' of his very considerable functions[40] (see appendix).

In addition to pronouncing it 'a very great honour', Mr Heseltine
said the new job 'has considerable potential'.[41] With him presiding
over it that was certainly true, especially as ex officio as deputy premier
he acquired the right, enjoyed by Willie Whitelaw under Margaret
Thatcher, of attending any Cabinet committee he chose.[42] When
Tony Bevins informed me of the scope of the Heseltine First Secretary
of Stateship following the lobby briefing,[43] it struck me that Heseltine's could be a 'Heineken' deputy premiership which 'could reach
parts no other Deputy Prime Minister has reached before'[44] in peacetime. Mr Heseltine could be heard enquiring initially if 'Rab Butler
had had enough to do' in 1962–3?[45] There was no doubt at all in my
mind that Mr Heseltine would have more than enough.

I spied him leaving Buckingham Palace the day he received his
seals of office as First Secretary (not used since Barbara Castle relinquished them in 1970). He waved at me, a trifle shyly, but with the
look of a man who had just won the lottery.[46] When the revised
Cabinet committee list was published just over a week later it became
even easier to understand why (see appendix). Mr Heseltine was to
sit on fourteen of the nineteen Cabinet committees (including all the
most important of the core ministerial groups on domestic, foreign,
European and economic policy); and he chaired four of them himself,
including the new Ministerial Committee on Competitiveness.[47]

Of all the new groups to emerge from the planning meeting
attended by the Prime Minister, the Deputy Prime Minister and
Leader of the House of Commons Tony Newton,[48] this was a pure
Heseltine phenomenon. As Peter Riddell rightly wrote: 'The committee will take over the work of six existing ministerial committees
and is similar to the industrial policy overlord proposed by Mr Heseltine in *Where There's a Will*, the book he wrote in his wilderness

years after resigning from the Cabinet in 1986. It will provide him with a crucial lever over many areas of government policy.'[49] With nineteen members, the new Heseltine group was almost the size of the full Cabinet itself, and could be seen as an attempt to create a kind of holding company incorporating many of the interlocking elements affecting the long-term vitality of the British economy – Mr Heseltine's grand obsession since first becoming a minister a generation earlier in 1970.

Another natural home for those Heseltinian talents was the Cabinet committee on the Co-ordination and Presentation of Government Policy. Almost from the moment he took over its chairmanship, Mr Heseltine began to call daily meetings at 8.30 in the morning. Given the importance of what his Cabinet colleague William Waldegrave calls 'the media-political complex . . . by which we are ruled', it is not surprising that Heseltine's use of that Committee led to the view in Whitehall that he was 'in effect setting the Government's agenda'.[50]

Given Mr Heseltine's preferment and the breadth and depth of his intended role, it may well be time, after over fifty years of sporadic experience of it, to recognize that though it remains a stranger to statute the office of Deputy Prime Minister is a feature of mid- to late twentieth-century British government. As Stanley Baldwin said in 1932:

> The historian can tell you probably perfectly clearly what the constitutional practice was at any given period in the past, but it would be very difficult for a living writer to tell you at any given period in his lifetime what the Constitution of the country is in all respects, and for this reason, that almost at any given moment . . . there may be one practice called 'constitutional' which is falling into desuetude and there may be another practice which is creeping into use but is not yet constitutional.[51]

There, in a single sentence from a man who had already been Prime Minister and was to be again, one can sense the fascination and the difficulty that enfolds anyone who sets out to fathom and map the depths and reefs of our extraordinary Constitution.

INTRODUCTION

The Hardware and Software of State

What's involved . . . is the repair of the software (the people involved, the political classes) and the repair of the hardware (the machinery of government, the political system).

Lord Bancroft, 1995[1]

A very peculiar constitution which no one intended . . . whereby the government of the day decides what the constitution is.

Vernon Bogdanor, 1995[2]

Politics is the final arbiter under an unwritten constitution.

Peter Clarke, 1985[3]

B ritish central government consists of five main elements: people, institutions, procedures, laws and public money. Lord Hailsham captured the second strand perfectly when he declared in his 1987 Granada Guildhall Lecture that 'nations begin by forming their institutions, but, in the end, are continuously formed by them or under their influence.'[4] His fellow parliamentarian Sir Kenneth Pickthorn distilled the third element with exemplary precision when he observed in 1960 that 'procedure is all the Constitution the poor Briton has';[5] while that grandest of old men, Mr Gladstone, had supplied the 'people' part long before when writing in 1879 that the British Constitution 'presumes more boldly than any other the good sense and the good faith of those who work it'.[6] Elements four and five require less descriptive refinement. Bonding the governing quintet is the notion of the Crown, the Queen in Parliament acting on the advice of Ministers of the Crown who comprise Her Majesty's Government, assisted by Crown servants (civil and diplomatic), who operate institutions created by Her Orders in Her Privy Council, which disburse services financed by taxes and duties raised by Her command through Her Board of Inland Revenue and Her Customs and Excise. Ours is a deeply monarchical system – and not just in name. As Sir David Keir put it: 'The King's prerogative, however circumscribed by conventions, must always retain its historic character as a residue of discretionary authority to be employed for the public good. It is the last resource provided by the Constitution to guarantee its own working.'[7] To apply Ian Bancroft's metaphor, both the hardware and the software of British government function in the Queen's name. An unwritten constitution may in many respects be an imagined phenomenon, but it has been impossible since the Restoration of 1660 to conceive of it as anything other than monarchy-infused – even though the personal powers of the Sovereign have been trimmed and trimmed again since the 'Glorious Revolution' of 1688, the whole process of royal containment speeding up progressively since the 1832 Reform Act began the process of removing the monarch's power to make or unmake ministries except in rare and special contingencies.

The fusion of software and hardware – in Buckingham Palace, in No. 10, in the Cabinet Room, in the Whitehall departments and in Parliament – imbues the approach of this study. That approach is also driven by history because, above all, the British Constitution is a continuous historical process rather than a matter of fixed points or legal settlements that hold until they are consciously undone and remade. This is absolutely plain to any scholar who has the slightest acquaintance with the working files of the guardians of the British Constitution preserved at the Public Record Office in a range of archives (from the Cabinet Office and the Prime Minister's Office to the Home Office and the Lord Chancellor's Office). It was well understood by Leo Amery when lecturing shortly after the Second World War. 'If', he said,

> by a constitution is meant a written document or series of documents embodying in statutory or declaratory form the principles and structure of our Government, then there is, in that sense, no such thing as the British Constitution. What we mean by the constitution is not any deliberate attempt to control and confine our political growth on the basis of a preconceived intellectual plan, reflecting the political theories of a particular group of men or the prepossessions of a particular age, but a *living structure* continuously shaped in the course of history by the interaction of individual purposes and collective instincts with the requirements of ever varying circumstances. [emphasis in original][8]

If John Griffith and Peter Clarke are right and the British Constitution *is* what happens, and what happens is primarily determined by *politics*, historical reconstruction is the key. This insight came rather late to me, some quarter of a century, in fact, after I sat down to read Bagehot that mid-sixties autumn evening in the library of St John's College, Cambridge. And it came courtesy not of Bagehot, nor indeed of John Griffith or Peter Clarke, but thanks to one of the prime guardians of the late twentieth-century British Constitution: Sir Robin Butler, Secretary of the Cabinet and Head of the Home Civil Service.

The initial trigger of the thought was a conversation in the Cabinet Office in July 1990 conducted for the purpose of gathering material for one of my 'Whitehall Watch' columns in the *Independent*. Looking ahead to the early 1990s (at that time Mrs Thatcher, though in trouble thanks to the poll tax and rumbling Euro-problems, did not seem in immediate danger), I asked Sir Robin what he, the Queen's Private Secretary, Sir Robert Fellowes, and Andrew Turnbull, at that time the Prime Minister's Principal Private Secretary, might do if the next election produced a hung result and they had to advise Her Majesty and those seeking to stay or to become her first minister on the use of her remaining personal prerogatives (the appointment of a Prime Minister and the dissolution of Parliament)?

'You try to make sure you get the documents in hand,' Sir Robin replied. 'A lot of things have been done in the past in the three weeks before an election. The documents are always in the cupboards.'[9]

'Always in the cupboards.' That phrase kept recurring to me. Finally, I made the connection. The contents of Sir Robin's cupboards would, one day, follow those of his predecessors to the Public Record Office. And, like as not, *their* documents would shape the appraisals and the contingency plans *he* would piece together with Sir Robert and Mr Turnbull – which, indeed, turned out to be the case; though not every gleaning available at Kew, it seems, passed under their purview in the run-up to the 1992 election.[10]

As the hugely respected former Clerk of the House of Commons, Gilbert Campion, liked to point out, to understand constitutional procedure and practice you have to grasp the continuous and living juxtaposition of the ancient and modern, the traditional and the novel in the British system. He was speaking of the 'traditional element' and the 'democratic element' in parliamentary procedure.[11] But the same applies to matters affecting the monarch's personal prerogatives. This approach, the historian's approach – asking what happened, when, why, how and with what consequences – is a thing of delight and frustration: delight at discovering a run of files, sometimes a solo document, that really does shed a beam of light that can be played over landscapes past and those still to come when it was written: frustration at the precariousness, the incompleteness, the haphazardness of it all. But pining for certainty where none exists – nor can exist, short of a gargantuan exercise in consultation, drafting and agreement – is futile and misleading. The search for our elusive Constitution is best treated as a kind of magical mystery tour in which fun, fascination and utility are blended in roughly equal parts, thanks to the rich interplay of history and politics, personalities and institutions, crises and defining moments which, sometimes out of the blue, place immense stress on both the hardware and the software of state as the latter take to the cupboards in search of past practice and future enlightenment. In such a spirit is this book written.

ONE

The Great Ghost

Constitution, Procedure and the Legacy of Walter Bagehot

To reform the House of Lords [in 1910] meant to set down in writing a Constitution which for centuries had remained happily unwritten, to conjure a great ghost into the narrow and corruptible flesh of a code. For this Constitution . . . was nowhere set forth in an Instrument. It had no visible body . . . Materialized, this spectral Constitution would have been a very monster, bearing a horrid mixture of features, from Norman French to early Edwardian; a monster flagrantly improvised, illogically permanent.

George Dangerfield, 1936[1]

I attach a memorandum on Questions of Procedure which deals with various questions of procedure affecting Ministers. This codifies the general principles of Ministerial conduct as they have evolved over many years and through successive Administrations. I ask all ministers to be guided by it.

Note by the Prime Minister attached to the first
Cabinet Paper circulated to the new Wilson
government, 19 October 1964[2]

Every minister when he gets there receives a document called *Questions of Procedure for Ministers* that isn't put before the Cabinet. It's a prime ministerial statement. I used to get these things and collective Cabinet responsibility is the core of it.

Tony Benn MP on *Questions of Procedure for Ministers*,
1995[3]

Bagehot . . . was one of the greatest political journalists of his – or indeed of any – age, equally skilled in the crafts of reporter, leader writer or editor; and it was by eschewing 'literary' pretensions and sticking to his trade that he achieved immortality. For it was in the course of describing the contemporary political scene, as he actually saw it, that he hit upon the secret of British politics – the difference between myth and reality.

R. H. S. Crossman, 1963[4]

For those in pursuit of our 'great ghost' of a Constitution, there can be a terrible temptation to wish – almost to believe – that somebody, somewhere, knows the phantom intimately almost to the point of compensating for its missing flesh and blood. Romantics might like to think the Sovereign herself is that person. For even though the monarch is primed by a network of discreet inside advisers on the beauties and mysteries of her Constitution, as Crown power would be the blood coursing through the 'ghost's' veins if it had any, might not the head of state *have* to be in a position of knowing what her wraith amounted to?

Given the protocol and convention surrounding the Queen's remarks on informal occasions, I shall have to be circumspect here. But in the early 1990s Her Majesty did drop in on a scholarly seminar which was in the process of discussing part of her Constitution. She was, indeed, well primed on its finer points, offering both important and droll asides upon it in the course of the conversation. As she left she delivered something akin to an immortal line on her 'great ghost': 'The British Constitution', she said, 'has always been puzzling and always will be.'[5]

Several reactions to this were possible from a would-be ghostbuster like myself, apart from genuine pleasure at hearing a classic sentence impeccably articulated. One, relief that Her Majesty was baffled like everyone else. If she does not know quite what her Constitution amounts to, one can feel in the very best of company at moments of personal confusion about its workings. Two, recognition of the importance of her acknowledgement of the fluidity surrounding the bundle of custom, precedent and procedure at the very heart of the Constitution. Three, a realization that, short of a huge drafting exercise succeeded by an endless production line of statutes to codify the 'great ghost' (in the most unlikely event that cross-party agreement could be reached on the essentials, let alone the details, of a written constitution), the puzzle, the magic and the mystery will remain. Four, acknowledgement that this raises significant questions for would-be reformers. Do you go with the grain or wait for a kind of constitutional 'big bang' precipitated by some unknowable trauma?

There was also a fifth and specific significance to Her Majesty's one-liner, for the seminar was discussing *Questions of Procedure for Ministers*, the document containing 134 paragraphs of guidance for the Queen's ministers which John Major declassified in May 1992, thereby fulfilling a manifesto pledge from the election campaign he had won the month before.[6] This was a hugely important break-through. Under his nine predecessors in No. 10, *QPM*, as this par-ticular constitutional artefact is known in Whitehall, had remained a Cabinet Paper, following the pattern set by Clement Attlee when he promulgated its first modern version in August 1945: it was, therefore, subject to the thirty-year rule for classified material. While writing my study of *Cabinet* in the mid-1980s, I had to make do with quoting Winston Churchill's 1952 version when addressing the importance of *QPM*s for Margaret Thatcher's ministers.[7] Mrs Thatcher herself was unmoved by my suggestion in early 1989 that she might see her way clear to releasing it, both as a contribution to open government and as a way of celebrating her ten years in Downing Street. Her successor proved far more sympathetic to my entreaties.[8]

My reasons as a Whitehall-watcher for pressing for the release of this document were not simply the appetite for a good story, though that was among them. I wanted it in the open because, first, it was at that time an instrument of prime ministerial power. As Tony Benn has pointed out, it had been presented to the Cabinet (usually after an election) as a fait accompli. Unlike other Cabinet papers, it was not up for discussion. Secondly, publication would enhance the notion of accountability in revealing the guidelines by which minis-ters are supposed to live and operate. If they remain a secret, how can we know when, and by how much, ministers transgress or fall short of requirements? Thirdly, as a believer in Pickthorn's dictum that 'procedure is all the Constitution the poor Briton has,'[9] I con-sidered it essential that, in so far as there is a procedure for the proper conduct of Cabinet government in Britain, it should be in the public domain.

Initially, the response to *QPM*'s publication was very muted in the media, and therefore in the political nation as a whole. Only when it featured on virtually every radio and television news bulletin on 28 November 1992 in relation to the issue of the Exchequer's assistance in paying legal expenses incurred by Norman Lamont in the process of evicting the then Chancellor's 'sex therapist' tenant, did *QPM* enter the press and public mind[10] – where it subsequently remained, thanks to the storm trail of personal misfortunes and resignations that afflicted some seventeen of Mr Major's ministers or Parliamentary Private Secretaries in the three years that followed its release.[11] Such coverage, though inevitable and understandable, did however distract attention from the deeper constitutional significance of *QPM*'s arrival in the public domain courtesy of Mr Major. Sarah Hogg, recently retired as the head of his Downing Street Policy Unit, was absolutely justified in complaining about this in a public lecture in March 1995. 'The British people', she said,

> do not have what one might call an official owner's manual on their system of government. But thanks to the present Prime Minister, they have a good deal more information than they did. John Major has been given far too little credit for what he has done to shed light on the working parts of government. This, I think, is partly because of the typically British, unglamorous nature of the important constitutional documents which he has – for the first time – made public.
>
> It has been said that 'procedure is all the Constitution the poor Briton has.' Within the last couple of years, the Prime Minister has caused to be published a crucial document with the downbeat title of *Questions of Procedure for Ministers*. *Questions of Procedure* are dos and don'ts for ministers – and much of the rather shallow attention they attracted focused on the personal bits, notably what presents they may or may not accept. But there is a great deal more on the rules of government and the handling of policy to be gleaned from *Questions of Procedure*. And its publication puts what has been called a Highway Code of government in the public domain.[12]

That word 'code' again. Is *QPM* a code? Or is it, as the former Cabinet Secretary, Burke Trend, put it to me on one unforgettable occasion, 'merely some tips for beginners – a book of etiquette'?[13]

Cabinet Office papers for 1964 declassified a decade after our conversation show that Trend took a rather different view of *QPM*'s significance in private. In a brief for Wilson on the day he became Prime Minister, Trend described *QPM* as 'an entirely non-Party document, which codifies the general principles of Ministerial conduct as they have evolved over many years. It has the authority of a good many Prime Ministers, of different party complexions; and it is revised, in the light of changes in practice, at regular intervals.'[14]

Confusion arises partly because *QPM* is a kitchen sink of a phenomenon whose contents range over matters from high politics (collective responsibility; the proper conduct of Cabinet business; relationships between ministers and civil servants) to what Sarah Hogg calls 'the personal bits' (acceptance of hospitality; the disposal of personal shareholdings for the duration of ministerial office) – Lord Trend's 'etiquette tips'. Lord Trend delivered his conception of *QPM* in the course of declaring: '*Questions of Procedure for Ministers* is not a constitution . . .'[15] Yet the early, postwar versions, with all of which Trend was familiar, were both shorter and overwhelmingly devoted to procedural-cum-constitutional questions. This was noticed by the Nolan Committee on Standards of Conduct in Public Life, which took a great interest in the content and status of *QPM* as part of its initial inquiry.[16] After perusing the old files on *QPM* from the Public Record Office which I had left with the Committee, having given evidence before it,[17] its assistant secretary, Martin Le Jeune, said of the post-1945 prototypes: 'How striking it is that *QPM* was once just that – *procedure*; nothing about gifts, hospitality, stocks and shares (at least not much) and all the other ethical matters that now feature.'[18]

My chief reason for lingering so long over *QPM* here, apart from its centrality to the proper conduct of government business and the proper personal conduct of government ministers, is to illustrate just how mercurially elusive even such a fundamental artefact of the postwar British Constitution is once one tries to establish its precise status. I had always assumed that *QPM* enjoyed the eminence of a constitutional convention. My own view of what *constitutes* a constitutional convention was guided by the classic definition propounded by the great constitutional lawyer of the late nineteenth and early twentieth century, A. V. Dicey, plus an overlay provided in the late 1970s by the constitutional historian G. H. L. Le May. Dicey defined a convention as expressing 'the understandings which make up the constitutional morality of modern England'.[19] Le May's delightfully practical definition sees constitutional conventions as 'the general agreements of public men about the "rules of the game" to be borne in mind in the conduct of public affairs'.[20]

QPM fits both the Dicey and Le May definitions perfectly. I had no hesitation, therefore, in answering 'yes' in December 1992 when one of the undergraduates on my 'Cabinet and Premiership' course at Queen Mary and Westfield College asked me, for the purposes of preparing an essay, if *QPM* was a constitutional convention. Sir Robin Butler, the current Secretary of the Cabinet and adviser to the Prime Minister on *QPM* and related matters,[21] was due to brief the course that same week, so I told Matt Sanders, my student, to ask the 'oracle' (as Mrs Thatcher liked to call Sir Robin's predecessor, Sir Robert Armstrong[22]) himself before writing his essay. This he duly did, and Sir Robin's reply took me by surprise. Of *QPM* he said:

> I don't regard it as having a constitutional force at all ... It would be perfectly possible for an incoming Prime Minister to scrap the whole thing and to devise entirely new rules. The fact that it has now been published, would, of course, lead to debate about that and he would, no doubt, be questioned about the reasons for the changes. But it is entirely at the discretion of the new Prime Minister to scrap this lot of rules and ... deal with the administration in the way that he chose.[23]

This was one of those magical moments when the 'great ghost' flitted before one's eyes, changing shape as it did so. Where else in the world could an intelligent 21-year-old undergraduate's question engineer a 180-degree shift in one's perception of such a central element of a country's statecraft?

If Dicey, appropriately wraith-like, had manifested himself in the

Old Treasury Board Room where Sir Robin sat that winter Friday afternoon in 1992, he might have reminded Sir Robin that his (Dicey's) definition of a constitutional convention had allowed for that very notion of discretion, describing as it did 'most' of the conventions of the British Constitution as 'rules for determining the mode in which the discretionary powers of the Crown (or of Ministers as servants of the Crown) ought to be exercised.'[24] And if Harold Wilson's first version of *QPM* from October 1964 had been available then (which it wasn't, only being declassified in January 1995), I would have reminded Sir Robin of its second sentence, which states: 'This [*QPM*] codifies the general principles of Ministerial conduct as they have evolved over many years and through successive Administrations.'[25]

Matters, however, did not rest there. A year or so later I rang Sir Robin to acquire his permission to quote him on *QPM*'s discretionary status in my inaugural lecture as Professor of Contemporary History at Queen Mary and Westfield, which he, to my great pleasure, was going to chair. (The course briefing had, naturally, been a private occasion.) I read him what he had said and he gave his permission to quote it, adding, on reflection, that 90 per cent of *QPM* was discretionary.

'The document itself', he explained, 'has a discretionary status, though it deals with some things which are not at the discretion of a Prime Minister to change, for example, the description of accountability to Parliament in paragraph 27.'[26] This alteration was itself of great significance, because paragraph 27 lay at the heart of the current Scott Inquiry into arms for Iraq, which was very much on Sir Robin's mind in January 1994 when our conversation took place. It read:

> Each Minister is responsible to Parliament for the conduct of his or her Department, and for the actions carried out by the Department in pursuit of Government policies or in the discharge of responsibilities laid upon him or her as a Minister. Ministers are accountable to Parliament, in the sense that they have a duty to explain in Parliament the exercise of their powers and duties and to give an account to Parliament of what is done by them in

their capacity as Ministers or by their Departments. This includes the duty to give Parliament, including its Select Committees, and the public as full information as possible about the policies, decisions and actions of the Government and *not to deceive or mislead Parliament and the public.* [emphasis added][27]

This paragraph is by any standards more than 'tips for beginners' or 'etiquette'. Accountability plus responsibility plus openness is – or should be – an absolutely fundamental constitutional requirement, especially as under British arrangements the executive and the legislature are fused in such a fashion that the balance of power is heavily tilted in favour of the executive, not least in the interpretation of the rules of the game (i.e. the Constitution).

Sir Kenneth Pickthorn, himself an authority on the history of the British Constitution, had this in mind in the debate on the 1959 Procedure Committee Report,[28] during which he delivered himself of his famous dictum. 'I want to say', he told the Commons, 'that this is the nearest thing to a debate on the Constitution which is possible in the House. Indeed, procedure is all the Constitution the poor Briton has, now that any Government which command [*sic*] 51 per cent of the House can at any moment do anything they like, with retrospective or prospective intention.'[29] This in itself was an intriguing pre-echo of Lord Hailsham's 'elective dictatorship' theory some sixteen years ahead of its actual expression.[30]

Returning to paragraph 27 of *QPM*, just over a year after deeming 10 per cent of the document to be non-discretionary, Sir Robin Butler seemed to be moving towards acknowledging that at least the immutable parts which Prime Ministers cannot reach were tantamount to constitutional conventions. On 8 March 1995 he told the all-party House of Commons Treasury and Civil Service Select Committee that

it has long been the role of the Cabinet Secretary to advise on *Questions of Procedure for Ministers* in general, that booklet which has now been published, and to advise the Prime Minister and Ministers individually on issues that arise in connection with that . . . These conventions applying to Ministers have accumulated over time and the Cabinet Secretary advises on them and keeps

a file, obviously, on the advice that is given and tries to be consistent in the advice that is given.[31]

I have sympathy with Sir Robin's imprecision about the conventional
and unconventional (as it were) here. It is characteristic not just of
the status of *QPM* but of so many of the fragments of custom,
practice and procedure which make up the British Constitution.

It is true, too, that Prime Ministers *have* changed the thrust and
tone of their *QPM* inheritance. Someone at some point between the
1983 and 1992 versions, for example, inserted the preamble which
injects a dose of real permissiveness into much of it (I suspect it was
Mrs Thatcher in the *marque* she circulated after the 1987 election,
of which I have yet to acquire a copy).

Compare the following opening sections and you will see what I
mean:

June 1983 version (Mrs Thatcher)

QUESTIONS OF PROCEDURE FOR MINISTERS
1. Throughout this memorandum Ministers comprehend all
members of the Government, including Assistant Government
Whips. They do not include Parliamentary Private Secretaries.[32]

The document, which has still to be declassified, then moves on to
deal with ministerial attendance at meetings of the Privy Council.

May 1992 version (Mr Major)

QUESTIONS OF PROCEDURE FOR MINISTERS
1. These notes detail the arrangements for the conduct of affairs
by Ministers. They apply to all Members of the Government,
but not Parliamentary Private Secretaries . . . They are intended
to give guidance by listing the rules and the precedents which
may apply. They must, however, be seen in the context of protect-
ing the integrity of public life. *It will be for individual Ministers to
judge how best to act in order to uphold the highest standards*. Ministers
will want to see that no conflict arises nor appears to arise between
their private interests and their public duties. They will wish to
be as open as possible with Parliament and the Public. These
notes should be read against the background of these general
obligations. [emphasis added][33]

Next comes the section on Privy Council meetings.

This addendum, with its significant DIY sentence on personal standard-setting, was brought to the attention of the Nolan Committee, who seemed most interested in it and later recommended changes to it.[34] Given that the 1983 and 1987 versions of *QPM* remain classified, it was not an amendment that had been noticed in public before.

Such historical and linguistic analysis of successive marques of *QPM* is not the stuff of mere antiquarianism or a kind of latter-day job creation scheme for scholars enjoying certain arcane appetites (though it is certainly fascinating and even fun in an obscure sort of way). It really matters, because *QPM* is all that Parliament and the public have to go on when their minds turn to the procedural and behavioural niceties of those set in ministerial authority. In this instance an important limb of the 'great ghost' is conjured into the 'narrow flesh' of a code which might prove all too corruptible in the self-serving hands of the powerful if permissiveness were to break out all over with prime ministerial blessing.

Such analysis – such a search for reality – is squarely in the tradition of Walter Bagehot that I began to absorb in Cambridge shortly after that World Cup summer of 1966, with Harold Wilson in No. 10 and the Beatles riding high in the charts. And Bagehot's is the ghost which will haunt (benignly) the pages that follow, because his depiction of the 'great ghost', in its mid-nineteenth-century manifestation, has achieved an undoubted immortality.

To be dubbed 'immortal' in a secular context is comparable only to canonization in the religious sphere – a condition to be bestowed with great discrimination and extreme infrequency. Why does Walter Bagehot, a journalist and a banker, unarguably occupy such a position in relation to that mercurial phenomenon, the British Constitution? After all, he dashed off the essays for what became his most celebrated work, *The English Constitution*,[35] in 1865–6 when, as one of his great admirers, A. J. Balfour, pointed out 'at home the generation of statesmen who fought over the first Reform Bill were dead or dying . . . Derby and Russell were about to leave the political stage; Disraeli and Gladstone were about to fill it,' while abroad 'the first of the three Bismarckian wars which made the German

Empire was over ... [and] ... the second took place while he was writing,' and 'in the United States the Civil War was finished and the constitutional disputes following on the murder of Lincoln were fresh in everyone's recollection.'[36] In other words, political conditions at the time Bagehot was writing were everywhere in flux.

Yet in late twentieth-century Britain we live in his shadow, almost his thrall, certainly whenever a scholarly pen begins to scratch out the words 'monarchy' or 'Cabinet' on the page. There was a Constitution *before* his series of articles began appearing in the *Fortnightly* in 1865 – the year in which Palmerston died and a new politics began to appear, along with those extensions of the franchise that Bagehot – no democrat he – feared so mightily;[37] and since his death at the young age of fifty-one in 1877[38] it has changed in several important ways as that franchise has been completed, the reach of the state and its apparatus has been extended far beyond any mid-Victorian imagination (even one as vivid as his) and the guardians of that state (whether recruited on the basis of heredity, competitive examination or the ballot box) have embraced an increasingly rich mixture of human capital. But still we turn to him first for the benchmarks against which we measure change or decay, or if we need a gamey quote to illuminate our contemporary texts.

So, too, have many of those set in authority over us in the years since 1945. In April 1963 Harold Macmillan's Cabinet repaired to Chequers for a strategy weekend. The Saturday afternoon session was devoted to a discussion on the need to modernize the government machine. This, noted that great Whitehall connoisseur R. A. Butler, 'did not get very far. I said that Walter Bagehot was still hard to beat.'[39] Macmillan himself declared some fifteen years later that Bagehot was 'extraordinarily up to date, extraordinarily modern'.[40] As Prime Minister Harold Wilson said of *The English Constitution*: 'If in one sense the Reform Act of 1867 rendered it out of date almost as soon as it was published, in another sense it will never be out of date.'[41]

Wilson was absolutely right about Bagehot. The first reason has to do with that very human emotion – pleasure. Bagehot wrote with a brio that always brings a glow, not least in an area where the opacity of the writing often matches the obscurity of the detail. His words, even now, rise off the page and walk to a very wide readership. (*The English Constitution* was reissued by Fontana as recently as 1993.)[42] The second reason has to do with the history of knowledge. He will always enjoy a prime position in the archaeology and anthropology of British scholarship because, as Sir Kenneth Wheare has pointed out:

> Bagehot *found* the English constitution. It took some finding: it was not by any means obvious; there was little to guide him. At the same time, in the modern sense, he *invented* the Constitution; he made of it a working and living structure. He had the gift of breathing life into it; he created it. It is not an exaggeration to say that before Bagehot wrote, there was no English constitution that people could recognise or apprehend as a living and working thing. And it was not a skeleton or museum piece that he assembled; he did not confine himself to the anatomy of the subject, he went far beyond anatomy and combined the physiology, the pathology and the psychology.[43]

Such a paean of praise, every word of which I would endorse, does not mean to say Bagehot was universally right, that those legendary powers of narrative and analysis caught whole the reality of even that transitional phase in British politics he was seeming to describe while it was a hot and happening thing. But, like nobody before or since, he showed there was magic in the constitutional mystery; that it wasn't dull or marginal; and, above all, that it mattered. Therefore it is not presumptuous to walk in the steps of Walter Bagehot in any promenade around the still largely secret (in the mysterious sense) garden of the late twentieth-century British Constitution; it is both necessary and indispensable to do so and is likely to remain so unless and until every significant strand of our constitutional DNA is captured in statute or code. That is as near immortality as you will find in the historical, the political science or the public law professions in our singular and baffling polity.

But why the special need for a constitutional health-check in the fading years of the twentieth century? Partly because the British, with rare and exceptional flashes of transient interest, tend to be profoundly casual about the rules of their political and governmental games. Any effort, therefore, to fan an ember of concern into something more flammable seems worthwhile – and an ember of concern there most definitely was in mid-1990s Britain, even though it found only indirect expression in the opinion surveys as a crisis of confidence in people and institutions at the time this book was begun. In later opinion polls it became more explicit.

The unprecedented unpopularity of the incumbent Prime Minister, whose satisfaction rating fell to the pollsters' all-time low when it touched 17 per cent in August 1994, may have had as much, if not more, to do with John Major than with public disquiet about the nature of the premiership *per se*.[44] But an ICM poll of March 1994, though it excluded the office of Prime Minister, told a disquieting story about lack of public confidence in public institutions generally and the public figures who people them. Asked 'Which institution do you trust?' those polled answered as follows, in descending order:

church	54%
police	44%
monarchy	32%
courts	23%
Civil Service	21%
Parliament	13%
government	11%

When the question was reposited as 'Which types of people do you trust?' the following table of esteem and disesteem emerged:

doctors	81%
nurses	79%
teachers	49%
police	41%
judges	27%
civil servants	20%
estate agents	6%
politicians	5%

Car salesmen and journalists propped up the rest with 3% apiece.[45]

When you extract from this data a kind of combined esteem rating for the golden pentagon of constitutional institutions to the illumination of which this volume is devoted – monarchy, premiership, Cabinet, Whitehall and Parliament – you find the central apparatus of the British state is a pretty tarnished affair. In short, in Jean Seaton's phrase, the British Constitution 'needs attention'.[46] In a nation without a written constitution and bereft of formal checks and balances, confidence is a crucial ingredient, one of the key bonding agents that holds (or should hold) the entire structure together. Another, as we have seen, is the notion of the Crown. Though monarchy outstrips all the other sides to our golden pentagon, it is only in terms of a relative lack of tarnish, not an abundance of sheen. And it is to this, the most ancient institution of state, that I shall turn first.

But before I do, a brief word is needed about method. Again, I shall walk quite deliberately in the steps of Walter Bagehot. In the very first paragraph of *The English Constitution*, he declared: 'an observer who looks at the living reality will wonder at the contrast to the paper description.'[47] For some time I have sought the 'reality' of the Constitution in the very private pieces of paper its guardians circulated among themselves about what 'it' was at particular times in relation to particular contingencies. For a brief moment in the spring of 1994 I thought I was within reach of a core archive that might help solve many a postwar constitutional puzzle. Taking the form of a loose-leaf folder that is almost as old as the postwar period itself, it is called the 'Precedent Book' and it lives in the Cabinet Secretary's private office overlooking the Prime Minister's lawn behind No. 10. I had caught fleeting references to it in files already released at the PRO.[48] Indeed, one or two of those files had been deposited in the 'Precedent Book' for the purposes of both posterity and future need. In June I wrote to Sir Robin Butler, asking him to declassify those bits of it that were more than thirty years old. It is necessary to quote his reply virtually in full, partly to explain why a breakthrough into reality of the kind which would have won Bagehot's approval was not to be, and partly to illustrate the heartbreaking, Noel Coward-like 'Some Day I'll Find You'[49] syndrome that afflicts all would-be discoverers of this magical entity we know as the British Constitution. The 'Precedent Book', Sir Robin informed me,

> is a loose-leaf collection of internal guidance notes, documents and precedents gathered together by the Cabinet Secretary's Private Office over the years and essentially for use within that office. It is in no sense a public record [a view with which I disagree, incidentally; *any* official piece of paper is a public record as it deals with public, not private, business] . . . much of the Precedent Book consists of precedents derived from personal information about the affairs of Ministers and ex-Ministers which as I am sure that you will appreciate should not be released.
>
> Other parts of it are entirely routine procedural matters such as a wealth of detail about how to format and distribute Cabinet minutes which are of no great historical significance. Overall I fear that the documents may have misled you in thinking that 'significant material' can be found in the Precedent Book and for the reasons I have given above, I am afraid that I do not think it is any more the sort of collection which could or should be put in the public domain than my filofax!
>
> I am sorry to have to send you a disappointing reply but I do not want either to build up your hopes or encourage you to start a campaign![50]

Disappointing it was. For, as Philip Ziegler once put it, the British Constitution, especially that patch of it where monarchy meets premiership, 'has worked on an extremely fluid basis of instantly invented precedents'.[51] But there it is. Unlike the prisoners in Beethoven's *Fidelio*, Sir Robin Butler's precedents cannot yet emerge blinking into the sunshine with me singing 'Freiheit!' beneath the Cabinet Secretary's window as they do so. I have, however, done my best with those files that are available.

TWO

Monarchy

The Gilded Sponge

There is far more toing and froing between Whitehall and the Palace than shows on the surface, which is suspiciously quiet. Sometimes a fish breaks to the surface, for example Tony Benn [as Postmaster-General 1964–6] and the postage stamps ... The Queen is a very small 'c' conservative, very pragmatic and is a supporter of consensus to her fingertips. If she does interfere it will be something trivial, like stamps, or where the sensible members of the body politic agree.

Philip Ziegler, 1995[1]

The Queen is quite good at change. Quite good.

Lord Charteris, Private Secretary to the Queen
1952–77, 1994[2]

You see, all the democracies are bankrupt now because, you know, because of the way that the services have been planned for people to grab ... I think the next generation are going to have a very difficult time.

HM the Queen to former US President Ronald
Reagan, on board the Royal Yacht off Miami, 1991
(a rare example of her personal views on policy reaching
the public domain)[3]

To understand how we're governed, and hence the power of the Prime Minister, you have to understand the power of the Crown. It's like the Trinity: God the Father is the Queen – she's just there and nobody knows very much about her; God the Son is the Prime Minister – who exercises all the patronage and has all the real power; and God the Holy Ghost is the Crown – the Royal Prerogative – and the Crown is a state-within-a-state, surrounded by barbed wire and covered in secrecy.

Tony Benn, 1994[4]

It is very hard for the political nation in Britain to discuss the monarchy in sensible terms. By most people and for much of the time it is accepted as simply being there, somewhat like the weather: rather baffling but a fixture and very much part of the scene, part of the specialness of being British and often a source of self-congratulation verging on the smug.

A decade ago, for example, the journalist Sir Peregrine Worsthorne could declare: 'These days the only efficient part of the British Constitution is the Monarchy' without raising a ripple of dissent from his audience of political scientists.[5] A few months earlier, in July 1984, the historian Lord Blake in a Gresham College lecture on the monarchy had told his listeners:

> I believe that the vestigial powers of the British monarch do matter and I believe that if they disappeared altogether the prestige of the monarchy would be subtly and marginally but nonetheless definitely diminished. On the other hand, they should be exercised, and they have been throughout the twentieth century, with the greatest tact and discretion.
>
> Apart from defeat in war, embroilment with 'politics' (in the widest sense of that word) has been the principal factor in bringing hereditary monarchies to an end. The wisdom and good sense of successive monarchs and their private advisers has prevented this danger in Britain. No doubt the preservation of monarchy, like that of liberty, requires eternal vigilance, but I see no reason whatever to believe that this will be kept any less in the future than it has been in the past.[6]

Again, few would have quibbled with that judgement in a year when, symbolically enough, striking miners' wives petitioned the Queen to intervene on behalf of their pit communities in the bitterest coal strike since 1926.[7]

Ten years on, thanks chiefly to the personal misfortunes of some members of the Royal Family, the heir to the throne in particular, waves of heated speculation about the durability of the House of Windsor afflicted the press.[8] Two factors, I suspect, stayed constant over that period. First, most of the Queen's subjects remained in near-complete ignorance of what those 'vestigial powers' of the monarch mentioned by Robert Blake amounted to. Secondly, mainstream political discussion continued to regard such matters as either unsuitable or too arcane for sustained treatment. The tone adopted by John Major himself spoke for this enduring tradition of complacency laced with imprecision when at a prime ministerial press conference in No. 10 on 16 January 1995 he described the monarchy as 'the central glue in the Constitution'.[9] On one level (the notion of Crown power), of course, it is. But Mr Major was not being narrowly technical on this occasion.

The most thoughtful commentators, however, did not take their line from the PM. As Peter Riddell of *The Times* had put it a few months earlier.

> Serious politicians are not supposed to discuss the monarchy. It is thought to smack of a lack of soundness and good judgement ... [but] ... In the Crown's own long-term interests, the fog over its political role needs to be lifted. That is an overdue subject for political debate. Contrary to Bagehot's view 125 years ago, its mystery is no longer its life.[10]

Absolutely right. Yet any serious attempt to dispel that 'fog' has to start with Bagehot and his famous aside that 'when there is a select committee on the Queen, the charm of royalty will be gone. Its mystery is its life. We must not let in daylight upon magic.'[11]

Walter Bagehot has mattered to the British Royal Family for a hundred years, ever since, in Queen Victoria's phrase, the man who became George V had 'a Professor from Cambridge to read with him'.[12] That 'Professor' was J. R. Tanner, Fellow of St John's College, Cambridge, an expert on maritime history and constitutional matters. In 1894 he instructed the then Duke of York on the kingly side of statecraft by setting him to read Bagehot's *The English Constitution* and inviting him to write a condensed version of the chapter on the monarchy. This the Duke dutifully did, the fruits of his labour remaining in the Royal Archives at Windsor.[13] In this didactic way

did Bagehot's famous trio of rights for a constitutional monarch –
'the right to be consulted, the right to encourage, the right to warn'[14]
– enter both the constitutional mainstream and the routine expectations of British kingcraft. The precise passage in George's 'Notes
on Bagehot's *English Constitution*' where this important example of
constitutional inoculation can be directly observed, complete with
the future King's underlinings, reads as follows:

> During the <u>continuance</u> of ministries. The Crown possesses, <u>first</u>
> the right to be consulted, <u>second</u> the right to encourage and <u>third</u>
> the right to warn. And these rights may lead to a very important
> influence on the course of politics, especially as under a system
> of party government, the monarch alone possesses a '<u>continuous</u>
> <u>political experience</u>'.[15]

As Kenneth Wheare said of Bagehot: 'By enumerating these three
rights as matters of fact, he invented or created them as rules of the
constitution. By that statement he ensured that no sovereign could
successfully claim more; I believe also', Wheare continued, 'that he
ensured that no sovereign could be granted less.'[16]

George V's second son Albert, the future George VI, received a
similar dose of Bagehot (though nobody expected *him* to have to live
by Bagehotian rules until Wallis Simpson helped bring, albeit briefly,
an entirely different set of principles to the conduct of kingship).
'Bertie' imbibed his dose at Trinity College, Cambridge. 'Dicey's
solid and uncompromising *Law of the Constitution* [being] relieved by
the brilliant and scintillating pages of Walter Bagehot', according to
his biographer, Sir John Wheeler-Bennett.[17] We also learn from
Wheeler-Bennett that the high-fibred George VI felt a special em-
pathy for Bagehot on the monarchy as the setter of a moral tone, as
'the head of our morality'.[18] 'To all dignity, its social value and its
essential morality – Prince Albert dedicated himself with a solemn
rectitude and an upright probity,' declared his biographer[19] – all of
which has a terrible poignancy as the monarchy endures a succession
of *anni horribiles* in the mid-1990s.

The Queen began learning her constitutional craft at the age of
twelve in 1938, Sir Henry Marten travelling the short distance from

Eton to Windsor Castle to instruct her. No notebooks or cribs are available to tell us which Bagehotian gems caught her imagination, but we know she 'read parts of it', as she put it to a leading British political historian in 1981.[20] The latest of a long line of royal biographers, Kenneth Harris, tells us that the Prince of Wales has scanned where his mother, grandfather and great-grandfather had read before him.[21] It is altogether ironic, therefore, to have to say baldly that Bagehot in his second most famous line on the British monarchy was plain wrong. 'It has not been sufficiently remarked', he opined in the mid-1860s, 'that a change has taken place in the structure of our society . . . A republic has insinuated itself beneath the folds of a monarchy.'[22] Bagehot doubted even then whether the two remaining personal prerogatives of the Sovereign – the sole power to dissolve a Parliament and the sole power to appoint a Prime Minister – were still live in practical terms, though he did acknowledge there were 'vestiges of doubt' about whether the monarch was duty bound to dissolve Parliament if the Cabinet so requested.[23] For Bagehot, the reality was that the Cabinet triggered general elections and Parliament chose Prime Ministers.[24] I think Bagehot was in error then and that his line of interpretation has never yet fitted the reality. (Though in the summer of 1994 he found a surprising ally in the person of Lord Hailsham, former Lord Chancellor and the longest-serving Cabinet minister in the postwar period, who declared 'we are a democratically governed republic with a wholly admirable hereditary head of State.'[25]) It is significant that five monarchs and nearly 130 years after Bagehot made his assessments, the current guardians of this particular piece of the Constitution reckon he remains in error.

In contrast, however, the Bagehotian trio of monarchical rights *has* become a fixed stratum of the constitutional geomorphology, reformulated as recently as 1986 by Sir William Heseltine, then Private Secretary to the Queen, as 'the right – indeed the duty – to counsel, encourage and warn her Government'.[26] The notion of a 'disguised republic' has never been a runner in the reality stakes. Furthermore, I am convinced, from studying the richer lodes of primary historical material now becoming available for the postwar period, that British historians since 1945 have very largely neglected the continuing political influence of the monarchy as practised by George VI and Elizabeth II. And it is this theme that will form the centrepiece of this chapter.

But first, a warning. Expect no dramatic revelations that the two postwar sovereigns affected either the content or the personalities of high political life to any great degree. The picture, a very British one, is full of what Douglas Hurd has called 'the nuances and ironies of the British Constitution'.[27] It deserves an important measure of adjustment nonetheless.

I was relieved, shortly after reaching this conclusion at the very time when sections of both the print and the electronic media were regularly raising the possibility of an undisguised republic in Britain, to find that my own rediscovery of Crown power as a factor was shared by a scholar, a politician and a biographer of premiers as eminent as Sir Robert Rhodes James. In the course of confiding a secret to an audience at the Royal Society of Arts in November 1993 (that three years earlier 'there was a real fear that after Mrs Thatcher had failed to secure the necessary majority on the first ballot [of the Conservative leadership contest] and was clearly heading for defeat on the second . . . she might recommend to Her Majesty an immediate dissolution of Parliament'[28]), Sir Robert's argument was that plainly a dissolution 'would certainly not have had the support of a majority of the Cabinet . . . and that the Queen was not bound to accept the advice of one member of the Cabinet, even the most senior one'.[29] Again, a view with which I concur wholeheartedly.

Sir Robert's memoir of those titanic last days of Mrs Thatcher is worth lingering upon. This section of his lecture came as a complete surprise to those whose duty it is to help the British Constitution sail safely through such stormy moments. It rang no bells for them.[30] Mrs Thatcher did, however, inform a bemused Russian television interviewer in Moscow shortly after her fall that she *had* briefly considered staying on as PM because you don't have to be a party leader to be a British Prime Minister.[31] She was right. From May to October 1940 Churchill was Premier, but not until after Neville

Chamberlain's retirement did he assume the leadership of the Conservative Party.[32]

Let me deal first with the remaining political-cum-constitutional
powers of the monarch (the areas of Bagehotian error) before coming
back to the routine activities of consulting, encouraging and warning
where Walter's prescriptions continue to prevail. The British like to
believe, and most do so genuinely, that the monarchy is above politics,
that the very essence of constitutional queencraft or kingcraft is that the
sovereign reigns but does not rule – that, in Bagehot's most famous distinction, the monarchy is wholly a part of the 'dignified' rather than the
'efficient' functioning of the state,[33] and is quite simply above the political
competition between those who would steer it. On one level, conventional wisdom has it absolutely right. The monarchy is not *party* political; but it does, if its famous reserve powers have any enduring vitality,
have real political functions which, even if only occasionally exercised,
are absolutely central to the British political process if their exercise
becomes even a possibility. For dissolving Parliament, thereby trigger-
ing a general election, or appointing a Prime Minister – decisions in
which the monarch would only become involved in conditions of
uncertainty where choices had to be made – are anything but marginal
activities. How the Sovereign made those choices would determine
the nation's politics and who occupied No. 10 Downing Street.

A number of questions, therefore, are posed by the so-called
'reserve powers' that are personal to the monarch.

1 Are they still live or have they fallen into effective, if
  unacknowledged, disuse?
2 If live, in what circumstances would they operate?
3 If operational, what principles would guide them?
4 Are the practice and principles of those powers sufficiently
  known, understood and accepted not just by the electorate
  but by those whose personal political futures might depend
  on the outcome of applied principle and practice?
5 Does the ecology of very late twentieth-century British
  politics require a clarification, perhaps even a reformation, of
  those 'reserve powers'?

The first question is truly Bagehotian. In *The English Constitution* he wrote: 'The Queen has a hundred ... [prerogative] ... powers which waver between reality and desuetude ... Some good lawyer ought to write a careful book to say which of these powers are really usable, and which are obsolete?'[34]

The penultimate official piece of paper, one of two that serve as a surrogate for Bagehot's 'good lawyer' on one of the 'reserve powers', the appointment of a Premier, had no doubt about its vitality. This document is part of that 'Precedent Book' which lies captive in the Cabinet Secretary's Private Office, but it has been declassified separately in the form it took when Sir Norman Brook's Private Secretary, Ronald Fraser, placed it there in January 1949. 'The choice of the Prime Minister by the King', it states, 'is not made on formal advice or submission' – from the outgoing Premier, that is.

> In many cases the choice is clear but the King has an absolute right in all cases to consult anyone he pleases. This right may of course be of the greatest value in cases where there is doubt about the choice; such as in the event of the death of a Prime Minister in office, the resignation of the Prime Minister for personal reasons, a complicated political situation and so forth. Nevertheless, as the King should not exercise, or appear to exercise, any political bias, he would normally choose as Prime Minister the leader of the party having the largest number of seats in the House of Commons.[35]

Savour the uncertainty lurking in those dry descriptive sentences – 'a complicated political situation'; the sovereign would 'normally' send for the party leader commanding the largest number of seats in the Commons. The certainty comes in the choice unarguably being the monarch's, a choice informed by an 'absolute right' to consult whichever of his or her subjects he or she pleases.

Since 1949 the use of those powers has arisen in at least six real or threatened contingencies:

1 in the spring of 1950, following the general election of February that year, when the majority of the Attlee government fell from 146 to six;[36]

2 in July 1953 when, with Churchill afflicted by a stroke and
    Eden under the surgeon's knife in the United States, the Palace
    was worried that the newly crowned Queen might have to
    send for Lord Salisbury as a caretaker Premier if Churchill
    perished;[37]
3 in January 1957 when, on Eden's resignation after the Suez
    crisis, the Queen had to choose between the claims of
    Harold Macmillan and R. A. Butler for the succession;[38]
4 in October 1963 when, on Macmillan's resignation, she had
    to do the same between the hapless Rab and the Earl of
    Home;[39]
5 in October 1964 when, as the election results came in
    overnight, No. 10 hastily prepared a 'Deadlock' file in case
    the result left neither main party with an overall majority;[40]
6 in March 1974 when Edward Heath, his majority gone after
    the first of that year's two elections, hung on over a weekend
    while attempting to do a deal with the Liberals.[41]

In addition to those occasions, most of which are relatively well
known, the Palace, the Cabinet Office and No. 10 engaged in intense
contingency planning in case the reserve powers should come into
play in the late winter and early spring of 1974 (lest Wilson lost an
early vote and sought a dissolution); in the winter and spring of
1978–9, as the Callaghan government staggered to its close; and in
the run-up to the last three elections – 1983, 1987 and 1992 – either
because Britain seemed about to revert to a 1920s-style three-party
system or, in the spring of 1992, because the opinion polls suggested
the strong possibility of a 'hung' Parliament.

What does that litany tell us? First, that the election of all party
leaders after 1965 – when the Conservatives finally abandoned what
Iain Macleod called the 'magic circle' that determined which Tory
leader would 'emerge'[42] – did not put paid to the personal prerogatives
of the monarch. It is always a profound mistake to write off Britain's
ancient Constitution because of some seemingly modern refinement.

Secondly, that the gilded guardians of our 'great ghost', the men
who stand at the points of the so-called 'golden triangle' (the mon-

arch's Private Secretary, the Prime Minister's Principal Private Secretary and the Cabinet Secretary) thought, and still think, that the 'reserve powers' of the Crown are most certainly active when it comes to calling elections and appointing Prime Ministers, even though no dissolution request from a Prime Minister has been refused by a monarch since before the Great Reform Act of 1832.[43]

Thirdly, that, so far, all the party leaders who have sought power at the thirteen general elections since VE Day have accepted the vitality of those powers and, privately, that they must conduct themselves within the 'tacit understandings', to use Sidney Low's marvellous phrase,[44] that accompany them by not placing the monarch in a position where he or she would become embarrassed or, still worse, party politicized. Certainly Messrs Major, Kinnock and Ashdown subscribed to this sub-theme of the 'good chap theory of government' (i.e. that a good chap knows what a good chap is expected to do and will never push things too far) ahead of the 1992 election, when it was made plain to each of them individually and privately that they must on no account embarrass the Queen in the event of a hung result and that they must agree a way forward among themselves before bringing it to Her Majesty for the Royal Household's equivalent of a 'good housekeeping' seal of approval.[45] Disagreements about the proper operation of the Royal Prerogative in certain contingencies nevertheless remained unresolved up to election day 1992 – and they have not been resolved since, as we shall see in a moment.[46]

There are several problems associated with 'doing a Bagehot' on the reserve powers by discovering and describing the 'living reality' of them in both mid and late twentieth-century Britain, though a scattering of files are available at the PRO from the late 1940s to the early to mid-1960s to enable the constitutional position to be pieced together from inside sources. The two most important ones date from March 1950, when Attlee feared the Labour government might see its thin majority disappear if the Conservatives moved certain amendments to the King's Speech, and from October 1964, when, in the event, Harold Wilson squeaked into No. 10 on an even slimmer majority than Attlee's fourteen and a half years earlier.

Let us examine the 1950 material first. From Cabinet Secretary Sir Norman Brook's 'no circulation' record of a Cabinet discussion of 9 March 1950 on the possibility of a King's Speech defeat (preserved by Attlee's Principal Private Secretary Denis Rickett, in the No. 10 files after Brook suggested 'you may like to have it by you in case a similar situation should arise at a later stage in this Parliament'[47]), we can reconstruct the genesis of what became a substantial contingency planning exercise in Buckingham Palace and the Cabinet Office as winter turned into spring.

The standard circulated Cabinet minute was blandly unrevealing:

> The Cabinet had some preliminary discussion about the situation which would arise if the Government were defeated in a division early in the lifetime of the Parliament. It was generally recognised that, from the point of view of the national interest, a very serious situation would result – especially as essential financial business had to be transacted by Parliament in March and April.[48]

The reality, rarely recorded in such detail as in the 'no circulation' account, ran like this:

> THE PRIME MINISTER said that the two Conservative amendments to the Address, both that on the Iron and Steel Act and that on Housing, would be pressed to a division; and he had been considering what advice he should tender to His Majesty if the Government were defeated in either of these divisions. He did not think it would be right to ask for a Dissolution so soon after the General Election, and he was inclined to think that his proper course would be to advise the King to send for Mr Churchill. The resulting Parliamentary situation would be unsatisfactory, for the Conservatives, being in a minority, would find it even more difficult to carry on the essential business of Government; but this situation would have been created by the Conservatives and he thought they should be forced to assume responsibility for handling it.[49]

One wonders what lessons about slim-majority brinkmanship a certain Harold Wilson, present at that meeting as President of the Board of Trade, might have learnt for future use between 1964 and 1966, and 1974 and 1976.

The government survived in the division lobbies in March 1950. But the wobble led Brook to commission research from his Private Secretary, A. R. W. Bavin, 'on the questions that would arise if the Government were defeated in the House of Commons'.[50] The opinions of experienced officials, such as Sir Alan Lascelles at the Palace and Sir Charles Harris in the Chief Whip's Office, were also sought. Constitutional authorities (Anson, Dicey, Lowell) were consulted on paper, as were deceased statesmen (Peel, Russell, Salisbury). Letters were sent to current scholars like Norman Gibbs in Oxford.[51] A huge and fascinating chart of 'Noteworthy Dissolutions since 1835' was prepared. Out of this cornucopic exercise came the grand conclusion 'that while there is some divergence of view among the authorities on the question whether the King can refuse a dissolution to a Prime Minister who asks for it, *the better opinion* is that the power still exists but that the prerogative could properly be exercised only in exceptional circumstances' [emphasis added]. That was the agreed position between the 1950 'golden triangle' and it remains the position of their gilt-edged successors today.

The 1950 Cabinet Office paper, 'Government Defeats in the House of Commons', which embodies the conventions affecting the use of the personal prerogatives, has a counterpart in the Royal Archives which the Palace is currently not prepared to release, even though a chunk of it, in the form of his Private Secretary's brief to George VI on the 'general strategical considerations', or options, open to him if Attlee fell on the King's speech, is reproduced in Wheeler-Bennett's official life.[52] But Sir Alan Lascelles did take up his pen to divulge the essence of his advice to the readers of *The Times*, stimulated by a flurry of speculative letters to that newspaper from a range of authorities including the former Lord Chancellor, Lord Simon,[53] and a future Home Secretary, Roy Jenkins.[54] Lascelles, writing under the pseudonym 'Senex' (wise old man), reflected his own and Cabinet Office thinking both in asserting the vitality of the remaining prerogatives and in stressing the limited, special and rare circumstances in which they might be used.[55]

It is worth comparing the two versions:

Cabinet Office version

It is difficult to imagine circumstances in which the King could properly refuse a dissolution to a Prime Minister with a clear majority in the House of Commons over all other Parties; for, if he did so, the Prime Minister would presumably resign and the King would have to send for the Leader of the Opposition who, though he accepted the office, on the view that the House of Commons had not outlived its usefulness, would in fact be unable to form a stable Government and would soon be defeated in the Commons. The King could hardly grant a dissolution to the second Prime Minister after he had refused it to the first.

A request for dissolution seems more likely to be refused to a Prime Minister in a minority in the House of Commons if it appeared that the Parties who together formed a majority were prepared to join forces to support an alternative Government. Even in these circumstances a dissolution could scarcely be refused unless the Parliament had been in existence a comparatively short time and appeared still to reflect the view of the electorate. If the King were to refuse a dissolution on those grounds and his judgement of the willingness of the other Parties to work together proved unfounded, so that the new Government was shortly afterwards defeated in its turn, it seems probable that he would then send for the Prime Minister who had first requested a dissolution and allow him a dissolution in due course.[56]

Lascelles was both terser and more comprehensible in stating the position.

Buckingham Palace version

It is surely indisputable (and common sense) that a Prime Minister may ask – not demand – that his Sovereign will grant him a dissolution of Parliament; and that the Sovereign, if he so chooses, may refuse to grant his request. The problem of such a choice is entirely personal to the Sovereign, though he is, of course, free to ask informal advice from anybody whom he thinks fit to consult.

Insofar as this matter can be publicly discussed, it can be properly assumed that no wise Sovereign – that is, one who has at

heart the true interest of the country, the constitution, and the
Monarchy – would deny a dissolution to his Prime Minister
unless he was satisfied that: (1) the existing Parliament was still
vital, viable and capable of doing its job; (2) a General Election
would be detrimental to the national economy; (3) he could rely
on finding another Prime Minister who could carry out his
Government, for a reasonable period, with a working majority
in the House of Commons.[57]

The 'Senex' letter was *the* insider source on the personal prerogatives for forty-one years – until, in fact, my BBC Radio 4 *Analysis*
producer, Simon Coates, and I persuaded Lord Armstrong
of Ilminster, who at different times in the 1970s and 1980s had occupied two of the three points of the 'golden triangle' in No. 10 and
the Cabinet Office, to come to the microphone and do a 'modern
Lascelles'. Sir Robin Butler later confirmed that the *Analysis* script
reflected the latest insider thinking in the Cabinet Office, the Palace
and No. 10.[58]

On the basis of the 'Senex' letter, the Armstrong transcript and
various private conversations I was able to indulge in a piece of
constitutional 'kremlinology' on the monarch's personal prerogatives
some time before the additional 1964 material was released at the
Public Record Office in January 1995. Here follows my attempt to
distil the essence of the monarch's reserve powers:

1 Only the monarch can dissolve Parliament, thereby causing
   a general election to be held.
2 Only the monarch can appoint a Prime Minister.
3 After an indecisive general election, the monarch is required
   to act only if the incumbent Prime Minister resigns before
   placing a Queen's Speech before Parliament or after failing
   to win a majority for that legislative programme in the
   House of Commons.
4 The overarching principle at such delicate times is that the
   Queen's government must be carried on and that the
   monarch is not drawn into political controversy by those
   politicians competing to receive her commission to form a
   government.

5 Normally an outgoing Prime Minister is asked to advise the
   monarch on the succession; but the monarch has to ask for
   that advice and, if given, it is informal advice which can be
   rejected rather than formal advice which must be acted
   upon.

6 After an inconclusive result, if the incumbent Prime Minister
   resigns the monarch will normally offer the first chance to
   form an administration to the party leader commanding the
   largest single number of seats in the House of Commons.

7 A Prime Minister can 'request' but not 'demand' a dissolution
   of Parliament. The monarch can refuse this. The
   circumstances in which this might happen would be, in Lord
   Armstrong's words, 'improbable'. But the power to withhold
   consent could be a check on the 'irresponsible exercise' of a
   Prime Minister's right to make such a request.[59]

8 The circumstances in which a Royal refusal could be
   forthcoming are, in Lascelles' words, if 'the existing
   Parliament was still vital, viable and capable of doing its job'
   or if the monarch 'could rely on finding another Prime
   Minister who could carry out [his/her] Government for a
   reasonable period, with a working majority in the House of
   Commons'.[60] (Lascelles, as we have seen, originally described
   a third circumstance in which a refusal might take place –
   that 'a General Election would be detrimental to the national
   economy' – but this had been dropped by the early 1990s;[61]
   an unintended nod, perhaps, to the volatility of the modern
   money markets and to Britain's perpetual economic
   difficulties though the timing of the Budget could still be a
   factor as it was during the contingency planning of 1950.)

All attempts to persuade the 'golden triangle' to come clean on
the current principles that underlie this particularly delicate aspect
of queencraft and statecraft have failed. The common line (which
has all the signs of being based on their own version of collective
responsibility) is that (a) no two sets of circumstances are alike and
(b) nothing must be done to diminish the flexibility which gives the

remaining reserve powers their precious elasticity.[62] In other words, the last 'vital and viable' powers of the British Crown are seen as part of the enduring glory of that British constitutional garden fostered lovingly and without plan by successive generations of head gardeners who have added a piece of shrubbery here or a ha-ha there.

Since I compiled my own taxonomy of the current 'reserve powers', however, the October 1964 'Deadlock' file has reached the public domain. This document was knocked up in the small hours of Friday 16 October when it looked as if neither party might enjoy an overall majority once all the counts were completed following the general election of the previous day. On the basis of a conversation a short while earlier with the Queen's Private Secretary, Sir Michael Adeane, and a scattering of photocopies of *The Times* for October 1922, when the Lloyd George coalition fell and Bonar Law asked for time before accepting George V's commission to form a government, Sir Derek Mitchell, Sir Alec Douglas-Home's Principal Private Secretary (and soon to be Harold Wilson's) dictated a memo entitled 'Deadlock. The Queen's Government Must be Carried On'. After considering how Sir Alec might seek help from the Liberals by offering Jo Grimond the post of Lord Privy Seal, the note went on to consider the Queen's choices if Sir Alec returned to No. 10 without a majority but not, as it were, unarguably defeated.

'She may', Sir Derek wrote of the Queen,

'(a) press him to stay on until defeated in the House;
'(b) press him to stay on in the hope that he may form a Coalition, or
'(c) send for someone who is not the leader of either major Party in the hope that some sort of compromise Government could be carried on until it were feasible to have another General Election.'[63]

All this comes with a fascinating little cover-sheet, a single page in Sir Derek's own hand in which the human (how to get Wilson to the Palace if he wins, whether he'll need morning dress, the need to take care of Mrs Wilson and to provide both with an evening meal; how to get Home away from No. 10 to Chequers if he loses) is mingled with high constitutional matters like the 'Deadlock' contingency.[64]

It transpired when the 'Deadlock' file for the 1959 election was discovered at the PRO[65] that Sir Derek had been drawing on the document prepared by his predecessor, Sir Tim Bligh, for Harold Macmillan on 5 October 1959.[66] The possibility of Jo Grimond being offered the post of Lord Privy Seal in the event of a hung result had been canvassed by Bligh, too, and the Queen's options were phrased in an identical fashion. But the 1959 contingency plan concentrated on the December 1923 general election and Baldwin's facing the Commons in January 1924 as the key precedent and guide for the conduct of No. 10 and the Palace in the event of a future hung parliament.[67]

Shortly after the 1964 'Deadlock' file was declassified, I contacted Sir Derek about this new and important historical-cum-constitutional artefact, suggesting it really was evidence of a back-of-the-envelope approach. 'It is, isn't it?' he replied. 'It bears out a lot of what you're always saying – the rush and the anxiety,' adding, characteristically, 'The nice thing about these files is that they are quite well done. Despite the rush, they read quite well.'[68]

Thanks to the release of Sir Derek's 'Deadlock' file, another Downing Street Principal Private Secretary of even more recent vintage, Sir Kenneth Stowe, was prepared to go on the record about the constitutional understandings as they had operated during his time with Harold Wilson, Jim Callaghan and Margaret Thatcher between 1975 and 1979. Sir Ken said:

> There is an assumption that everybody will conduct themselves in the same spirit. And this is the important constitutional point – the Queen's government must be carried on. The Prime Minister must have the confidence of the House of Commons . . .
>
> There are three principles involved:
>
> 1 The Queen's government must be carried on.
> 2 The Prime Minister appointed by the Sovereign must be able to command a majority in the House of Commons.
> 3 The Prime Minister must be confident of leading or

> commanding the support of the majority party in the
> House of Commons.

These are the three points of a triangle and they give you an
indestructible basis to confront any situation that arises.[69]

Sir Ken, ever sensitive to the human factor, acknowledged the real
basis supporting his 'triangle' – the 'good chap theory': 'The "good
chap theory" is shorthand for saying that there is a consensus among
anyone with responsibility for the governance of the United Kingdom – that the government shall be carried on in a certain spirit
and an orderly way which brings you back to that triangle which is
the basis of that spirit and that order.'[70]

Shortly after the 'Deadlock' file was declassified I showed it and the
Mitchell–Stowe commentaries to my MA students. One of them,
Pamela Baxter, caught the Britishness of it to perfection. 'It's like
discussing different ways of making a cup of tea,' she said. 'But it's
not that. It's about the making or unmaking of governments.'[71] Quite
so. We really do need, despite Bagehot's caveats, to let daylight
in upon this particular piece of our magical constitutional identity,
however charmingly its essence may be expressed by its former
guardians and operators.

It is my belief that if Bagehot could suddenly materialize in mid-
1990s London and resume his walks from Belgravia to Whitehall
via Buckingham Palace he would recognize the utility of such an
approach. Why? For half a dozen reasons:

1 That the 'reserve powers' of the Crown are (or should be)
  in the 'efficient' working section of the Constitution rather
  than its 'dignified' heritage museum.
2 That the possibility of electoral volatility, stemming from a
  two-and-a-half – if not a three-party system, with much
  regional variation thrown in each polling day, means that the
  chances of 'hung' results, and therefore of some element of
  real choice reverting to the Queen's commission, should be
  recognized by the 'golden triangle' and planned for. It is
  certain, and fully appreciated by the 'triangle', that if Britain
  moved to any kind of proportional representation for

elections to the Westminster Parliament the Monarch's role would be substantially enhanced as no single party has attracted more than 50 per cent of the votes cast since before the Second World War.

3 That the general principles which inform that planning should be discussed with the party leaders on the basis of that most ancient of private networks, the Privy Counsellors, and published with a content and in a fashion that commands general assent.

4 That the personal misfortunes of some members of the Royal Family and the percussive effect of the continuing arguments about the Royal finances mean that the constitutional functions of the monarchy must be kept separate from the debate about money and private lives. Neither the Queen nor the institution she embodies should in any way be placed at risk of even apparent politicization if it can be avoided by forethought and prior discussion. Just one hung election result in which the Royal choice left a part of the political nation aggrieved would be immensely damaging.

5 At the last election, disagreement remained on the precise working of the 'reserve powers' in what one participant to the very private discussions called two 'nightmare scenarios'. (1) What would happen if the outgoing Prime Minister (i.e. John Major) still had the largest number of seats after the election, even though his majority had gone, and wished to hand over the leadership of the party to someone else (e.g. Douglas Hurd)? Should the Queen wait until the Parliamentary Conservative Party had chosen a new party leader, or should she send for Neil Kinnock straight away and ask him to try to form a government? (2) What would happen, with the same post-election arithmetic, if the Conservatives managed to persuade the Liberal Democrats to help keep Labour out by refusing to support them in Commons votes? Would Labour acquiesce in this outcome? Allied to these two 'nightmares' was a third: what would the

Queen have done if Major had requested another election without facing the Commons?[72]

6 Bagehot, surely, would have taken such threats to continuity, stability and constitutional balance very seriously. And, finally, I hope he would have seen the fact that these questions were live and being discussed privately but very seriously by real politicians and real crown servants in the run-up to the election of April 1992 as convincing evidence that Britain neither was, nor ever had been at any point since 1867, a 'disguised republic'.

There is a way of resolving these uncertainties of which I hope Bagehot would approve. It is this. Even though the 'golden triangle' remains unconvinced about the need to consult with a view to fashioning agreed general principles that might be applied to admittedly unforeseeable contingencies (and there is no sign that the current Prime Minister would offer a hostage to fortune by initiating discussions himself with Tony Blair or Paddy Ashdown on a Privy Counsellor basis), Mr Blair and Mr Ashdown should simply ask for them. It would be very difficult to refuse. After all, the Constitution does not belong to the government of the day. It has to do first and foremost with the rules of the game under which our competition for political power takes place. In other words, as a totality it belongs to all 42 million of us who have the vote. And the rubric surrounding the 'reserve powers' of the monarch belongs not to the Queen, the Prime Minister and the 'golden triangle', but to all those who legitimately aspire to capture the state by open and democratic means. These particular constitutional power-lines really should be brought to the surface for all to see and inspect. Ours, after all, is the era of transparency and regulation.

Finally in this chapter, I turn to that other piece of pure Bagehotry – the right of the monarch to be consulted, to encourage and to warn. Here the historians, my fellow professionals, must be the ones to probe and push, not the politicians. The Tuesday evening session between Premier and Sovereign is about the only governmental meeting that never leaks – partly because no one else is there and no minutes are taken. Ignorance, therefore, of its tone, pitch and content has been nearly complete. Historians, being human, tend not to write about things about which, for lack of evidence, they cannot know. And things that are not written about tend to be ignored. For the postwar period, this is gradually beginning to change; and for once, the old scholarly cliché 'more research is needed' is justified. Some of the so-called 'audience notes' prepared for Mr Attlee's weekly sessions with the King (which give us a pretty good idea of the areas in which George VI chose to exercise his Bagehotian rights[73]) are declassified, for example, though those for the present reign are still retained (even though No. 10 and the Palace reviewed the position in 1992–3).[74] The hundred-year rule applied to most Royal-related material on Whitehall files was reduced to thirty years by the *Open Government* White Paper of 1993.[75] A genuine, though not a complete, opportunity now exists to piece together something of the ebb and flow of that 'most special relationship' between George VI, Elizabeth II and their Premiers.[76]

I have reason to think that passivity will not be found to be the norm. George VI (though I do not believe his influence, promoted though it was by two corners of the 'golden triangle' of 1945, Bridges and Lascelles, was decisive in Bevin's going to the Foreign Office rather than Dalton[77]), did pepper Attlee with his reservations about the intrusiveness of the state in the lives of his subjects thanks to the retention of many instruments of the wartime siege economy into the peace; and he was no believer in nationalization.[78] Though in favour of the principle of a National Health Service,[79] the King thought Gaitskell was right to place charges on teeth and spectacles in 1951 and told him so.[80] He did not, however, raise a squeak about the NATO treaty trenching on the prerogatives of peace and war when briefed on it by Ernest Bevin, a great Palace favourite;[81] and he was a stickler for his right to be consulted, flying into what his family called a 'gnash' if he thought his ministers were keeping him in the dark.[82]

His daughter, too, though a 'gnash-free zone' by comparison with her father, did have strong views about certain matters: Suez was one example (though Eden gave her no chance to express her concerns *fortissimo* at their autumn audiences in 1956).[83] Jim Callaghan has gone public on her influence on Rhodesia when he was Foreign Secretary,[84] and the former Australian Prime Minister, Bob Hawke, has blown the gaffe on the difficulties on matters of domestic policy in her relationship with Mrs Thatcher.[85] Already the Public Record Office files show how swiftly and fully informed she was even early in her reign on such delicate matters as nuclear weapons.[86]

One of my favourite vignettes from the present reign, provided by a very private but well placed source, is of Her Majesty's reaction to one of Harold Wilson's honours lists. When the roll of proposed honorands was placed before her she raised her eyes from a particular name and said to the Downing Street Private Secretary: 'Please remind the Prime Minister there is always time to think again.' That is what constitutional monarchs are for; even though in this instance the Prime Minister did not 'think again'.[87]

Another reason for sensing the existence of historical fruit still to be harvested from the Palace–No. 10 nexus is Her Majesty's own characterization of the weekly meetings as occasions when

> They unburden themselves or they tell me what's going on or if they've got any problems and sometimes one can help in that way too. They know that one can be impartial ... I think it's rather nice to feel that one's a sort of sponge and everybody can come and tell one things. And some things stay there and some things go out of the other ear and some things never come out at all. One just knows it ... And occasionally you can be able to put one's point of view which, perhaps they hadn't seen it from that angle.[88]

Indeed, the Queen's discretion is legendary. She is much more than a mere gilded sponge. If Nigel Lawson's testimony is any guide, she can offer a kind of catharsis by Royal appointment. In his memoirs Lord Lawson wrote: 'I recall telling the Queen, the one person to whom I could unburden myself in complete confidence, during my usual pre-Budget audience with her the following Monday, that I thought the 1988 Budget would be my last, because the Prime Minister was making the conduct of policy impossible.'[89] In fact, he did manage one more budget before he could take no more.

Still more reason to suspect the existence of a royal factor where personality and politics mingle at the apex of the British system of government came to light as the Queen's seventieth birthday approached in 1996. The journalist Graham Turner tempted some very experienced figures into telling him about the Queen's influence for the birthday portrait he prepared for *The Daily Telegraph*.[90] One senior civil servant, musing for Turner on the very special relationship between the monarch and her premiers, said: 'they know it would be very bad news for them politically if it got around that the Queen did not approve of government policy. I can certainly remember occasions when Mrs Thatcher said "The Queen wouldn't like that, so we can't do it." In that sense, the Queen is important to them politically.'[91]

Turner, in a richly revealing section of his article, distilled the human chemistry that has always been so important when the Sovereign deals with his or her ministers. Of the present Queen he wrote:

> Ministers . . . clearly hold her in considerable awe. 'I've been shouted down by Mrs Thatcher and it's very unpleasant,' said a member of the present Cabinet, 'but I'd much rather have that than take the Queen's disapproval. I just wouldn't want to take those eyes and those folded arms' . . . A suggestion to the Prime Minister about an appointment is accepted. 'Aha! so it worked,' she will murmur mysteriously.
>
> An 'Are you sure?' about a proposed honour provokes a rethink. And, when decisions have been taken at relatively low levels of government, the Queen has merely to 'express an interest' for that decision automatically to be reviewed at a higher level. The Queen, however, uses her influence sparingly.
>
> 'To an amazing extent,' says Douglas Hurd, 'she doesn't choose to exert it. Whether controversial opinion has been squeezed out of her or whether it's strict discipline on her part, it's almost uncanny the way in which she holds back. Queen Victoria, after all, was intervening the whole time.'[92]

Turner, too, exhumed some fascinating material on the Queen's difficulties with Mrs Thatcher, described to him by a former minister as 'a strange exotic beast' Her Majesty did not entirely understand. Just before Graham Turner embarked upon his trawl for revealing indiscretions, a huge official one had taken place courtesy of the thirty-year rule. The 1965 papers produced a gem which at least one highly placed figure in royal circles believes should not have been exposed to the light of day.[93]

Shortly after the unilateral declaration of independence by the Smith regime in Southern Rhodesia in November 1965, Harold Wilson developed the idea of despatching Lord Mountbatten, Chief of the Defence Staff, to Salisbury, Rhodesia, in an RAF Comet decked out as the Queen's Flight. Mountbatten would convey a KCVO (an honour in the Sovereign's personal gift) for her beleaguered Governor, Humphrey Gibbs, and would bestow it after his virtually unannounced arrival, thereby boosting the morale of the loyal and casting down the spirits of those who had seized independence illegally. Mountbatten indicated to Wilson (a) that he would be willing to undertake the mission and (b) that he would like to take one or two members of the Royal Household with him.

As a result, on the evening of 17 November 1965, Wilson's Principal Private Secretary, Sir Derek Mitchell, telephoned his opposite number at Buckingham Palace, Sir Michael Adeane, to convey Mountbatten's wishes. It was Mitchell's candid 'Note for the Record' of this bizarre (and soon to be aborted) enterprise whose release occasioned surprise a generation later.[94] On receiving Mitchell's message, 'Sir Michael Adeane went a little broody and said he would like to have a few hours to think about the proposition as a whole.' Just over three hours later Adeane rang Mitchell

> and said that he had discussed the matter fully with the Lord Chamberlain and that he and Lord Cobbold had raised the matter with The Queen. The Queen Herself had stressed that, although She had been attracted by the idea when it was mentioned to Her by the Prime Minister at his Audience on Tuesday, November 16, She had only given Her agreement to its being explored. If the Prime Minister wished to pursue the proposal She would want very definite advice, in terms, in writing and preferably publishable. Moreover, since this was a matter in which She was involved personally, it must be recognised by the Prime Minister that a negative answer might be returned.[95]

This was a breathtaking historical fragment almost worthy, at first glance, *of* Queen Victoria – a document which indicated a far from passively compliant Sovereign. That she might veto her premier *and* go public about it seemed barely credible. Certainly nothing like this had been declassified before for Queen Elizabeth's reign.

Explanation was required from seasoned guardians familiar with the gilt-edged relationships at the summit of government. The first came from a figure who knew all the *dramatis personae* well. Speaking of the mid-1960s Palace he said: 'They didn't trust the Prime Minister, of course. And Adeane and Cobbold certainly didn't trust Dickie [Mountbatten] who clearly wanted to do it flying in a Comet dressed up as the Queen's Flight.

'This [document] is Private Secretary talking to Private Secretary and Adeane is determined at all costs to protect the Queen constitutionally. Adeane and Cobbold were a pretty cautious pair. Reading it it's so unreal now.'[96]

'But,' I suggested, 'it's unusual for the Queen to contemplate giving a negative to Advice with a capital "A" coming from her Prime Minister.'

'That is unusual,' came the reply. 'But,' he added, 'if a Prime Minister wants the Queen to do something he doesn't just send in a proposal containing Advice with a capital "A". First of all, he sends in informal advice with a lower case "a" which enables the Queen to say "I wish you wouldn't." That's what was happening here over Rhodesia.'

'Can you think of any other occasion in the postwar period like this?' I asked.

'Absolutely not.'

'But the negative answer?'

'It's because the Queen is involved,' he explained. 'The KCVO is her decoration and it's the Queen's Flight. It touches her personally.'[97]

For a seasoned figure from a later generation the Rhodesia episode represented 'a classic case of the Queen's eyebrow being raised in a gentle way – a good case of the Queen exercising one of her Bagehotian rights [her right to warn]'.[98]

Yet in this very area of minister–monarch relations, however, Bagehot's search for the 'living reality' was unsuccessful. Had Bagehot been taken into Gladstone's confidence about his sessions with Victoria, that chapter in *The English Constitution* would have read very differently and might have depicted the relationship as trauma by Royal appointment rather than catharsis.[99] If even a fragment of the great lady's diary had been leaked to *The Economist*, her desire not just to harass but to influence (to put it no higher) would have become the common property of the nation.

It is known that the present Queen keeps a diary, managing about six hundred words most days. It is also known that she is a very shrewd and very funny observer of character and episode. It is also thought that nobody apart from Her Majesty has ever read her diaries; and almost certainly nobody will until her official biographer is appointed and granted access to them after her demise.[100] For me, as a disciple of Bagehot and the search for 'reality', these diaries are, and will remain, on the monarchical patch of the modern British Constitution, *the* most desirable bits of paper – a potentially fascinating running commentary on the 'most special relationship' since February 1952. Not long ago, I confided my craving to a very seasoned courtier. 'I have never seen them,' he said, 'but I suspect you would be disappointed and that they are just like her father's – about the weather.'[101] I live in hope (a) that they are not and (b) that it is a very long time indeed before they appear in public print. Sponges, especially royal ones, are one of the few commodities in respect of which high state secrecy is both necessary and desirable. And deferred gratification is the most intense of pleasures.

If, as I powerfully hope, Her Majesty's diary stretches beyond the output of her Meteorological Office, what might we discover from the extracts inserted in her official biography, in the manner Sir John Wheeler-Bennett adopted in his life of her father? Undoubtedly a monarch who always kept to the constitutional proprieties, 'encouraging' and 'warning', in Bagehot's terms, only when a Prime Minister made it plain he or she wished her to (though Her Majesty, I understand, is very good at pursuing a line of questions, in the Socratic manner, which give an indication of her concerns).[102] Possibly, too,

corroboration for Bob Hawke's hints about her distress at some of
the more socially divisive measures of 1980s British government.
Lord Charteris, a very well placed source indeed, despite the customary caveat, confirmed for me in 1994 that Her Majesty's views are
very much part of the warp and woof of the postwar settlement
at whose high-water mark (the famous era of 'Butskellism'[103]) she
ascended to her throne. 'You might say', he explained,

> that the Queen prefers a sort of consensus politics rather than a
> polarized one, and I suspect this is true, although I can't really
> speak from knowledge here. But if you are in the Queen's posi-
> tion, you are the titular, the symbolic head of a country, and the
> less squabbling that goes on in that country, obviously the more
> convenient and the more comfortable you feel. Therefore, I sus-
> pect – and I think it's only natural – that politics which are very
> polarized are very uncomfortable to the Sovereign. I think that
> must be so.[104]

For Her Majesty, this experience must have been rather like Alan
Bennett's brilliant characterization of the Royal Family's general
frustration – 'it's like being in opposition all their lives.'[105] If there
is any trace of this in the Queen's diary, and if, to any degree at
all, those views crossed that most sensitive constitutional membrane
between Her Majesty and her Premiers in the period since 1952, it
will feed the argument about the nature and extent, at some points
the very existence, of that fabled 'postwar consensus'[106] which, like
the argument about the true powers of the monarchy, is a debate
that will never (and should never) die – and the monarchy debate
will not cease unless, heaven forbid, we convert ourselves into a
republic (probably not even then).

Historians should not succumb to the temptations of forecasting.
It is not their trade. The past is not that kind of a guide. But, breaking
trade practice, I will venture to predict that whatever else Britain's
constitutional landscape may look like around the year 2020, there
will be a Windsor on the throne and that his name will be Charles
III or William V. For all the personal vicissitudes of some members
of the Royal Family and the ebb and flow of republican sentiment,
few have taken on board the sheer complexity of turning ourselves

into a republic. That great swathe of governmental activity which takes place under the Royal Prerogative would have to be put on a statutory basis. An Abolition of the Monarchy Bill, as a constitutional measure, would by convention have to be taken on to the floor of the House of Commons at every stage. It would paralyse the legislative timetable of any government that introduced it for at least two years and it would split the country from top to bottom. And would it be worth it? Would you trade Her Majesty the Queen for any of our defunct politicians? For believe me, the run-off for the Presidential Palace would probably be between Lady Thatcher and Lord Owen. It is simply not going to happen.

All the same, I did wonder if my good friend and source of constant constitutional stimulus, Tony Benn, might be on to something when he warned the Lord President of the Council in 1994 that he would use the Privy Council's proclamation of the next monarch to block the accession by objecting (an intention he first disclosed to the students on my 'Cabinet and Premiership' course during an impromptu seminar in the back garden of his Holland Park home on 30 April 1993). His hope was that his objection at the accession Council would invalidate the words of the Accession Proclamation, which declares: 'We therefore ... do now hereby, with one voice and consent of Tongue and Heart, publish and proclaim ...' Mr Benn, a Privy Counsellor since 1964, informed Tony Newton, the Lord President: 'I am writing to let you know that when the Privy Council is summoned to proclaim a new Monarch, after the death or abdication of the Queen, it is my solemn intention to express my opposition to the Proclamation and thus prevent it being issued by writing my objection on the draft proclamation and signing my name.'[107] Tony Benn's belief, of course, is that Parliament should elect the head of state.[108] Did his fashioning of the custom and practice of our monarchical past mean he had found, at its very heart, a truly effective republican instrument? It did not.

Tony Newton replied as follows:

> As you know, the right of succession was set out in the Act of Settlement of 1701. The arrangements enshrined in that Act could be changed only by Act of Parliament. The position there-

fore remains that the Heir Apparent would succeed immediately
and automatically to the Throne on the death of the Sovereign.

It would be for you to judge whether you felt able to accept a
Summons to a meeting of the Privy Council and, should you
accept, whether or not to sign the Proclamation. The registering
of an objection in the terms you have suggested would, however,
have no legal effect on the Proclamation itself, let alone on the
Accession, which would already have taken place.[109]

I stand by my prediction, even though Tony Benn, in the light of
Tony Newton's letter, swiftly started work 'on a draft for an Amendment to the Act of Settlement'.[110] We may or may not be a 'disguised
republic'; I think *not*. But I doubt very much that we shall become
a real one in my lifetime.

THREE

Premiership

Shadow and Substance

[The Prime Minister] is undoubtedly the most important member [of the Cabinet] but not a Monarch.

Clement Attlee, 1965[1]

I remember one summer evening in '21, sitting with Maynard Keynes and talking ... I said 'Has it ever occurred to you that Lloyd George has designs on the Constitution?' 'Oh,' he said, 'so that has passed through your mind too, has it?'

G. M. Young, 1952[2]

Heath himself once told me the moment when he decided that he could not serve under Margaret Thatcher. On a flight from Geneva to Paris, he read an interview with her in which she said there would be no room in her government for people who disagreed with the central thrust of policy.

John Cole, former BBC Political Editor, 1995[3]

It must be a conviction government. As Prime Minister I could not waste time having any internal arguments.

Margaret Thatcher, February 1979[4]

There are other heads of government whose powers are much greater ... [but] ... There is no headship of government in any country of comparable importance ... which bears the same combination of duties or demands the same qualities; those of national leader, negotiator, debater, orator on solemn occasions, representative of a constituency, manager of a party, executive head of the government, minister responsible for the Civil Service, the intelligence services and security.

David Dilks, 1992[5]

It's never a misfortune to become Prime Minister, it's always the greatest thing in your life. It's absolute heaven – I enjoyed every minute of it until those last few months of the 'Winter of Discontent'.

James Callaghan, 1991[6]

There is but one front door in the United Kingdom that has a BBC Television camera trained permanently upon it: No. 10 Downing Street. The only film we have, for example, of the moment of impact on the morning the IRA mortar bombed No. 10 when the Gulf 'war cabinet' was at work in the Cabinet Room (mercifully cutting short, as one insider put it to me, David Mellor's account of how as Chief Secretary to the Treasury he had been taking a begging-bowl labelled 'HMG' around the oil-rich Gulf kingdoms[7]) is the picture being filmed by that constantly running camera jumping in sympathy with the shock-wave. Legend has it that after Michael Heseltine's surprise departure from the Cabinet over Westland in January 1986, when the cameras only caught up with him as he strode, ever Corinthian, down Downing Street on his way back to the Ministry of Defence, it was decided that a continuously rolling camera was a small price to pay as insurance for capturing the great moments of our political time.

That front door, probably still the most famous in the world, is part of our national identity. We feel quite familiar with the person who – as First Lord of the Treasury, not as Prime Minister[8] – crosses and recrosses its threshold in the sense that they constantly fill our newspaper columns and television screens whatever their place on the overwhelming–underwhelming spectrum. And it is in this arena that we semi-consciously measure our Premiers since they made themselves into television personalities somewhere between Anthony Eden's party election broadcasts in the spring of 1955 and Harold Macmillan's enticing of General Eisenhower into No. 10 to do a joint world statesman routine as part of what political scientists would now call the 'long campaign' before the 1959 general election.[9]

Such familiarity with the incumbents and the place means, I suspect, that most people reckon they have a fairly good idea of what the country's top (non-hereditary) public job involves. But how much do we *really* know about what being Prime Minister means? Nearly a decade ago Anthony King, who has done as much as any scholar to illuminate the British premiership,[10] declared: 'Why, one asks, is the academic literature on the prime ministership so thin?'[11] Thin it is, certainly in comparison to the shelves that groan with studies of the United States presidency. Professor King's is a difficult question to answer, though it may have something to do with the illusion of familiarity with the office that we all acquire, beginning in the days of our youth when we start to compile a map of expectation in our minds about the premiership that is usually powerfully shaped by the first Prime Minister to whose ways we became accustomed in our formative years (Macmillan in my case).

But illusion it is. Let me illustrate this by adapting the famous question the Victorian child put to his father on espying the Empress of India: 'Dad, what is that lady for?' Ask 'What is the Prime Minister for?' and it is, and always has been, very difficult to answer the question – even in Mrs Thatcher's time when, one suspects, her answer might have been: 'to do everything as I can't rely on anybody else.' What, in fact, she did say, after the most dramatic fall in British political life since Neville Chamberlain's, was: 'I think sometimes the Prime Minister should be intimidating. There's not much point being a weak, floppy thing in the chair is there?'[12] If the testimony of several of her former ministerial colleagues is anything to go by, this is a near-perfect reflection of the tone and spirit of her opening remarks at many a Cabinet and Cabinet committee meeting – my own favourite being Malcolm Rifkind's recollection of the morning she came in to a ministerial meeting, 'banged her handbag down on the table and said: "Well, I haven't much time today, only enough time to explode and have my way!" ' (It was on the same programme – the television version of Kenneth Baker's memoirs – that Kenneth Clarke recalled her actually demanding at a meeting: 'Why do I have to do everything in this government?')[13]

Answering, as it were, the little boy's enquiry is a first-order question for those who would seek to understand the nature and scope of the British premiership. Only when a stab has been made at that – again in the grand Bagehotian tradition of seeking 'reality' while dispelling conventional wisdom where it fails to fit that reality – will it be possible to see how well modern Premiers have lived up to the requirements of their job and what might be done to give them a fighting chance of doing so more effectively in the future. And here, though it may sound like special pleading from me, the historian's craft is indispensable. Harold Wilson never uttered a truer word when in 1976 he described the job he had just left as 'a calling that must be one of the most exciting and certainly one of the best organised – organised by history – in the democratic world'.[14] Tony King put the same point another way. 'The person', he said, 'who walks for the first time through the door of No. 10 as Prime Minister does not create or re-create the prime ministership: the job, to a considerable extent, already exists.'[15] That is why (and this is not either the historians' trade union or intellectual snobbery at work here) it really does help if Walpole's lineal successors do have both an accurate and a real sense of their office and its past before they call their first Cabinet to order.

I was pleased, therefore, to read Sir Nicholas Henderson's diary entry for 20 December 1975 as it records that on a visit to the Paris Embassy, the Foreign Secretary and soon-to-be Prime Minister, James Callaghan, 'had brought with him for bedtime reading Robert Blake's book, *The Office of Prime Minister*.[16] Callaghan, who did not know until the following week, when tipped off by Harold Lever, that Harold Wilson's departure might not be too far away,[17] swiftly read the mind of HM Ambassador, who, no doubt, was clearly fascinated by the conjunction of *that* book and *those* hands. ' "God forbid I should ever have to be in Harold's shoes," Callaghan protested when he saw that I had caught sight of the title,' Henderson recalled.[18]

There is much argument about how one carbon-dates the emergence of the office of Prime Minister, a debate into which I shall not enter here. For me, as I suspect for Bagehot, the first *modern* Premier is Robert Peel. Bagehot warmed to Peel and was a connoisseur of his premiership. One of the best essays Bagehot ever penned was on 'The Character of Sir Robert Peel'[19] and it brought forth from him some of his finest lines on statesmanship and governance, including the dictum 'a constitutional Statesman is in general a man of common opinions and uncommon abilities'.[20] To that I would have added then, as now, 'and uncommon energies too' – because, from Peel to

Major, the sheer bone-tiring slog of the job is a consistent theme. The latest fragment of evidence to come my way for addition to the great mosaic of 150 years of prime ministerial 'overload' involves a private conversation in early 1963 between a pair of connoisseurs of both Peel and the premiership – Harold Macmillan (who was Prime Minister) and Rab Butler (who, perhaps, thought he ought to be). Butler's papers record that on 8 January 1963 'we had a short talk on the awfulness of going into business [rich pickings there for followers of Martin Wiener's thesis about the decline of the industrial spirit in Britain[21]] and that politics despite its dangers was the greatest game in the world. He said as PM "sometimes the strain is awful, you have to resort to Jane Austen." '[22]

Unlike Macmillan, who cultivated deliberate distractions (or, at least, feigned to), Peel was a glutton for work. Listen to his breakdown of what the job involved just before he vacated No. 10 as delivered to a promising protégé of his by the name of W. E. Gladstone:

> There is the whole correspondence with the Queen several times a day, and all requiring to be in my own hand, and to be carefully done; the whole correspondence with peers and members of parliament in my own hand, as well as other persons of consequence; the sitting seven or eight hours a day to listen in the House of Commons. Then I must, of course, have my mind in the principal subjects connected with the various departments . . . and all the reading connected with them . . . Then there is the difficulty that you have in conducting such questions on account of your colleague whom they concern.[23]

Mr Gladstone knew that 'learning from Nellie', to use a vulgarism from a later age, was hugely important for a post that not only was bereft of a job description but remained without mention on any official piece of paper until either 1878, when Disraeli signed the Treaty emerging from the Congress of Berlin as 'First Lord of Her Majesty's Treasury, *Prime Minister of England*',[24] or, if you will only accept a wholly British document, until December 1905, when a Royal Proclamation awarded 'the Prime Minister' a place in the order of precedence on state occasions one behind the Archbishop of York.[25] So, depending upon one's degree of pedantry, either Disraeli or Sir Henry Campbell-Bannerman wins the palm as the first *officially* recognized British Prime Minister. Not until 1917, with the Chequers Estate Act, did the office find itself noticed by statute.[26]

Gladstone, writing around the time Disraeli presumed to flaunt the title in the service of his country abroad, declared that 'Nowhere in the wide world does so great a substance cast so small a shadow; nowhere is there a man who has so much power with so little to show for it in the way of formal title or prerogative.'[27]

Peel, in fact, had elaborated a little on the functions of the Prime Minister four years after briefing Gladstone on its intricacies. In 1850 he told a House of Commons Select Committee on official salaries:

> You must presume that he [the PM] reads every important despatch from every Foreign Court. He cannot consult with the Secretary of State for Foreign Affairs and exercise the influence which he ought to have with respect to foreign affairs, unless he be master of everything of importance passing in that department. It is the same with respect to other departments: India, for instance; how can the Prime Minister be able to judge of the course of policy with regard to India, unless he be cognisant of all the current important correspondence? In the case of Ireland and the Home Department it is the same. Then the Prime Minister has the patronage of the Crown to exercise . . . ; he has to make inquiries into the qualifications of persons who are candidates; he has to conduct the whole of the communications with the Sovereign; he has to write, probably with his own hand, the letters in reply to all persons of station who address themselves to him; he has to receive deputations on public business; during the sitting of Parliament he is expected to attend six or seven hours a day . . . for five or six days a week; at least he is blamed if he is absent.[28]

Bagehot, as astute as ever, culled from Peel's testimony some important lessons about the condition of the mid-Victorian premiership. 'The necessary effect of all this labour', Bagehot wrote in that celebrated essay on Peel's character in 1856,

is that those subject to it have no opinions. It requires a great
deal of time to have opinions . . . That leisure which the poets say
is necessary to be good, or to be wise, is needful, for the humbler
task of allowing respectable maxims to take root respectably . . .
Our system, indeed, seems expressly provided to make it unlikely.
The most benumbing thing to the intellect is routine. You see this
in the description just given which is not exhaustive. Sir Robert
Peel once asked to have a number of questions carefully written
down which they asked him one day in succession in the House of
Commons. They seemed a list of everything that could occur in
the British Empire, or to the brain of a member of Parliament.
A premier's whole life is a series of such transitions. It is rather
wonderful that our public men have any minds left . . .[29]

Bagehot was describing what political scientists over a century
later depicted as 'overload'. Peel himself had had a good stab at this
when he said in 1845: 'I defy the minister of this country to perform
properly the duties of his office . . . The worst of it is that the
really important duties to the country – those out of the House of
Commons – are apt to be neglected.'[30] Bagehot, for his part, was
strong on both the causes and the consequences of tired minds trying
to do too much. In another essay on 'The Premiership', written in
1875, two years before he died, Bagehot attempted to capture the
further increase in workload over the quarter of a century since Peel
had outlined the problem before the Commons Select Committee
and had urged them to 'ascertain the progressive increase of business
in each department, caused in part by the advent of "the penny
post" '.[31] In doing so, Bagehot also drew up a useful job description
for the premiership which led him to doubt 'how long Mr Disraeli's
frame can stand such fatigues as these'.[32] For Bagehot detected

a process which has gone on augmenting from 1850 till now, till
it must make the miscellaneous work of a Prime Minister most
teasing and vexing. And independently of that, and considering
only the principal points, if we consider what it must be to lead
the House of Commons, to consult with, and often control, colleagues; to be chairman of the Cabinet; to compose the quarrels
of the Cabinet; to write to the Queen [this is the era before

Cabinet minutes were taken, remember] in the careful, delicate way necessary in dealing with a superior; to dispense the most critical patronage; to form some kind of idea of the legislative plans proposed and contemplated – we shall wonder how any man can be equal to so much.[33]

That, by my calculation, is seven chief functions of the Premier circa 1875. But Bagehot, in that uncanny way of his, goes on to pre-echo the findings of both the Haldane Report of 1918[34] and Ted Heath's 1970 White Paper on *The Reorganisation of Central Government*[35] by pointing out the need for a strategic analytical capacity over and above the numbing routine. Even the 1875 list, he declared,

> is scarcely all, for the Prime Minister is at the head of our business, and, like every head of a business, he ought to have *mind in reserve*. He must be able to take a fresh view of new contingencies, and keep an animated curiosity as to coming events. If he suffer himself to be involved in minutiae, some great change in the world, some Franco-German war may break out, like a thief in the night, and if he has no *elastic thought* and no *spare energy*, he may make the worst errors. [emphasis added][36]

'Mind in reserve', 'elastic thought', 'spare energy' – these phrases have a certain salience inside the late twentieth-century 'Cabinet circle', to borrow a phrase of Churchill's.[37] Bagehot rounded off this prescient passage with one of his most famous bons mots: 'A great Premier must add the vivacity of an idle man to the assiduity of a very laborious one.'[38] Not a bad aspiration for an academic, too, come to think of it.

Three years after Bagehot committed these vibrant one-liners to the pages of *The Economist*, Gladstone displayed his own thoughts on the nature of premiership in the pages of the *North American Review* as part of a comparison of the British and American ways of government entitled, interestingly enough, 'Kin Beyond Sea'.[39] Gladstone was a great dissembler on this theme: no advocate he of any prototypical argument about prime ministerial government. For him, it had to be a 'Government of Departments',[40] and, like several of his successors, he tended to stress how puny were the powers of the monarch's first minister. In his Anglo-American comparison he said: 'The head of the British Government is not a Grand Vizier. He has no powers, properly so called, over his colleagues: on the rare occasions, when a Cabinet determines its course by the votes of its members, his vote counts as only one of theirs.'[41] Immediately, however, he contradicted himself by homing in on the Prime Minister's power to hire and fire, a power Enoch Powell a century later likened to those of Henry VIII ('conversation in the Cabinet is a conversation influenced by the knowledge that we all have to hang together . . . [but] . . . it's like having a debate with Henry VIII in the chair . . . I was conscious that he [Harold Macmillan, PM 1957–63] had the axe down by his chair').[42] Ministers, Mr Gladstone said plainly, 'are appointed and dismissed by the Sovereign on his advice'.[43] And, if knowledge is the currency of power, the Grand Old Man had the measure of the Prime Minister's share of that particular treasury too:

> In a perfectly organised administration, such for example as was that of Sir Robert Peel, in 1841–6, nothing of great importance is matured, or would even be projected, in any department without his personal cognisance; and any weighty business would commonly go to him before being submitted to the Cabinet. He reports to the Sovereign its proceedings, and he also has many audiences of the august occupant of the Throne.[44]

Gladstone takes note, too, of what in today's argot we would call the Premier's 'self-destruct button' but which I, and I suspect he, would prefer to be seen as the Sampson-in-the-Temple prerogative: 'As a rule', he wrote, 'the resignation of the First Minister, as if removing the bond of cohesion in the Cabinet, has the effect of dissolving it.'[45]

Neither his contemporaries nor his colleagues were deceived by this Gladstonian camouflage. Morley, in his famous 1889 life of Walpole, was widely regarded as describing Cabinet life under Gladstone rather than the man commonly accepted as first holder of the office of Prime Minister. Indeed, he admitted as much to Asquith.[46]

Morley depicted the Prime Minister as 'the keystone of the Cabinet arch' and went on to deploy a Latin phrase that has rung down the years ever since:

> Although in Cabinet all its members stand on an equal footing, speak with equal voices and, on the rare occasions when a division is taken, are counted on the fraternal principle of one man, one vote, yet the head of the Cabinet is primus inter pares, and occupies a position which, so long as it lasts, is one of exceptional and peculiar authority.[47]

Indeed, Morley continued, 'the flexibility of the Cabinet system allows the Prime Minister in an emergency to take upon himself a power not inferior to that of a dictator, provided always that the House of Commons will stand by him.'[48]

Add to the late nineteenth-century reality of Cabinet Room life as sketched by Morley the fact that from 1870 Gladstone ended the practice whereby Cabinet members other than the Prime Minister could call meetings of what Sidney Low was later to call 'the most powerful committee in the world',[49] and you have what I think amounts to the first unarguably fully modern premiership. Peel was the model (Rosebery was right to describe him as 'in name and deed that functionary, so abhorred and repudiated by the statesmen of the eighteenth century, a Prime Minister');[50] but Gladstone turned precedent into procedure, adding an important prerogative to the armoury of premiership – the power to summon or not to summon a meeting of the Cabinet.[51] 'Agenda setting', we would call it today.

A Premier's inheritance is most certainly 'organized by history'; but, as a history-maker himself or herself, a new Prime Minister can add to this particular piece of the national heritage, which grows like coral or, in a possibly apter metaphor, like a stately home which acquires additions and alterations with each succeeding generation as if it were a kind of Hatfield House. On the subject of Hatfield, we know what the Marquess of Salisbury thought a Premier should be, thanks to his rather catty remarks about other holders of the office to his nephew A. J. Balfour, himself a future Prime Minister. Salisbury did not care much for the top job. His heart lay always in the Foreign Office, where the Cabinet would meet, symbolically enough, when Lord S. held both posts simultaneously. As Balfour put it: 'He knew his capacity as Foreign Secretary; he knew that the country had need of his services, and he gladly gave them. But as Prime Minister he was required also to do other work equally important, but much less congenial and though he did it, he did not always do it gladly.'[52] It was in a discussion about Disraeli at Hatfield in May 1880 that the Marquess ventured his notions of what premiership should be by using Disraeli as an exemplar of what its holder should not be. 'As a politician', Lord S. said,

> he [Disraeli] was exceedingly short-sighted, though very clear-sighted. He neither could, nor would, look far ahead, or attempt to balance remote possibilities . . .
>
> As the head of a Cabinet his fault was want of firmness. The chiefs of Departments got their own way too much. The Cabinet as a whole got it too little, and this necessarily followed from having at the head of affairs a statesman whose only final political principle was that the Party must on no account be broken up, and who shrank therefore from exercising coercion on any of his subordinates.[53]

Interestingly enough, it was the apparently languid Balfour who as Premier not only sharpened up the machinery of government by creating the Committee of Imperial Defence and by putting himself in its chair,[54] but also ended the uncertainty about a Prime Minister's absolute power to hire and fire ministers[55] – though it was not until Lloyd George's time that it was finally established that only a Prime Minister can ask the Sovereign for a dissolution of Parliament.[56]

It is striking that most of the first-hand sources on what a Prime Minister is for have come from holders of the office musing on their predecessors. There is a kind of freemasonry or trade unionism about this. Harold Wilson begins his account with the famous quote from Asquith's memoirs that 'the office of the Prime Minister is what its holder chooses and is able to make of it.'[57] Asquith in his turn looked to Rosebery;[58] and Rosebery looked to Peel.[59] In more recent times, James Callaghan has told me that experience as a junior minister, with occasional Cabinet attendance, under Attlee and full Cabinet service under Wilson helped shape his own Downing Street craft.[60] Of all of them it is Rosebery, though Premier for only a very short span a century ago, who set himself most directly to answer the question: 'What is a Prime Minister?'[61] His answer is worth savouring at length, not least for the strange pre-echo of relatively recent events with which he concluded. The title of Prime Minister, Rosebery declared,

> expresses much to the British mind. To the ordinary apprehension it implies a dictator, the duration of whose power finds its only limit in the House of Commons. So long as he can weather that stormful and deceptive ocean he is elsewhere supreme.[62]

Shades of Morley there.[63] But, Rosebery continues,

> the reality is very different. The Prime Minister . . . is technically and practically the Chairman of an Executive Committee of the Privy Council, or rather perhaps, of privy councillors, the influential foreman of an executive jury. His power is mainly personal, the power of individual influence. That influence, whatever it may be, he has to exert in many directions before he can have his way. He has to deal with the Sovereign, with the Cabinet, with Parliament and with public opinion, all of them potent factors in their various kinds and degrees.[64]

But even in the 1890s Rosebery knew well where the locus of real constraint lay:

> A machinery liable to so many grains of sand requires obviously all the skill and vigilance of the best conceivable engineer. And yet without the external support of his Cabinet he is disarmed. The resignation of a colleague, however relatively insignificant, is a storm signal.[65]

That passage is the strange pre-echo of events in Whitehall and Westminster in November 1990, the dramatic change in the political weather pattern brought about by Sir Geoffrey Howe's resignation and the storm which blew Margaret Thatcher out of Downing Street, the crucial moment being the evening of 21 November when between a half and two-thirds of the Cabinet told her she could not go on – the night she unforgettably described as 'treachery with a smile on its face'.[66] In a rather rambling way, she caught this perfectly in a television interview eight months later. 'It was just very strange,' she said. 'Have you seen a situation slip away from you? I'm a politician . . . I can sense it. And when some people whom I expected to be absolutely staunch had very different views, said, "Look, I will support you, but I don't think that it is a foregone conclusion," then . . . No general can fight without a really good army behind.'[67]

Eavesdropping on former Prime Ministers is fascinating and adds to the stock of knowledge. But, in the end, it is infuriatingly imprecise, and goes only so far towards the piecing together of that elusive job description for the British premiership. I have something of a taste for the sweet and the sour in scholarly life – political science plus archive, allowing as accurate a sense of the past as possible to inform the here-and-now. Cabinet and premiership is an area that cries out for this as the debate, now on its zimmerframe, between the Prime Ministerial School and the continuing detectors of Genuine Cabinet Government all too often collapses into competitive anecdote at what Anthony King has called 'the level of a bar room brawl'.[68] My preferred approach not just to this controversy, but to British constitutional matters generally, has been to raid the files at the Public Record Office to see what the keepers or guardians of the Constitution in the Cabinet Office, No. 10 and Buckingham Palace – the enduring 'golden triangle'[69] – *thought* it was at any given moment.

In Mr Attlee's time, according to the collective wisdom of Whitehall and the Palace in the era of Edward Bridges, Norman Brook and Alan 'Tommy' Lascelles, as recorded in the 1947–9 file on the 'Function of the Prime Minister and his Staff',[70] it was something like this. (This is my summary, not the precise wording of the document.)

1 Managing the relationship between the monarch and the government as a whole;
2 hiring and firing ministers;
3 chairing the Cabinet and its most important committees;
4 arranging other 'Cabinet business', i.e. the chairmanships of other committees, their membership and agendas;

Above The King in the garden of Buckingham Palace with his new Labour
Ministers in 1945. Left to right: Herbert Morrison, Clement Attlee,
HM the King, Arthur Greenwood, Ernest Bevin (a great Palace favourite)
and A. V. Alexander.

Below 'One's a sort of sponge and everybody can come and tell one things':
the Queen in No.10 with her premiers James Callaghan,
Alec Douglas-Home, Margaret Thatcher, Harold Macmillan,
Harold Wilson and Edward Heath.

Above H. H. Asquith paying off a taxi: 'Power, power? You may
think you are going to get it but you never do.'
Below Peter Brookes's view of Scott – but the report itself
had limited political impact.

"*Once you've put it down, you can't pick it up.*"

Above Clement Attlee in the Cabinet Room with Francis Williams: 'Ministers are not mere creatures of the Prime Minister.'

Right Sir Alan ('Tommy') Lascelles: his letter to *The Times* in May 1950 became the standard constitutional text on the monarch's personal powers for over forty years.

Above Sir Derek Mitchell (centre in cardigan) watches Harold Wilson briefing the press at Heathrow: Mitchell's single sheet of paper took care of all the possibilities on election night 1964.

Opposite page 'The Queen's government must be carried on' inside her 'back-of-the-envelope' nation: Derek Mitchell's drill for the 1964 election (held on 15 October), drawn up in the middle of the night when the results declared showed the outcome might be inconclusive.

Key: for details of the 'Deadlock' memorandum see pages 63–4.
Timings taken from the last transfer of power in October 1951.
(Council = Privy Council needed for the swearing-in of new ministers.)

MA = Sir Michael Adeane, the Queen's Private Secretary
HW = Harold Wilson, whose home was in Hampstead Garden Suburb
BP = Buckingham Palace
Mrs W = Mary Wilson
ADH = Sir Alec Douglas-Home
Agnew = Sir Godfrey Agnew, Clerk of the Privy Council
FW = Freddie Warren, Private Secretary to the Chief Whip
HB = Herbert Bowden, Labour's Chief Whip

Taken from Public Record Office, PREM 11/4756

— 51 file

— Deadlock note — in case

— 16/10   1951   Attlee went to Palace   5·30   Fri
           WSC   5·45

                 Council at 3 p.m.   Sat

                          announcement from No 10
                            " time.

                   MA   tel. HW ? at Hampstead
                        No 10 car   ↓
— Talk to Agnew   BP

F.W — HB   phone no ?   ' morning dress for this
                      (subsequently lounge suit (as Attlee))

                    alone in car   ? police
                       ↓ No 10
     ? Chequers   ← ADH   then telek Mrs W

                          ? evening meal

Above Sir Norman Brook (left) and Harold Macmillan in September 1962, showing the strain of the burden of government which Brook persuaded Macmillan to have examined in 1957.

Below Ted Heath briefing the press as Prime Minister, flanked by Sir Donald Maitland, his Press Secretary (left), and Sir William Armstrong, Head of the Home Civil Service (right). Armstrong produced the first draft on the functions of the postwar premiership in 1947.

5 overall control of the Civil Service;
6 the allocation of functions between departments, their creation and abolition;
7 relationships with other heads of government;
8 a specially close involvement in foreign policy and defence matters;
9 top Civil Service appointments;
10 top appointments to many institutions of 'a national character';
11 'certain scholastical and ecclesiastical appointments';
12 the handling of 'precedent and procedure'.

To those dozen late-1940s functions I would, had I (though less than three months old when the file began to do the rounds in Whitehall in 1947) been invited in to help, have added the following:

1 special responsibility for the secret services;
2 the making of nuclear weapons policy;
3 managing relations with opposition leaders;
4 preparing the 'War Book' in case the country found itself engaged once more in serious hostilities;
5 responsibility for the overall load on government and Whitehall efficiency generally;
6 managing the 'special relationship' with the United States (as part of that heads of government section);
7 managing changes in the United Kingdom's constitutional relationship with the Empire and/or its former members.

To the best of my knowledge no modern equivalent of that 1949 document exists in the Cabinet Secretary's cupboard. If one did, what would it look like? Between Attlee and Major those functions have increased in a fashion that would leave Peel, Gladstone, Salisbury, Balfour and Asquith (and even Lloyd George) breathless, though they would have been surprised that their successors after the Second World War no longer led the House of Commons (Attlee appointed Morrison Leader of the House in 1945). I have made an attempt at constructing a mock-up, grouping these grossly expanded functions into bundles.

Constitutional and procedural

1 Managing the relationship between government and monarch;
2 managing the relationship between the government and the opposition on a Privy Counsellor basis;
3 establishing the order of precedence in Cabinet;
4 interpretation and content of procedural guidelines, both for ministers and for civil servants (including the final say in whether they should appear before parliamentary committees);
5 changes to Civil Service recruitment practices;
6 classification levels and secrecy procedures for official information;
7 requesting the Sovereign to grant a dissolution of Parliament.

Appointments

A caveat here: by 'appointment' I mean the recommendation of an appointment to the Queen, in whose name all these things are done.

1 Appointment and dismissal of ministers (final approval of their Parliamentary Private Secretaries and special advisers);
2 appointments to the headships of the intelligence and security services;
3 top appointments to the Home Civil Service and, in collaboration (with the Foreign Secretary) to the Diplomatic Service plus (with the Defence Secretary) to the armed forces;
4 top ecclesiastical appointments, plus a handful of regius professorships and the mastership of Trinity College, Cambridge;
5 top public-sector appointments and top appointments to Royal Commissions and committees of inquiry;
6 the award of peerages and honours (except for those in the gift of the Sovereign).

Conduct of Cabinet and parliamentary business

1 Calling meetings of Cabinet and its committees; fixing their agendas;
2 calling 'political Cabinets' with no officials present;
3 deciding issues where Cabinet or Cabinet committees are unable to agree;
4 granting ministers permission to miss Cabinet meetings or to leave the country;
5 ultimate responsibility (with the Leaders of the Houses) for the government's legislative programme and the use of government time in the chambers of both Houses;
6 answering questions twice a week (when the House of Commons is sitting) on nearly the whole range of government activities.

Organizational and efficiency questions

1 Organization and staffing of No. 10 and the Cabinet Office;
2 size of Cabinet; workload on ministers and the Civil Service; the overall efficiency of government;
3 the overall efficiency of the secret services, their operations and their oversight;
4 the creation, abolition and merger of government departments and executive agencies;
5 preparation of the 'War Book';
6 contingency planning on the civil side (with the Home Secretary), e.g. for industrial action that threatens essential services or for counter-terrorism;
7 overall efficiency of the government's media strategy.

Budget and market-sensitive economic decisions

1 Determining, with the Chancellor of the Exchequer, the detailed contents of the budget (by tradition, the full Cabinet is apprised of the full contents of the budget statement only on the morning before it is delivered; but since the inauguration of the 'combined budget' in November 1993, a Cabinet committee shapes the content of the public

expenditure component of the budget ahead of its final compilation);

2 determining which ministers (in addition to the Chancellor) will be involved, and in what fora, in the taking of especially market-sensitive economic decisions such as the level of interest rates.

Special foreign and defence functions

1 Relationships with heads of government (e.g. the nuclear and intelligence aspects of the US–UK 'special relationship');
2 representing the United Kingdom at 'summits' of all kinds;
3 with the Defence Secretary, the use of the Royal Prerogative to deploy Her Majesty's forces in action;
4 with the Foreign Secretary, the use of the Royal Prerogative to sign or annul treaties, recognize or derecognize countries;
5 the launching of a UK nuclear strike (with elaborate and highly secret fall-back arrangements in place in case the Prime Minister and the Cabinet were wiped out by a bolt from the blue in a pre-emptive strike: the so-called 'Decapitation' scenario or 'Headless Chickens' scenario, depending upon the level of *comédie noire* prevailing in Whitehall).

Symbolically enough, the last act a British Prime Minister would take is not a matter for the Cabinet but one for the PM alone.[71] The Polaris or Trident missile would erupt from the Atlantic thanks to a prime ministerial decision made by the Premier under the Royal Prerogative in the name of the Queen.

This is not a bad list of powers for a politician whose job is mentioned, almost in passing, in but a handful of statutes and who did not exist officially until 1905. Morley was right: those powers are not inferior, in an emergency, to those of a dictator, provided (the nuclear strike apart) that the Cabinet first, his or her Party second, Parliament third and the electorate (a long way fourth) can be carried. Modern commentators have echoed Morley on this. Anthony King concluded in 1991 that the British Prime Minister 'is probably able to be more powerful inside his or her own government than any head of government anywhere else in the democratic world',[72] while twelve years earlier Tony Benn had declared that it was time 'to transform an Absolute Premiership into a Constitutional Premiership'.[73]

Two interlocking thoughts are stimulated by that potent yet paralysing audit of functions which fall to a modern British Prime Minister almost irrespective of party and whether they crave a big state, a little state or something in between. First, should they have so much personal power? Second, can any one human frame stand the workload and pressures which accompany them, not least the now near-constant foreign travel? Peel thought the job was beyond a single person 150 years ago when the apparatus of government really did accord with Lasalle's notion of the 'night-watchman state',[74] and he certainly did not have to visit those countries and colonies whose lives he so assiduously monitored through despatches from Her Majesty's Ambassadors and Governors-General.

The rating of superpowerdom slipped from the United Kingdom when India won its independence in 1947, if not earlier. But the hangover of greatpowerdom (or 'the itch after the computation' as a senior figure in the British Intelligence community put it to me[75]), still strongly conditions the contents of a British Premier's diary in the late twentieth century. *The Economist* calculated in the summer of 1994 that Mr Major's

> trip to the Hague and Berlin on September 7th and 8th was his 63rd foreign expedition, excluding holidays, since he became Prime Minister in 1990 ... Mr Major has spent all or part of 164 of his 1,381 days in office outside Britain. And that of course does not include the days spent on foreign affairs in No. 10; the telegrams, the meetings, lunches, dinners and receptions for visitors from faraway countries of which he generally knows little.[76]

Much of this tally, of course, depends on whether you now count European affairs as wholly foreign. As *The Economist* pointed out, some two-thirds of these trips are to other member states of the European Union, and it noted a new tradition of Euro-summitry creeping in beneath the regular and even the 'special' European Councils, a new tradition (if there can be such a thing) 'of two bilateral summits a year with the Germans, two with the French and one with the Italians'.[77]

Weighing and juggling those bundles of prime ministerial responsibilities, foreign and domestic, leads me to the conclusion that even a politician of truly 'uncommon abilities', with a well-stocked 'reserve mind' capable of truly 'elastic thought' plus a physique throbbing with 'spare energy' to match the experienced little grey cells and an alimentary canal robust enough to cope with the gastronomic demands of first ministership[78] would be hard pressed to meet the modern job specification exhausting week upon punishing year, despite the Rolls-Royce service in No. 10 and the alleged comforts of the RAF's charming old VC10 when Downing Street is in transit (though, sensibly, No. 10 concluded a 'bargain basement' deal with British Airways to acquire Concorde to zip Mr Major across the Atlantic and back for his 'special relationship' patch-up session with President Clinton in April 1995[79]). The model of a modern Prime Minister would be a kind of grotesque composite freak – someone with the dedication to duty of a Peel, the physical energy of a Gladstone, the detachment of a Salisbury, the brains of an Asquith, the balls of a Lloyd George, the word-power of a Churchill, the administrative gifts of an Attlee, the style of a Macmillan, the managerialism of a Heath and the sleep requirements of a Thatcher. Human beings do not come like that.

Is part of the solution to reduce that workload – to ease it in such a way that the dangers of an overmighty as well as an overburdened premiership are mitigated simultaneously through a more sensible sharing of power and load within what is already supposed to be a 'collective executive',[80] to borrow the phrase of Lord Hunt of Tanworth, the former Secretary of the Cabinet? Isn't this, after all, to reprise the child's question about Queen Victoria, what Cabinet government is meant to be for? It is to that truly ancient entity – far more venerable than any notion of a 'sole' or a 'prime' minister – that I shall turn in the next chapter.

FOUR

Cabinet

The Necessary Shambles

The central directing instrument of government, in legislation as well as in administration, is the Cabinet. It is in Cabinet that administrative action is co-ordinated and that legislative proposals are sanctioned. It is the Cabinet which controls Parliament and governs the country. In no other country is there such a concentration of power and such a capacity for decisive action as that possessed by a British Cabinet, provided always that it enjoys the support of a majority in the House of Commons.

Leo Amery, 1947[1]

The word 'Cabinet' is not a term of art; it is indeed unknown in Constitutional law.

H. H. Asquith, 1926[2]

The essential principle of our British system is that of collective responsibility. Ministers are not mere creatures of the Prime Minister, but for the most part, elected representatives, Ministers responsible to the Crown, parliament and the electorate ... An approach to one-man Government is in my view a mistake.

Lord Attlee, 1960[3]

Her style of government was a subject of permanent fascination to her ministers. They had never met such a bossy woman ... Margaret Thatcher had quickly moved away from the *prima inter pares* doctrine of premiership. There were times when she seemed unable to treat her colleagues as grown-ups, much less as equals.

John Cole, former BBC Political Editor, 1995[4]

Thanks to the regular picture of their one o'clock dispersal down the steps of No. 10 every Thursday lunchtime (not a minute later, lest the waiting journalists smell a crisis[5]), we are almost as familiar with the 'idea' of the Cabinet as we are with the 'job' of Prime Minister. But probe an inch below that familiarity and, as usual, you find ambiguity, fluidity and uncertainty.

Living as we do under a system of government without precise rules for the conduct of affairs that are formally agreed and made public – a system largely free of both regulations and referees – it is very difficult, at any given moment, to know what norms of behaviour and procedure are thought to be proper and necessary for the exercise of genuine Cabinet government. It is rather like Ben Pimlott's characterization of the great 'postwar consensus' debate. 'The British postwar consensus', he wrote, 'could be defined, not entirely flippantly, as the product of a consensus among historians about those political ideas that should be regarded as important, and hence to be used as touchstones of the consensus.'[6] When engaged upon tackling the never-ending problem of trying to pin down the fluid and elusive relationship between the Prime Minister and the Cabinet (a subject which, as Sir Claud Schuster vividly and accurately put it, 'like the procreation of eels, is slippery and mysterious'[7]), we can find ourselves relying very heavily on the *obiter dicta* of experienced and widely respected figures – insiders talking about an insiders' system and contributing powerfully thereby to its continuity and preservation.

The notion and the practice of Cabinet government are very susceptible to this tendency. It was, for example, at a significant moment at the height of the Westland crisis that Douglas Hurd, then Home Secretary, declared one Sunday in conversation on television with Brian Walden: 'I think it is very important that people should see that we are under Cabinet government. I think that is what people prefer and want to know about . . . they want to see that it is Cabinet.' (This was a near-perfect echo of Gladstone's declaration in 1884 that 'in the public mind and in ordinary practice the Cabinet is viewed as the seat of ultimate responsibility.'[8] Hurd's was a threefold message. It was addressed in the first place to a political nation alarmed by the bonfire of conventions which quite plainly had characterized the Westland affair up to that point,[9] and in the second place to a certain viewer in No. 10 who enjoyed her own special media relationship with Mr Walden and who had famously announced her intention of running 'a conviction government';[10] and finally, in his scholarly way, Mr Hurd was signalling that certain constitutional bequests from the past had a utility far higher than mere antiquarianism, indeed, that they were an essential requirement if our political system was to be kept clean and decent and efficient.

The use of the word 'efficient' instantly conjures up the spirit of Walter Bagehot. For, in penetrating the mid-Victorian Cabinet Room, he believed he had discovered 'the efficient secret of the English Constitution',[11] in contrast to the *'dignified* parts ... those which excite and preserve the reverence of the population',[12] in particular the monarchy. Has this central component of the Bagehotian analysis held firm? Compare two disquisitions on Cabinet government from a pair of supremely intelligent observers, separated by nearly a century and a half though linked by a shared tendency towards Whiggishness. First, naturally, Bagehot himself, writing in 1867. For him,

> The efficient secret of the English Constitution may be described as the close union, the nearly complete fusion, of the executive and legislative powers ... The connecting link is the Cabinet. By that new word we mean a committee of the legislative body selected to be the executive body ... A Cabinet is a combining committee – a hyphen which joins, a buckle which fastens, the legislative part of the State to the executive part of the State. In its origin it belongs to the one, in its functions it belongs to the other ... The committee ... by virtue of that combination, is, while it lasts and holds together, the most powerful body in the state.[13]

Next Nigel Lawson, the former Chancellor of the Exchequer, talking in March 1994 at an Institute of Historical Research seminar:

What most people think of as the Cabinet is really the least important part of being a member of the Cabinet . . . that is the pictures they see on television of ministers trooping in for the weekly Cabinet meeting on Thursday mornings and trooping out again. When I was a minister I always looked forward to the Cabinet meeting immensely because it was, apart from the summer holidays, the only period of real rest that I got in what was a very heavy job. Cabinet meetings are ninety percent of the time a dignified [rather than an] efficient part of Cabinet government.[14]

Even allowing for the fact that nowadays Cabinet committees are as much a part of Cabinet government as is the full Cabinet itself (and that he was describing the ecology of Mrs Thatcher's 'conviction Cabinet'), Lawson's remarks do indicate that things have changed since Bagehot attempted his composite of Cabinet life in the days of Peel, Derby, Disraeli and Lord John Russell.

Toss in a third quotation from John Wakeham, who sat with Lawson in Mrs Thatcher's Cabinet and survived her demise as PM to deliver this description of Cabinet life under John Major, and you will see that there is life left yet in an ancient debate:

We have a system of Cabinet government. The Prime Minister is *primus inter pares*; he is the Minister who chairs the Cabinet . . . executive powers – either under Royal Prerogative or Act of Parliament – formally rest with the Ministers of the Crown who run government departments. They ought to be in the lead in their policy areas. The Prime Minister has very few formal powers. The most important is to appoint the right people to his Cabinet and give them the right jobs to do . . . because of the doctrine of collective responsibility, the process of Cabinet government has to work by building consensus. Colleagues must be able to support collective decisions. It is not possible to conduct business by putting them in a position where the only options they have are to submit or resign.[15]

Who *can* he have had in mind? Finally, in a Bagehot-style bonding metaphor, Lord Wakeham declared in the same lecture, delivered at Brunel University in November 1993: 'Many commentators who bemoan what they see as the decline of the Cabinet as a decision-taker fail to appreciate its significance as the cement which binds the government together.'[16]

These extracts show that the debate about prime ministerial versus Cabinet government in Britain may be on a zimmerframe, but it's a zimmerframe of fire: the argument still glows! This, however, has been a hugely question-begging opening section. What is this 'Cabinet government' around which the argument swirls, this 'Cabinet system' whose 'gradual growth and final establishment', according to the former Unionist Prime Minister, A. J. Balfour, 'has been of greater importance than anything in our constitutional history since the Revolution settlement – greater, for instance, than the series of Reform Bills which began in 1832 [I have to differ with A. J. B. here]' until it became 'embedded in the very centre of constitutional practice'? Balfour's view was reprised by another equally self-conscious Conservative intellectual, Lord Hailsham, in his 1987 Granada Guildhall Lecture, when he reached into his bag of hyperbole and described Cabinet government as 'one of the permanent gifts conferred by British political genius on the science and art of civilized government'.[17]

For that great cartographer of the mid-century British Cabinet, Sir Ivor Jennings, it was simply the sun around which the entire constitutional constellation revolved:

> The Cabinet is the core of the British constitutional system. It is the supreme directing authority. It integrates what could otherwise be a heterogeneous collection of authorities exercising a vast variety of functions. It provides unity to the British system of government. If, therefore, a constituent assembly were to set out in a written document the present British Constitution, as it is actually operated [that will be the day, given that we can't even see the Precedent Book[18]], the Cabinet would be provided for in a prominent place.[19]

Interestingly enough, Jennings put the Cabinet first in his hierarchy of importance, with the Prime Minister a close second:

In the Cabinet and, still more, out of it, the most important person is the Prime Minister. It is he who is primarily concerned with the formation of a Cabinet, with the subjects which the Cabinet discusses, with the relations between the King and the Cabinet and between the Cabinet and Parliament, and with the co-ordination of the machinery of government subject to the control of the Cabinet. He, too, would be given a prominent place in a written Constitution.[20]

In taking this line, Jennings is very much in accord with Arthur Balfour's notion of Cabinet government as *the* crucial phenomenon in Britain's constitutional arrangements, even though, as Balfour continued, 'It never became a Party watchword; it was never clamoured for by a mob; it has never been recognised by statute; nor can any man tell us exactly when it became fully effective.'[21]

My preferred tactic when searching for the British Constitution – plundering the insider files of its guardians – is not entirely successful when it comes to the working notions of Cabinet government in the postwar period. The nearest thing we have is a lecture prepared for the BBC's European Service by Lord Hankey in the spring of 1946. Hankey, the first Secretary of the Cabinet, designer of the Cabinet Secretariat and, with Lloyd George, the joint creator of the modern Cabinet system,[22] circulated his text to his successor, Sir Edward Bridges, and to Sir Albert Napier, Permanent Secretary at the Lord Chancellor's Office, saying he would 'be grateful if [they] would glance through it to see if it contains anything that is constitutionally incorrect or objectionable'.[23]

After quoting G. M. Trevelyan's *History of England* on Sir Robert Walpole, 'who did most to evolve the principle of the common responsibility of the Cabinet, and the supremacy of the Prime Minister as the leading man at once in the Cabinet and in the Commons',[24] Hankey declared (with official approval):

The main features of that description – the common responsibility of the King's principal Ministers, who are all Privy Counsellors, for the policy of the Government and for one another's actions; the supremacy of the Prime Minister; their collective responsibility to Parliament and especially to the House of

Commons, which alone can vote the money to carry out their policy – remain the guiding principles of the British constitution.[25]

Significantly enough, the Lord Chancellor's Office file in which this time-honoured wisdom is preserved is entitled 'Principles of Cabinet System and the Work of the Cabinet Secretariat'.[26]

In the absence of a definitive insider file (or as definitive as one can ever find in the British system of government), my own preferred path to the inner core of Cabinet government is to see it as a process, as a way of doing business – a view with which some ex-insiders have considerable sympathy. Among scholarly seekers of this Holy Grail of the British Constitution, it was Colin Seymour-Ure, reacting to the experience of the first Wilson Cabinets of 1964–70, who first developed such an approach. Professor Seymour-Ure argued that 'the importance of the Cabinet as an institution appears to have diminished to the point where it ought properly to be described as no more than *primus inter pares* among other government committees, just as the Prime Minister used to be called *primus inter pares* among his colleagues.'[27] I do not subscribe to this 'parity of importance' idea. Formal Cabinet committees are qualitatively different from other ministerial groups or interdepartmental committees – a subject to which I shall return in a moment in the context of Nigel Lawson, Mrs Thatcher and the Exchange Rate Mechanism debate of the mid- to late 1980s.[28] It is, however, in a supplementary thought of Colin Seymour-Ure's – 'that the Cabinet is becoming a *principle* of government'[29] – that I think one finds the key insight (though I would not agree with the rest of this sentence, in which he goes on to say that the Cabinet is now 'barely an institution at all').[30] And, intriguingly enough, one finds this train of thought sustained by some of the best-placed, most acute, toughest and least starry-eyed of Cabinet government's inside observers.

Sir Frank Cooper, former Permanent Secretary at the Northern Ireland Office and later at the Ministry of Defence in the 1970s and 1980s, captured Seymour-Ure's ruling principle in three words: 'discussion before decision'.[31] His friend and colleague Lord Hunt of Tanworth, who, as Sir John Hunt, was Secretary of the Cabinet under four Premiers (Heath, Wilson, Callaghan and Thatcher), said in a public lecture on election day 1983: 'I accept that Cabinet government must always be a cumbrous and complicated affair and that this is a price well worth paying for the advantage of shared discussion and shared decision, *provided the system can keep up with the demands put upon it* [emphasis added]'[32] – this last being a theme to which I shall return in chapter 7.

Hunt's depiction, interestingly enough, was phrased in very similar terms to Lord John Russell's complaint about Cabinet government at the time of the Crimean War, when he described it as 'a cumbrous and unwieldy instrument . . . It can furnish suggestions, or make a decision on a measure submitted to it, but it cannot administer'.[33] Speaking of Cabinet government under Jim Callaghan over 120 years later, caught in the coils this time of a financial crisis as the government had resort to the International Monetary Fund in the autumn of 1976, Lord Hunt produced as candid a description-cum-defence of the British way of central government at its apex where politics and administration meet as one is ever likely to hear from the lips of one of its traditional guardians. 'It is cumbersome. It is difficult. It has all sorts of disadvantages and it is possible it may need to change,' he told an Institute of Historical Research seminar in the autumn of 1993. It might be something of a 'shambles', but 'it has got to be, so far as possible, a democratic and accountable shambles.'[34]

Lord Hunt was defending the system whose chief mechanic he had been from 1973 to 1979 against an attack on its core principle – collective responsibility – from the former Labour minister, Edmund Dell, who had argued that the experience of the 'IMF autumn' had exposed once and for all that principle for what it was – a myth, which ought to be replaced by a new notion, 'collective tolerance', under which the Cabinet would leave such complicated and technical decisions as the readjustment of the British economy and its external finance to those who know and those who matter in the Cabinet, primarily the Prime Minister and the Chancellor of the Exchequer.[35]

Collective responsibility is the superglue, the ultimate bonder of Cabinet government. This was expressed rather well in one of my favourites among the confidential documents which occasionally came my way when I was a daily journalist. Entitled 'Talking about the Office', it used to coach Cabinet Office civil servants on the cover stories to spin at parties when asked what they did. My version was an early 1980s one, and, mercifully, it is now redundant thanks to John Major's decision to release the list of ministerial committees of the Cabinet,[36] including even details of the Cabinet Office's central intelligence machinery.[37] 'Talking about the Office', however, declared, accurately enough up to that point, that:

> It has always been maintained by successive administrations that disclosure of the process by which Government decisions are reached weakens the collective responsibility of Ministers, which is what welds the separate functions of Government into a single Administration. [That still holds, but the next section does not.] The first rule, therefore, is that even the existence of particular Cabinet Committees should not be disclosed – still less their composition, terms of reference, etc.[38]

The degree to which collective responsibility still remains as the crucial speck of DNA that determines the physiognomy of central government can be gauged from *Questions of Procedure for Ministers*. It was quite plain, too, from the 'collective responsibility' section of *QPM*, that the new openness would only go so far. The two key paragraphs read as follows:

> 17. The internal processes through which a decision has been made, or the level of Committee by which it was taken, should not be disclosed. Decisions reached by the Cabinet or Ministerial Committees are binding on all members of the Government. They are, however, normally announced and explained as the decision of the Minister concerned . . .
> 18. Collective responsibility requires that Ministers should be able to express their views frankly in the expectation that they can argue freely in private while maintaining a united front when decisions have been reached. This in turn requires that the privacy of opinions expressed in Cabinet and Ministerial Committees should be maintained.[39]

As with Cooper and Hunt on the essence of collective Cabinet government itself, Hunt's predecessor Burke Trend (another

Cabinet Secretary to have served four Premiers)[40] caught collective responsibility in a single succinctly colloquial comment. Pondering on Cabinet government in the aftermath of one of its most spectacular failures in the postwar period – the Westland affair of 1986 – Lord Trend said: 'One would have thought that it was easy enough to understand. Twenty or so individuals sit round a table and try to agree on the solution to some difficult problems, on the basis that they are accountable for their decisions; that it is therefore better to hang together than to hang separately; and that hanging together implies being pretty reticent about their methods of doing business.'[41]

As for those 'difficult problems', *QPM*, in the only official working definition we have of what the Cabinet is for (to return to the little boy's enquiry about Queen Victoria), states under the heading 'Cabinet and Ministerial Committee Business' that:

> 3. Cabinet and Ministerial Committee business consists, in the main, of –
> (i) Questions which significantly engage the collective responsibility of the Government because they raise major issues of policy or because they are of critical importance to the public.
> (ii) Questions on which there is an unresolved argument between Departments.[42]

Notice how the key strand of DNA – collective responsibility – is woven into this undramatic but highly important statement of procedural priority. Notice, too, the emphasis upon the need to apply collective, i.e. Cabinet and *not* prime ministerial government, to 'questions which . . . raise major issues of policy or . . . are of critical importance to the public'. That is an inclusive statement with no caveats or exceptions.

The next paragraph of *QPM*, on 'Ministerial Committees', anoints these, too, with the chrism of collective discussion – with what John Hunt has described as the principle of the 'collective executive'.[43]

> 4. The Cabinet is supported by Ministerial Committees which have a two-fold purpose. First they relieve the pressure on the

Cabinet itself by settling as much business as possible at a lower
level; or failing that, by clarifying the issues and defining the
points of disagreement. Second, they support the principle of
collective responsibility by ensuring that, even though all important questions may never reach the Cabinet itself, the decision
will be fully considered and the final judgement will be sufficiently
authoritative to ensure that the Government as a whole can be
properly expected to accept responsibility for it.[44]

So important was this notion of parity of authority between full
Cabinet and some Cabinet committees that, before John Major's
day, it used to be deployed as the chief excuse for not divulging the
existence of Cabinet committees, let alone their membership and
terms of reference.

In February 1978 Jim Callaghan circulated a Prime Minister's
minute – one of the most potent pieces of paper in Whitehall – to his
colleagues on this theme. Past refusals 'to publish details of Cabinet
Committees or to answer Questions in the House about them' had,
he said, 'led to some allegations in the Press about Whitehall obscur-
antism but little interest or pressure in Parliament itself'.[45] After this
unintentionally eloquent tribute to the lack of the scrutiny appetite
on the part of our legislators, Callaghan went on to note: 'there is
however now some evidence that Select Committees would like to
interest themselves in the Committee system and may be seeking to
evade the present convention.'[46] He put the 'pros' and 'cons' of the
case for disclosure before coming down against.

The wording of the crux of the 'con' case was interesting as it
repeated verbatim the philosophical core of the insiders' case for
secrecy which had featured in every edition of the then still secret
Questions of Procedure for Ministers, from the first of the modern
versions of it (Attlee's August 1945 marque) at least up to Wilson's
1966 edition, of which, though it remains technically secret under
the thirty-year rule, I have acquired a copy. The key passage reads:
'the method adopted by Ministers for discussion among themselves
of questions of policy is essentially a domestic matter, and is no
concern of Parliament or the public.'[47] The Callaghan version of the
traditional Cabinet 'ode to secrecy' told his colleagues:

It is important ... to understand the reasons for the current practice of non-disclosure. They are as follows: the Cabinet Committee system grew up as the load on Cabinet itself became too great. It allows matters of lesser importance to be decided without troubling the whole Cabinet; and major issues to be clarified in order to save the time of the Cabinet. The method adopted by Ministers for discussing policy questions is however essentially a domestic matter, and a decision by a Cabinet Committee, unless referred to the Cabinet, engages the collective responsibility of all Ministers and has exactly the same authority as a decision by the Cabinet itself. Disclosure that a particular Committee had dealt with a matter might lead to argument about the status of the decision or demands that it should be endorsed by the whole Cabinet.[48]

As we have seen, this barbican of the old order stands firm in today's *QPM* even under Mr Major's new openness regime.[49] It is the next bastion of Callaghan's Prime Minister's minute that has crumbled:

publishing details of the Committees would be both misleading and counter-productive. The existence of some could not be disclosed on security grounds; others are set up to do a particular job and then wound up. The absence of a Committee on a particular subject ... does not mean that the Government do not attach importance to it; and the fact that a particular Minister is not on a Committee does not mean that he does not attend when his interests are affected.[50]

But John Major's more open style does not mean that collective responsibility has in any way been corroded as *the* governing principle in the Cabinet Room. It is enshrined in his 1992 version of *QPM*. It was the centrepiece of the public reaffirmation that consensus Cabinet had replaced conviction Cabinet in Lord Wakeham's very significant lecture on 'Cabinet Government' at Brunel University in November 1993.[51] And it has, in practice, conditioned Mr Major's personal style of government in the Cabinet Room most of the time on most issues. For example, on the single most destabilizing issue within his Cabinet – Europe – he has deployed it with great care. For example, on the question of qualified majority voting in the Council of Ministers, the Prime Minister at the end of March

1994 let every Cabinet member have his or her say before summing up in favour of the compromise proposal put forward by the Foreign Secretary, Douglas Hurd.[52]

But, as with all premierships, the blend of the prime ministerial and the collective components in the practice of Cabinet government is never entirely consistent. The 'back to basics' campaign with which Mr Major greeted the new political season in the autumn of 1993 'had not been properly discussed with the Cabinet';[53] and a year earlier, the fissile issue of pit closures, for fear of leaks,[54] did not even go to the Prime Minister's Cabinet Committee on Economic and Domestic Policy, created after his 1992 election victory for the specific purpose of considering 'strategic issues relating to the government's economic and domestic policies'.[55] It is this *strategic* angle which goes to the heart of the matter about modern Cabinet. It is the efficiency question which Bagehot would undoubtedly have posed if he were today directing the editorial content of his old magazine from *The Economist*'s tower in St James's just across the Park from the Cabinet Room. John Hunt, too, went straight for it when he said that the disadvantages of Cabinet government were worth it 'provided the system can keep up with the demands put upon it'.[56]

And the DNA of collectivity, that example of 'British political genius' of which Lord Hailsham spoke,[57] very much remains the daily sanction of constitutional impeccability bequeathed by history or the '*cake* of custom', as Bagehot would have put it.[58] Significantly, John Hunt made this the thrust of his defence in the autumn of 1993 against Edmund Dell's argument that collective responsibility was now a dangerous myth.[59] 'There are', Hunt conceded, 'big questions over collective responsibility at the moment, but I don't think it is a myth.' Collective responsibility, he said,

> goes back a very long way and starts with some point where the King lost his power of being chief executive under the Hanoverians and was not replaced by a chief executive. And you had, first of all in the King's closet, but then, separately, in 10 Downing Street, this collective executive forming . . .
>
> It does go back to this constitutional thing that in this country

we do not elect a Prime Minister, we elect a Parliament and from that Parliament the majority party forms a government with a Prime Minister at the head of it. And Parliament vests all power in individual departmental ministers: nothing in the Prime Minister who has no constitutional position.[60]

It is worth lingering on John Hunt's words, because any reform attempt that wishes to go with the grain of constitutional and historical experience needs to ensure that the pursuit of efficiency does not cut against accountability and the diffusion of power at the top.

But, first of all, what of the arguments suggesting that late twentieth-century Cabinet government has fallen victim to a version of the disease Mancur Olson describes as 'institutional sclerosis'?[61] Some, naturally, have to do with the kind of human factors that cannot be remedied unless we sought a Cabinet of Younger Pitts – the fact that, as a private memo from a scientifically trained senior civil servant put it in the mid-1980s:

> Psychologists know that small children have a low tolerance of information; this increases in adolescence to a maximum of forty-five minutes, which is why lectures last that span. It then decreases as people get older and more important until the tolerance of information of important people in industry and of Cabinet ministers reduces to that of a six-year-old.

This, he concluded worryingly, means: 'They can take no more than five minutes or three sheets of A4.'[62]

An audit of concern from knowledgeable insiders, both ministers and officials, serving and retired, would produce, in addition to that grim assessment of innate cognitive capacity, conclusions something like these:

1 A full Cabinet of twenty plus is too large a body for taking measured decisions on anything but the crude politics of an issue.
2 It is certainly too large for processing and judging information of any technical complexity or intellectual difficulty.
3 There is a lack of agreed data, with individual departments competing with others to have their version of the problem

and the options, if any, for a solution, accepted as the accurate
picture of reality.

4 There is a lack of any real technical or professional expertise
on the part of most ministers, especially on scientific matters,
in what are almost invariably governments of amateurs.

5 There is a general and all-pervasive problem of overload, with
an almost constant lack of 'reserve minds', 'elastic thought' or
'spare energy', to revert to the Bagehotian criteria, which
expresses itself, among other manifestations, in an excessive
ministerial concentration on departmental as opposed to
Cabinet responsibilities and in what Nigel Lawson has called
a 'creeping bilateralism' – deals struck with the Prime Minister
without the proper involvement of Cabinet.[63]

Tired minds and untrained minds are at a great disadvantage when
it comes to the conduct of 'government by discussion' (i.e. Cabinet
government), which Bagehot saw, in his intriguing volume on *Physics
and Politics*, not just as 'an instrument of elevation'[64] but, with its
concomitant, 'tolerance' (which is 'learned in discussion'[65]), as the
prime distinguishing characteristic between 'customary societies'
where 'bigotry is the ruling principle'[66] and a 'modern community'
capable of 'elastic action'.[67] In other words, in an open society practis-
ing proper Cabinet government, TINA, that silly acronym of the
1980s for 'there is no alternative',[68] is the democratic and secular
equivalent of a sin against the Holy Ghost.

To be fair to some postwar Premiers, there has been intermittent
recognition of the problem of institutional sclerosis in the Cabinet
Room and occasional attempts to do something about it. They have
usually focused on the creation of 'overlords' or 'co-ordinating ministers', or the establishment of 'inner cabinets' of various kinds with
varying degrees of formality or informality.[69] Sometimes, too, the
data problem has been examined, with new outriders harnessed to
the creaking central machinery of state such as the Central Economic
Planning Staff created in 1947,[70] Churchill's revival of his wartime
Statistical Section in 1951,[71] the fabled Central Policy Review Staff
commissioned in 1971 by Ted Heath,[72] the reinvention of a Prime

Minister's Policy Unit by Harold Wilson in 1974[73] (Lloyd George's Prime Minister's Secretariat being the precursor)[74] and, in a slightly different way, the Prime Minister's Efficiency Unit launched by Mrs Thatcher in 1979,[75] which, among other things, looked at 'The Conventions of Government'.[76]

Most solutions, whether targeted at the human or the data aspect of the problem, tend to be reprises or remixes of previous attempts – the latest new/old runner being the idea of an 'inner cabinet' pressed by Nigel Lawson, both in his memoirs and on the seminar circuit.[77] This is an idea on which I want to concentrate here, as it could be a serious and potentially valuable runner for twenty-first-century British central government, especially if it is linked, genuinely and fruitfully, with a revived notion of the 'think tank' in a way that does nothing to jeopardize the valuable aspects of 'government by discussion'.

Lord Lawson is neither a constitutional purist nor an avid tinkerer with the machinery of Cabinet government. He does nevertheless recognize that the informal, ad hoc group of ministers he persuaded Mrs Thatcher to convene in November 1985 on the desirability of Britain's joining the Exchange Rate Mechanism of the European Monetary System was not a proper Cabinet committee and that, therefore, 'it was not a meeting that had any constitutional significance.'[78] Finding herself in a minority within it, therefore, did not prevent the Prime Minister setting her face against ERM membership for almost another five years. He contrasts this episode with the case of the poll tax, which *did* have its own proper Cabinet committee treatment, passing 'through rigorously all the text books said it should and more' but still proving 'the most disastrous single decision which the Thatcher Government took'.[79]

For Lawson the lesson is as much political as administrative, human as governmental. And it took the departure of one man from the Thatcher government – Willie Whitelaw at the turn of 1987–8 – to convince him finally that the hour of the 'inner cabinet' had come once more. As he told the IHR seminar:

> You all remember Margaret Thatcher's celebrated remark, 'every prime minister needs a Willie'? ... Certainly the fact that

there was somebody who discussed things with her ... did help ... The process of government definitely deteriorated in the third Thatcher Parliament after Willie Whitelaw had departed ... Perhaps we want, as it were, an institutionalized Willie, and that is why I come to my conclusion about an inner cabinet.[80]

On the same occasion, Lord Lawson sketched out a potential membership for his idea of a Lord Whitelaw-by-another-means to avoid the 'gulf' that sometimes 'grows between a Prime Minister and senior colleagues, particularly after a considerable time in office when there is also a danger of this departmental deformation happening ... [and] ... therefore it is desirable to have some ministers who are going to think more widely than simply as heads of their own departments with their own particular issues to push'.[81] There was, too, he added, 'a right number for a real discussion, unlike the Cabinet which is unwieldy, impossible'.[82] The Lawson-model 'inner cabinet' would be six-strong.

The Lawson inner cabinet
- Prime Minister
- Chancellor of the Exchequer
- Foreign and Commonwealth Secretary
  plus
- 'Three other members who would be the weightiest, most senior members of the government of the time, whatever office they happened to hold.'[83]

Lord Lawson's discussant at the IHR was Lord Armstrong of Ilminster, who as Robert Armstrong had been Principal Private Secretary to Edward Heath and Harold Wilson and Cabinet Secretary to Margaret Thatcher. Also present was Sir David Pitblado, former Principal Private Secretary to Attlee, Churchill and Eden. Together they formed as close to a human collective memory for postwar Cabinet and premiership as you could find. This trio took a quick and critical canter through previous attempts to crack the problem Lord Lawson had identified, starting with Churchill's system of 'supervising ministers',[84] or 'overlords', as they became known. 'Well, that didn't work,' commented Sir David, though 'it did divide up responsibilities. Possibly the wrong people [Lords Woolton, Cherwell, Leathers and Alexander[85]] were put into it . . . Ministers are responsible for their duties in Parliament . . . and these things really need to be backed up with collective responsibility.'[86] 'Also', added Lord Armstrong, 'ministers that were being overlorded greatly disliked it . . . and on the whole they were responsible to Parliament [as] Cabinet ministers.'[87]

They then considered formal 'inner cabinets', such as Wilson's successive versions from 1966 to 1970 in a variety of disguises (the 'Strategic Economic Policy Committee', the 'Management Committee', the 'Parliamentary Committee').[88] 'It started off well,' said Lord Armstrong, who had witnessed the 'experiment', as he called it, from the Treasury, 'but the trouble was if you have a formal inner cabinet like that, it becomes a matter of disgrace to a minister who is not on it and therefore a matter of intense manoeuvring to get on to it. And, successively, Mr Wilson conceded membership of [it] to people to whom it ought never to have been conceded.'[89]

Finally, they turned to informal 'inner cabinets'. Lord Armstrong had seen this kind in operation between 1970 and 1974: 'Mr Heath undoubtedly had a small group of ministers who were particularly close to him. They weren't called the "inner cabinet". They had no formal status in the machine and you can argue about who exactly was in it at any one time.'[90] The Foreign Secretary (Home) and the Chancellor (Barber) were not, so it certainly didn't fit the Lawson model. In Armstrong's judgement, 'It wasn't a formal inner cabinet . . . it . . . was an association based as much on personal friendship as political alliance – as on any position that any of them held at that time.'[91]

While I'm all for freeing up the minds of senior ministers for the tougher, long-term issues that truly demand first-class intellectual and political imagination, it seems to me that the 'overlords' idea is not worth repeating. In effect, Churchill conceded this when he abandoned the experiment after two years. The seasoned Cabinet Secretary, Norman Brook – fulfilling to perfection Hugh Dalton's depiction of British senior civil servants as 'congenital snaghunters'[92]

– warned him at the outset of all the problems that did eventually accrue in a memo of 15 November 1951:

The conception of a super-Minister, responsible for supervising the work of other Ministers of Cabinet rank, is fraught with serious difficulties, both constitutional and practical. Thus

(a) It is difficult to reconcile with the doctrines of Ministerial responsibility. Each Departmental Minister is personally accountable to Parliament for the policy and administration of his Department: and this responsibility would be blurred if, on all matters of major importance, he was subject to the directions of another Minister.

(b) It is inconsistent with the principle that policies and plans should be formulated by those who have the executive responsibility for carrying them out.

(c) It rests upon the assumption that policy can be divorced from administration. In fact the two are inextricably intertwined: policy cannot safely be formulated in vacuo: it should be founded on experience in administration, and should be capable of modification in the light of practical experience.

(d) It is contrary to our traditions of Cabinet Government that one Minister of Cabinet rank should be subordinated to another. This new relationship would be likely to give rise to frictions.

(e) Among officials, difficulties would certainly arise if staff attached to the super-Minister attempted to dictate to the Departmental staffs who have greater knowledge and experience of the subjects which they handle.

(f) Advocates of a system of supervising Ministers claim that it would enable a few senior Ministers to concern themselves with broad issues of policy, undistracted by the details of administration. Even if this were desirable (see (b) and (c) above), it seems doubtful whether it would be achieved in practice. For once it was announced that the responsibility for final decision rested with the super-Minister, Members of Parliament would insist on referring to him all matters

> which they considered important and would be reluctant to
> accept a final answer from the Departmental Minister.
>
> This lead would be followed by local authorities, industry and
> individual members of the public concerned with the subjects
> falling within the jurisdiction of the super-Minister. He would
> thus be drawn into the details of administration – and might well
> find himself, in the end, doubling the work of the Departmental
> Minister (and, incidentally, providing himself with a staff for that
> purpose). Meanwhile the position of the Departmental Minister
> would have been undermined.[93]

Brook took the same line as Attlee (who had been an 'overlord'
enthusiast before the war[94]) did later in the Commons: that co-
ordination was better carried out through the mechanism of Cabinet
committees, the names of whose chairmen were not made public.[95]
This system, Brook told Churchill, 'was developed under the wartime
Coalition Government and has since come to be accepted as a normal
piece of Government machinery' and the chairmen of such committees 'can play a co-ordinating role in the formulation of policy without undermining the responsibility of the Departmental Ministers
to Parliament'.[96] Those arguments would, I think, recrudesce (and
justifiably) if 'overlordships' were recreated nearly half a century on
– as indeed Paul McQuail has shown they did in 1969–70 during
the internal Whitehall discussions which went into the making of
the giant new Department of the Environment.[97]

Informal 'inner cabinets' suffer from quite the reverse problem.
They are so insubstantial that few people in Whitehall, let alone
Parliament, know they exist. Evanescence rarely arouses fuss. Nor
can an inner cabinet, in this instance, amount to more than useful
chats among political intimates about political strategy or individuals.
Such things have their place; but there is nothing co-ordinating
about them in terms of moving policy on. Their wiring within the
machine is not so much hidden as non-existent.

What, then, of the Wilson model? The papers for his Strategic
Economic Policy, Management and Parliamentary Committees have
not yet reached the PRO, so we cannot judge their internal impact.
I have my doubts about their efficacy, both in terms of effective links

with the rest of the central government machine when such an 'inner cabinet' makes or shapes policy and in respect of the analytical back-up available to them – quite apart from the swirls of resentment they caused among excluded ministers. The Lawson idea, however, *is* promising, though it will need refinement if it is to be a runner with a chance of 'taking' as a graft on to the existing Cabinet culture with a robust and sustained future ahead of it. It needs, too, to avoid the shortcomings of John Major's Economic and Domestic Policy Committee, which is a back-up free zone in terms of extra analytical input which could increase its chances of adding value.[98]

The question that needs to be addressed is this: How is one to construct an inner cabinet with the personal effectiveness of an informal one, avoiding the resistances and resentments engendered by formal inner cabinets or a superstructure of 'overlords', and yet furnished with valuable extra briefing, while preserving the constitutional niceties alongside the high political and administrative status such a body would acquire? The answer, I suggest, on the basis of the British experience since 1945, is a new Cabinet Strategic Policy Committee, an SPC, embracing foreign, defence, economic and domestic questions with real strategic implications for the country and the government as a whole. It would be served by a revived Central Policy Review Staff, which would have a special, but not the sole, briefing input to the new SPC. The SPC would look something like this:

The Hennessy Strategic Policy Committee
- Prime Minister
- Foreign and Commonwealth Secretary
- Chancellor of the Exchequer
- Home Secretary
- Defence Secretary

    plus

- up to three (preferably two) other senior ministers.
- If there is a Willie Whitelaw figure chairing several Cabinet committees, he or she should be included.

● Between them, the members of the SPC should chair all the
more important Cabinet committees.

This model, I suggest, would represent a modernizing innovation,
but one which goes with the grain and preserves the need for shared
discussion before decision, enabling such discussion to happen more
thoughtfully and effectively *and* guarding against creeping prime
ministerialism. Not only should the Cabinet, not No. 10, be the
most powerful single body in the state for both accountability and
power-sharing reasons, it needs to be so organized as to be continuously and efficiently effective in achieving its collective, restraining
purpose. Overmightiness at the top has to be resisted.

For the same reason the distinguished social philosopher Ernest
Gellner pushes the virtue of civil society on a wider canvas. Civil
society, says Gellner, rests on 'the idea of institutional and ideological
pluralism, which prevents the monopoly of power and truth';[99] a
society in which 'it is *not* clear who is boss'.[100] This is precisely the
point Bagehot was making about tolerance and openness to argument
in advanced as opposed to custom-caked societies, 'as . . . the mere
putting up of a subject to discussion is a clear admission that that
subject is in no degree settled by established rule and that men are
free to choose in it'.[101]

So important are both the spirit and the principles of collective
Cabinet government that it would be a definite advantage if they
could be spelt out in the kind of job description I have already
attempted for the monarchy and the premiership – especially if a
future experiment were to be undertaken with some kind of inner
cabinet. I would begin with the terse, caveat-free definition of the
Cabinet's centrality which is enshrined in the guidelines on *Cabinet
Committee Business* circulated by the Cabinet Office to all departments,[102] plus two key paragraphs from *Questions of Procedure for
Ministers*, before ranging more widely:

The purposes of Cabinet government
1 'The Cabinet reconciles Ministers' individual responsibilities
with their collective responsibility. It is the ultimate arbiter
of all Government policy.'[103]

2 Cabinet and Cabinet committee business consists chiefly of questions which significantly engage the collective responsibility of government because they raise major issues of policy or because they are of critical importance to the public or matters on which there remains disagreement between government departments.

3 Cabinet must at all times act as a necessary restraint upon a potentially overmighty premiership.

4 It must bring wider political considerations to bear on technical and administrative matters (this is especially important on big, science-related procurements or when a 'war cabinet' is in operation).

5 It must blend as genuinely and effectively as possible the width of opinion represented by the coalitions of views which make up Britain's two main parties in such a way that outcomes can be accepted by the Cabinet as a whole. (John Major put this point rather well when he told his fellow heads of government at the Group of Seven summit in Halifax, Nova Scotia, in June 1995: 'I am a coalition government on my own.')[104]

6 It must strive to treat issues in the round, with Secretaries of State being capable of raising their eyes above their narrow ministerial concerns in what Gladstone once called a 'Government of Departments'.

7 It must ensure that the decencies, probities and accountabilities of British public and political life are maintained in relation to:
   (a) Parliament;
   (b) the public in its dealings with government departments and agencies;
   (c) the raising and disbursement of public money;
   (d) the non-partisan deployment of the apolitical Civil Service.

In short, Cabinet counts; which is why it was so important, constitutionally, that the most striking 'boss' prime ministership of the postwar period, Mrs Thatcher's, should have ended with nearly two-thirds of her Cabinet telling her she could not go on, as this was the crucial moment when she realized that her pyrotechnic command premiership was finished. For in the end she was undone by that very same conflict she detected during her first days as a Cabinet minister twenty years earlier when she sensed very powerfully 'the opposition between my own executive style of decision-making and the more consultative style to which they [the senior civil servants] were accustomed'.[105] It was a tension Margaret Thatcher never resolved – and probably never wanted to, because she thought those seeking to soften her line, on whatever issue, were either feeble or misguided.

John Biffen, one of her long-purged ministers, caught it perfectly when he said she thought 'she was a tigress surrounded by hamsters'.[106] Thank God for Wednesday 21 November 1990 – the Night of the Hamster. And here's to Cabinet government – albeit in a more efficient form.

FIVE

Whitehall

Gyroscope of State

Englishmen have always distrusted 'officialism', and they have none of that respect for the public functionary which prevails on the continent of Europe. The civil servant . . . has been regarded rather as a necessary evil than an object of admiration or affection.

Sir Sidney Low, 1904[1]

Well, the Prime Minister has had a very difficult time, I'm sure. What I say is, 'Thank God for the Civil Service.'

King George VI, swearing in Aneurin Bevan and John Wilmot as Privy Counsellors, July 1945[2]

The Civil Service is a bit like a rusty weathercock. It moves with opinion then it stays where it is until another wind moves it in a different direction.

Tony Benn, 1995[3]

I recognize the 'weathercock' symbol. The Civil Service is dedicated to the status quo. It only changes with a tremendous breath of air – the War; probably the Thatcher period. It's not politicization in the party sense. It's thought colonization.

Ian Beesley, former chief of staff of Mrs Thatcher's Downing Street Efficiency Unit, 1995[4]

We have not been politicized, but, after sixteen years of Conservative administration, every senior civil servant I know is wishing for a change of government next time.

Top Whitehall figure I, spring 1995[5]

It's getting just like 1964 in Whitehall with everyone looking forward to a Labour government. But if it comes, it will be very hairy, just as in 1964, after so many years, not of politicization, but of one party's thought patterns. I just hope the Labour ministers appreciate that we haven't been politicized and that we are not Thatcher's children. But so few of them know us.

Top Whitehall figure II, spring 1995[6]

I want the government to change because I wish to live in a liberal democracy.

Senior civil servant, winter 1994–5[7]

Unlike monarchs, Premiers and Cabinet ministers, senior civil servants are not usually the stuff of legend, table talk or gossip in pub and club. They are, to borrow the cruel phrase of my friend and former ace pressure-grouper, Des Wilson, scarcely 'household names in their own household'.[8] Yet they matter, and have done since they developed as a great fixture of state from the mid-nineteenth century. They are, after all, the chief human instrument of state power, the 'software' of the system, to revert to Ian Bancroft's metaphor.[9] Without them, the conversion of politics into policies, decisions into programmes, simply would not happen.

It is surprising, therefore, given his mission to search out and explain the realities of government, that Walter Bagehot was relatively silent on the Civil Service. There is no separate chapter on Whitehall in *The English Constitution*; his observations on the bureaucracy in his greatest single work are confined to a smallish section of the chapter 'On Changes of Ministry'.[10] These few pages, however, contain some nice touches. For example: 'It is an inevitable defect, that bureaucrats will care more for routine than results ... [they came] ... to imagine the elaborate machinery of which they form a part, and from which they derive their dignity, to be a grand and achieved result, not a working and changeable instrument.'[11] Touches of a 1980s Rayner efficiency scrutiny here posing its series of prior questions: Do we have to continue carrying out this piece of business, and, if so, could the private sector take it over? If not, can we do it better?[12]

Bagehot had a touch, too, of a kind of prototypical public choice theory: 'Not only does a bureaucracy ... tend to under-government, in point of quality; it tends to over-government in point of quantity. The trained official hates the rude, untrained public. He thinks that they are stupid, ignorant, reckless ...'[13] Pretty scathing stuff about what Lord Radcliffe would nearly a century later call one of the great 'standing armies of power'.[14] But it was high-class abuse, as these things go; and, like so many of its critics, Bagehot had a kind of grudging regard for the British Civil Service. In a *Saturday Review* article on 'Thinking Government' in 1856, he wrote: 'There is such a thing as the pomp of order. In every public office there is a grave official personage, who is always neat, whose papers are always filed, whose handwriting is always regular, who is considered a monster of experience, who can minute any proceeding, and docket any document.'[15] We may not warm to them, but every organization needs people like that. They are, at risk of sounding sexist, the continuity girls of any system.

Bagehot might have given the Civil Service the chapter it deserved if he had written *The English Constitution* half a decade later, after the 1870 Order in Council that created a permanent career public service, recruited free from political or personal patronage on the sole basis of ability as revealed through that great Indian Civil Service method – competitive examination. Bagehot had been scornful of the idea of competitive examination for everyone in the clerical grades,[16] but he was a firm supporter of it for the young men coming into the senior levels. Writing within days of the promulgation of that Order in Council – the crowning work of Gladstone and Lowe in public service reform[17] – Bagehot declared:

> If this Order in Council gives to the permanent civil service at once intellectual distinction and a popular origin – for when all privilege is abolished, and any man of whatever birth up to a particular standard of intellectual culture has a chance of success, no one can call its origin other than popular – it will create a lasting barrier against any political abuse of patronage in the future, for which we may well be thankful.[18]

By and large it has proved a barrier, and most of us are grateful for it. Not bad for a single Order in Council issued under the Royal Prerogative. Whether it is sufficient any longer is a matter to which I shall shortly turn. But the principle of 1870 resounds even now through mid-1990s documents. Both the Government's Civil Service White Paper, *Continuity and Change*,[19] released in July 1994, and the House of Commons Treasury and Civil Service Committee's report on *The Role of the Civil Service*, published the following November,[20] begin with unequivocal reaffirmations of it. And both cite directly the Northcote–Trevelyan Report of 1853 whose principles Gladstone and Lowe finally put in place seventeen years later, though not in the statutory form Northcote and Trevelyan recommended. The White Paper put it this way:

> The Government, like its predecessors, is wholeheartedly committed to sustaining the key principles on which the British Civil Service is based: integrity, political impartiality, objectivity, selection and promotion on merit and accountability through Ministers to Parliament. They are as important to good government in the future as they have been in the past . . .
>
> The Civil Service in the United Kingdom has a long tradition of non-political appointments and the Government is committed to continuing this system. The Northcote–Trevelyan Report first established that appointments should be made on the basis of merit rather than patronage and the Civil Service Commissioners were appointed to oversee fair and open competition and selection on merit.[21]

The Select Committee report actually opens with, if anything, an even more effusive paean of praise to the settlement of 1870:

> The British Civil Service is a great national asset. Since the 1870s, it has been the permanent and impartial instrument of administrations. Governments have always seen it as their duty to preserve its efficiency and honesty for their successors. The Civil Service's commitment to the highest standards of performance and conduct is a guarantee of constitutional and financial propriety and good government. Wherever the boundaries are drawn between public and private sectors, there are certain crucial values which must underly public administration. The values of impartiality, integrity, selection and promotion on merit and accountability are as important today as they were in the last century.[22]

There have, of course, been lapses from the ideals of 1870. Fears of creeping politicization in the 1980s had their pre-echoes – though, as in the Thatcher years, they were usually associated with individual officials rather than the senior Civil Service as a whole, the relationship between Neville Chamberlain and Sir Horace Wilson being the most famous of this century,[23] with the Margaret Thatcher–Charles

Powell example the most discussed and notorious of recent times.[24] Life in No. 10, where politics and administration meet and blur, has always been the danger zone. As Sir Charles Powell himself put it, Downing Street is such a small place that a Prime Minister has to feel the staff are on his or her side. Your loyalty has to be to the PM. Departmental ties have to be cut: 'Because it is so small you have to live by your wits. There's bound to be a different atmosphere from the Ministry. You have to take some things on your shoulders.'[25]

I don't accept the simplicity or the inevitability of the Powell line. The argument turns on what those 'some things' should and should not be. Anything plainly *party* political should, I am convinced, be in the latter category – which is why I was somewhat disturbed to find from the No. 10 papers on the timing of the 1964 general election, when they were declassified in January 1995, that that fine public servant, Sir Tim Bligh (Principal Private Secretary to Sir Alec Douglas-Home as to Harold Macmillan before him) was intimately involved in such intensely political matters to the extent of advising in December 1963 that a March election would give the Conservatives the greatest chance of victory in 1964 as the economy was likely to sour thereafter.[26] A civil servant briefing a Premier on the 'best time' (to use Bligh's words) to hold an election is simply beyond the conventions of Northcote–Trevelyan and 1870 however they are interpreted. I shall return to the politicization question later.

The most important feature of the nostrums of 1870 is that both government and Parliament continue to regard them as the crucial speck of DNA that should continue to determine the life of our public service. Indeed, when William Waldegrave and his then Permanent Secretary in the Office of Public Service and Science, Richard Mottram, trod their milk-round of Cabinet ministers' offices while the Civil Service White Paper was in preparation, they were surprised (very surprised in some cases, I would imagine) not just by the unanimity revealed about political impartiality, but by the strength of feeling with which these high-minded views were expressed.[27]

It is important to concentrate on these factors, the grand principles of a *grand corps*, because they are the essence of the British Civil Service as a profession, whatever the current configurations of the public service and in whatever capacity public servants are pursuing their calling, whether it be as Secretary of the Cabinet or the Prime Minister's Principal Private Secretary, or the administrative assistant across the counter from the 'customer' (as they're now called) in the Benefits Agency or Employment Service local office, or the tax-gatherer in the Inland Revenue or the seeker after drugs traffickers in the Customs and Excise. The state, after all, has gone through several transformations in size, scope and shape since Northcote and Trevelyan laid down their pens. Yet the ethic has prevailed as a kind of gold standard. And my friends in the bureaucracy branch of the international management consultancy trade tell me that this is what ministers and officials in recently de-tyrannized nations seek most avidly – the secret of an uncorrupt, rational, politically clean Civil Service, something they believe the British specially, if not uniquely, possess.[28]

I recognize, however, that in a decentralized and fragmented public service it will be harder for such an ethic to infuse state service; and I am sure it has been – and will remain – virtually impossible to contract out the public service ethos in its widest sense, with those activities that have been market-tested and extruded never (or probably never) to return, as Sir Peter Levene, Mr Major's efficiency adviser, acknowledged before the Treasury and Civil Service Select Committee.[29]

This process is well developed; the centralized mid-twentieth-century British Civil Service is already parcelled up into what its former Head, Lord Bancroft, calls 'a lot of civil services' clustered around a small, almost nineteenth-century-style core of departmental policy advisers, bringing with it what he sees as 'the danger of disintegration.'[30] The balkanization of the public service since the inauguration of the 'Next Steps' executive agencies in 1988[31] and, most potently of all, since the process of market testing began under the 1991 White Paper, *Competing for Quality*,[32] was particularly vividly illustrated by the following exchange between that most assiduous of veteran Whitehall-watchers, Labour MP John Garrett, and Sir

Robin Butler, Head of the Home Civil Service, during the Treasury and Civil Service Committee's session on 23 November 1993:

> MR GARRETT: Is it not the case that we are in the process of moving from a unified Civil Service of some thirty main departments to a Civil Service which consists of thirty ministerial head offices, about a hundred and fifty executive agencies and units, hundreds of quangos, like TECs [Training and Enterprise Councils], trusts and corporate bodies, and thousands of contracts with private contractors, all of whom are trying to make a profit? Would you agree with that description?
>
> SIR ROBIN: Yes, I do not think that that is an inaccurate description.[33]

Significantly, the Cabinet Secretary went on to say: 'nor do I think there is anything that is contrary to the traditions of the Civil Service which is in it.'[34]

'The traditions of the Civil Service.' What are they? It's time to send for the little boy who wondered what Queen Victoria was for. Sometimes it is revealing to put that question cold to those who have grown up in that tradition and, in one way or another, have sought to apply it all their working lives.

One of the most accomplished and most admired (rightly) of our postwar public servants, on whom I quite recently sprung the question, replied quietly, and with an appropriately mandarin smile, 'To run the country.'[35] As a good Trollopian, as an afterthought he sent me the following declaration of Lady Laura Standish's in *Phineas Finn*, published in 1869, sixteen years after the Northcote–Trevelyan Report was completed: 'Every question so handled by [the Prime Minister] has been decided rightly according to his own party, and wrongly according to the party opposite. A political leader is so sure of support and so sure of attack that it is hardly necessary for him to be even anxious to be right.' This, naturally, is the cue for the Civil Service. 'For the country's sake,' Trollope continued with a dash of Bagehotry, 'he should have officials under him who know the routine of business.'[36] Shades of Evelyn Sharp and Dick Crossman, or Appleby and Hacker, a century before Crossman confided his resentments to his diary[37] and Jay and Lynn converted them into the brilliant pastiche of *Yes, Minister*.[38]

Next I put the question to the incarnation of the successor generation to my anonymous retired Permanent Secretary: Ian Bancroft, a postwar recruit to the Treasury, part, as he has put it himself, of the generation who 'began their official lives believing that everything was achievable'.[39] Asked 'What is the Civil Service for?' Lord Bancroft said: 'To act as a permanent piece of ballast in the Constitution on the basis that you have what can be a very volatile legislature and an equally volatile ministerial executive. Sometimes, therefore, you need a degree of balance and permanence.'[40]

Savour those two words 'balance' and 'permanence': the notion of the Civil Service as a kind of gyroscope of state. 'Someone', Lord Bancroft continued, 'who can say "Oi! We've been here before." '[41] Here is another thought to savour – the Civil Service as collective memory. This is very important in a state without a written constitution where precedents and procedure are all, and where, by convention, ministers cannot look at the files of previous administrations (unless they were members of it or the former Premier gives permission[42]), but civil servants can. Lord Bancroft rounded off his top-of-the-head *tour de force* by returning to his ballast metaphor: 'and, occasionally, ballast in the sense that if ministers run out of ideas, the Civil Service should be able to generate (or to get ministers to generate) some kind of kick-start to the engine.'[43]

Finally, to complete my triptych, I put the 'little boy' question to a very senior figure at the heart of the mid-1990s Civil Service. He said: 'It's for the effective support of ministers in the administration of government within the law. This is likely to be best achieved by a permanent, politically impartial Civil Service dedicated to the provision of objective advice.'[44] How this would have won the approval of Northcote and Trevelyan or Gladstone and Lowe. It might even have inspired from Mr G. a reprise of his great line from 1879, which found favour with today's Treasury and Civil Service Select Committee,[45] that the British Constitution 'presumes more boldly than any other the good sense and good faith of those who work it'.[46]

Needless to say, the 1870 settlement has been under great pressure since the early 1970s when Sir William Armstrong, rightly or wrongly, was portrayed as Mr Heath's Horace Wilson,[47] and the growing polarization of British politics in its most ideologically adversarial postwar phase made it difficult for Ian Bancroft's notion of balance to flourish as it began to suffer from a particular form of stress which became acute in the Thatcher years under a Premier who could not see a manifestation of consensus without launching into an anathema.[48] Though the ideological temperature may have lowered since November 1990, the growing distance in time since the last change of governing party and the development of a British version of what Giovanni Sartori has called a 'predominant party system'[49] has put the Civil Service through an experience probably beyond Gladstone's imagination in 1870, given the swings and roundabouts of office since he had entered the Commons in 1832. Place this alongside the new public management, the fostering of what Sir Terry Heiser has called a 'can do' ethos among senior officials,[50] and the fragmentation of the traditional central apparatus of state, and you have to confront the Bagehotian question, whenever the axioms of 1870 are intoned: Does the reality fit the aspiration any longer?

Even the government's White Paper has the feel of a deal about it – one neatly signalled by its title, *Continuity and Change*. Ministers, I suspect, bought the soothing Northcote-and-Trevelyanish 'continuity' only because the 'change' section brimmed with new managerial abrasives in line with Citizen's Chartery, market testing, performance-related pay and the associated jargon and acronymia of sub-management-school babble which will bring so much dry amusement to historians of government when they revisit Command Paper no. 2627 in the decades to come.

The question is, will the deal hold? Does it hold, even within the 46-page compass of *Continuity and Change*? Doesn't the newly created 'Senior Civil Service'[51] with its new contracts (theoretically 'indefinite' up to retirement age at sixty, but punctuated by 'specified periods of notice'[52]) carry with it the danger of those whose faces or views do not fit the current minister's personal or political tastes being removed quite easily from the department concerned under the camouflage not only of the standard face-savers but the new rubric of contractual relationships? Even here, the nature of the deal is apparent. It is plain that ministers wished to go over completely to fixed-term contracts for the whole Senior Civil Service, but were persuaded by their officials to settle for this kind of half-way house.[53]

There is a danger of ministerial patronage of the kind that could lead to a crumbling of the old career/politically neutral model – but only if a 'one of us' climate is already in place. This is the key. For if the virus of politicization was already rampant, nothing in the White Paper or the personnel practices of the public service or the nostrums of 1870 could resist the contagion.

Is that climate already established? I think not. There was more than a trace of it in Mrs Thatcher's No. 10 in the days of Powell–Ingham influence. Sir Charles, and his boss, resisted the determined efforts of both the Cabinet Secretary and the Head of the Diplomatic Service (stimulated by these very dangers) to prise him back into the Foreign Office mainstream.[54] His and Sir Bernard's giving 'cover' to the leak of the Solicitor-General's letter at the time of Westland in 1986 is well known and much discussed.[55] And Sir Geoffrey Howe's memoirs are very eloquent about the crucial intervention by Ingham which helped persuade Mrs Thatcher not to accept Mr William McCall's very sensible and practical offer of a no-strike deal from the Civil Service unions at the time of GCHQ de-unionization in 1984.[56] That apart, there was not, I believe any serious politicization even in the high days of Mrs T. and her 'ism'. There were problems, however, associated with having an ideological government (by British standards) in office for so long. In part, these have to do with an increasing lack of familiarity with other kinds of thinking in the ministerial suites. For example, if you joined the Department of the Environment after May 1979, you could be quite senior now. Yet you will not be able to recall a time when local government was seen by ministers as potentially part of a solution rather than always part of the problem. Politically sensitive departments were aware of this familiarity gap in the run-up to the 1992 election. More than one laid on seminars at which the old sweats briefed the young and high-flying on what it was like to work for Labour ministers. One such exercise even drew up a glossary of terms to be banned from the vocabulary of the private office if the government changed.[57]

Allied to this there was – and remains – a human problem. Most senior Whitehall people, certainly after fifteen years, would settle for a quiet life by *not* serving up analysis and advice unpalatable to the now very familiar thought patterns of the ministerial class. Even before the end of Mrs Thatcher's first term, Lord Bancroft had noticed that 'the grovel count' in both ministers *and* civil servants was 'much higher than normal'.[58] He went, I think, to the core of the alleged politicization question when he saw it as a 'subtle' and 'insidious' problem. 'The dangers', he explained, 'are of the younger people, seeing that advice which ministers want to hear falls with a joyous note on their ears, and advice which they need to hear falls on their ears with rather a dismal note, will tend to make officials trim, make their advice what ministers want to hear rather than what they need to know.'[59]

In one respect, I have some sympathy with those whom it would be wrong to see as 'grovellers' but who, nonetheless, have been criticized by name for being too accommodating of ministerial wishes, including those who have been portrayed as failing to steer Mrs Thatcher and her ministers away from the reef of the poll tax. Sir Terry Heiser, Permanent Secretary at the Department of the Environment, was even depicted in Labour Shadow Cabinet circles as being a keen Thatcherite, when anyone who knew him was aware he was anything but.[60] In their superb book on this sorry episode, David Butler, Andrew Adonis and Tony Travers upbraid top DoE officials generally and Heiser in particular for not warning more strongly of the tax's defects in detail and about its lack of overall viability.[61]

Heiser, certainly one of the 'can do' breed of official favoured by some Conservative ministers, is temperamentally inclined to pursue ministers' wishes with zest. He does not believe it is an official's function to conform to Hugh Dalton's 'congenital snaghunter' stereotype or to be a 'Mr Wait-a-minute', as Jim Callaghan liked to put it during his No. 10 days.[62] The real culprits, if one wishes to play the singularly unfruitful 'I-name-the-guilty-men' game, are ministers who sat on the E(LF) (Economy, Local Government Finance) Cabinet Committee, who, as Nigel Lawson's memoirs graphically show, failed through timidity, tedium or incomprehension to subject the poll tax proposals to the scrutiny they deserved, not least as that tax might have ended all their political careers.[63] What really count, however, are not the opinions of scholars and commentators, but those of the Cabinet, and the Prime Minister in particular, after a change of government. If *they* think the Civil Service has been politicized – that Whitehall has turned into Bluehall – they will act accordingly, and evidence to the contrary (and the nostrums of 1870) will be to no avail.

For these reasons, I regret the passing of the consensus on most of the Whitehall managerial reforms, the Next Steps agencies in particular, which had held up to the 1992 election. A year before that election John Smith, as Shadow Chancellor, had accepted the philosophy behind 'Next Steps' and indicated that Labour would continue with that programme,[64] exactly as its *Civil Service* framers wished. Sir Peter Kemp, the project's manager, had said: 'We are building for the state . . . not just for any particular government'; Sir Robin Butler explained that the Next Steps system 'allowed for an incoming government to reshape the agencies by altering their framework agreements'.[65] However, Nigel Lawson, interestingly enough, as we learned from his memoirs, was eventually persuaded of the value of Next Steps largely as a way of reshaping public businesses so that they could be more easily privatized at a later date.[66]

It was the injection of serious market testing into that system, in effect overriding the freedom of agency chief executives to run their public businesses the way they wished (albeit within certain limits), which marked the beginning of the end of the cross-party consensus when *Competing for Quality* was published in the autumn of 1991. As the 1992 election approached, however, Robin Butler was able to persuade Neil Kinnock of the general fitness of the Civil Service to work for a Labour government and that if there had been a politicization problem it was confined to No. 10. It may not be so easy next time; particularly as Sir Robin's role as the interpreter of *Questions of Procedure for Ministers*, in his capacity as the Prime Minister's propriety adviser, has been called into question by some senior Labour figures in the context of the Aitken/Ritz affair.[67]

Would it be so bad if patronage in the pre-1853 style were restored to ministers when it came to senior Civil Service appointments within the policy-making areas of their departments? I think it would. Politicians possess one asset (and one only) in abundance – prejudice. They do not need reinforcement in this area over and above from the single special adviser they are allowed at the moment.[68] Quite the reverse. The senior Civil Service may have its faults when it comes to policy advice (a matter to which I will turn in a moment). But crude partisanship and a weakness for what Victor Rothschild unforgettably described as 'the promises and panaceas which gleam like false teeth in the party manifestos'[69] are not among them. Someone somewhere within the system needs to be in a position to speak truth unto power, and to do that you need a form of old-style academic tenure. Hence my defence of a neutral, permanent, career Civil Service – which is not at all the same thing as maintaining that this kind of taxpayer-funded British equivalent of the Dutch Order of the Golden Fleece should enjoy any kind of monopoly supply on the analysis or advice which flows across ministers' desks.

Despite the welcome restatement of the nostrums of 1870 in the first half of *Continuity and Change*, the tang of unease that has grown sharper since the Treasury and Civil Service Committee began its inquiry in the spring of 1993, thanks to the Scott Inquiry, the growing preoccupation with sleaze, worries about the 'quango state' and the ever-fading memory of what it was like to have Labour ministers in charge of Whitehall departments, leads me to the firm conclusion that a new underpinning is required for those five mid-Victorian values. I am not alone in this. The Public Accounts Committee made the same point very powerfully in January 1994 in its report on the conduct of public business and the proper uses of public money.[70]

I have long regretted that Mr Gladstone did not follow the specific recommendation of Northcote and Trevelyan that the new meritocracy should be reinforced and protected by an Act of Parliament to prevent either 'imperceptible' or 'avowed' abandonment of the career service principle by future governments.[71] It seemed to me a strangely unfinished piece of business, and nothing could better buttress the reaffirmation of those principles than the replacement by a mid-1990s Parliament of their prerogative status by substituting a Civil Service Act for the existing Orders in Council. I was therefore delighted when the Treasury and Civil Service Committee proposed exactly this in November 1994. Its precise formulation was very shrewd. In essence it took the key elements of a career Civil Service as outlined by Sir Robin Butler in his evidence to them – 'impartiality, integrity and objectivity ... plus ... selection and promotion on merit'[72] – and converted them into a code,[73] recommending that the code itself should, as a last resort, permit recourse by a concerned public servant to a strengthened Civil Service Commission whose enhanced role would be established by statute.[74] Though the government fell short of accepting the idea of an Act, while keeping an 'open mind' about the possibility,[75] its acceptance of both the code and an enhanced Civil Service Commission (thereby overcoming Sir Robin's initial doubts about the need to do much more than bring the existing codes together in one place[76]) was, I am sure, made possible by Giles Radice and his colleagues on the Select Committee *not* seeking to change existing constitutional understandings and by their wise decision to recommend an existing and appropriate piece of machinery as the instrument of implementation in the shape of the Civil Service Commission.

To be fair to the government, it is plain from the wording of its reply to the Select Committee – *Taking Forward Continuity and Change*, to give it its proper title – that it was chiefly its molten majority, or semi-majority, in the Commons that prevented it from accepting the idea of a Civil Service Bill for fear that backbenchers, including perhaps the Conservatives' own at that time unwhipped ones, might try to tack on changes which could change our constitutional arrangements. Referring to itself, the government admitted in the White Paper:

> It acknowledges the view that additional authority would be conferred on the proposed Civil Service Code, including the new role envisaged for the [Civil Service] Commissioners, by a statutory

approach and that such legislation if based on cross-party consensus could be an effective means of expressing and entrenching general agreement on the non-political nature of the Civil Service; and it recognises that the Select Committee recommended narrowly-based legislation on these lines on the basis that it could command wide support. The Government would welcome further discussion of such an approach.[77]

Mr Blair and Mr Ashdown, if they had been sensible, would have sought such discussions swiftly on that most venerable yet efficient of circuits, the Privy Counsellors network. But two months after the White Paper had appeared, the Labour leadership had still to reply to the government's invitation.[78]

The Select Committee's draft code is worth careful absorption for two reasons. First, it was plain that, give or take an entirely acceptable change of the occasional word, as suggested in the government's reply,[79] it would, after a period of further consultation, form the basis of the code that will be laid before Parliament either as an Order in Council or as a Bill. Secondly, its first ten paragraphs are as good a definition of what the Civil Service is for as you could hope to find:

1. The constitutional and practical role of the Civil Service is, with integrity, honesty, impartiality and objectivity, to assist the duly constituted Government, of whatever political complexion, in formulating policies of the Government, carrying out decisions of the Government and administering services for which the Government is responsible in the interests of the public.

2. Civil servants are servants of the Crown. Constitutionally the Crown acts on the advice of Ministers and, subject to the provisions of this Code, civil servants owe their loyalty to the duly constituted Government.

3. Civil servants should serve the duly constituted Government in accordance with the principles set out in this Code and recognising
   - the duty of all public officers to discharge their public functions reasonably and according to the law;
   - the duty to respect, comply with and obey the law of the

land, international law and the provision of international
treaties to which the United Kingdom is a party and not
to imperil the due administration of justice;
- those duties which may arise as members of professions.

4. This Code should be seen in the context of the duties and
responsibilities of Ministers set out in *Questions of Procedure for
Ministers* which include:
- the duty to give Parliament and the public as full
  information as possible about the policies, decisions and
  actions of the Government, and not to deceive or mislead
  Parliament and the public;
- the duty to give fair consideration and due weight to
  informed and impartial advice from civil servants, as well
  as to other considerations and advice, in reaching policy
  decisions; and
- the duty to comply with the law of the land;
together with the duty to familiarise themselves with the contents
of this Code and not to ask civil servants to act in breach of it.

5. Civil servants should conduct themselves with integrity, fair-
ness and honesty in their dealings with Ministers, Parliament and
the public. They should make all information and advice relevant
to a decision available to Ministers. They should not deceive or
mislead Ministers, Parliament or the public.

6. Civil servants should endeavour to deal with the affairs of the
public efficiently, and without maladministration.

7. Civil servants should endeavour to ensure the proper, effective
and efficient use of public money within their control.

8. Civil servants should not make use of their official position or
information acquired in the course of their official duties to
further private interests. They should not receive benefits of any
kind from a third party which might reasonably be seen to
compromise their personal judgement or integrity.

9. Civil servants should conduct themselves in such a way as to
deserve and retain the confidence of Ministers, and to be able to
establish the same relationship with those whom they may be
required to serve in some future Administration. The conduct of

civil servants should be such that Ministers and potential future Ministers can be sure that that confidence can be freely given, and that the Civil Service will conscientiously fulfil its duties and obligations to, and impartially assist, advise and carry out the policies of the duly constituted Government.

10. Civil servants should not misuse information which they acquire in the course of their duties or seek to frustrate the policies, decisions or actions of Government by the unauthorised, improper or premature disclosure outside the Government of any confidential information to which they have had access as civil servants.[80]

The Government's response to the Select Committee, however, does represent a significant advance, and not just in its recognition that existing safeguards against ministerial misuse of the Civil Service, such as paragraph 55 of *Questions of Procedure for Ministers* (which, as noted in chapter 1, Sir Robin Butler described as having a largely 'discretionary status'[81]) and the Armstrong memorandum on *The Duties and Responsibilities of Civil Servants in Relation to Ministers*,[82] were inadequate for late twentieth-century purposes. For the reply to the Select Committee accepts implicitly that Parliament should have some say in the cultivation, even the replanting, of the once secret garden of the British Constitution. We have come a long way from the days when Sir Norman Brook in the Cabinet Office minuted Sir Edward Bridges in the Treasury in May 1952 to the effect that 'it is unwise to enter any discussion in Parliament about the relations between Ministers and their official advisers. I do not think that the House of Commons should be encouraged to go behind the principle that it is the Minister himself who is personally responsible to Parliament.'[83] The days of private government protected largely by what Clive Priestley has called 'the good chap theory' have finally gone. Late twentieth-century Britain, regrettably perhaps, has not produced a climate in which all the unspoken decencies can flourish unaided and unmonitored.[84]

Such developments, too, are a welcome change from the preoccupation with management that has dominated Civil Service reform since 1979, important though this has been. I remain a keen supporter of the Next Steps agencies but a sceptic about most market testing when it reaches beyond the contracting out of basic services and a convinced opponent of it when any hands, other than those of Crown servants under discipline, are applied to any activity where the state possesses coercive powers over the Queen's subjects, whether it be in the capacity of tax-gatherer or gaoler or law enforcer. Yet despite all the upheavals since Labour left office, one gap continues to yawn in any assessment of Whitehall practices suitable for treatment – the policy analysis capacity of the inner core. Ted Heath was the last Premier to address this seriously with his *The Reorganisation of Central Government* White Paper in 1970.[85] There have been no Rayner scrutinies and no charters in this area. And, very significantly, action here was one of the Treasury and Civil Service Select Committee's suggestions that the Government's White Paper turned down flat. 'We recommend', said the Select Committee, 'that the [Prime Minister's] Efficiency Unit carries out a scrutiny of the effectiveness and efficiency of the work of Ministers and support for Ministers.'[86] 'The Government does not propose to task the Efficiency Unit to conduct a scrutiny of the effectiveness and efficiency of the work of Ministers,' came their mistaken and shortsighted reply.[87] Even the most vigorous reforms have their no-go areas.

It is almost as if ministers were fearful of sharpening up Mr Gladstone's monsters, an impression reinforced by the slaughter of the intellects which has become part of the programme of fundamental expenditure reviews with the Treasury itself in the vanguard.[88] Ever since a Conservative politician with a fine political lineage of his own told me that it was the British way to have not-so-bright Etonians in ministerial suites telling sharp Wykehamists in Permanent Secretaries' offices what to do, I have harboured the suspicion that those who deployed their time at university in pursuit of union fame or political club fortune have been rather in awe of their contemporaries more devoted to the library and the life of the mind, producing, perhaps, a reluctance to widen the grey cell gap any further through the creation of, say, an enhanced Civil Service College or a renewed search for top-flight in-house advice mechanisms. From my observations of it, the national resource represented by the Whitehall pool of talent has not been used to maximum advantage since 1979 – far from it; and this is both a waste of public money and public servants and a real contributor to poor morale in the senior ranks.

On balance, however, the Civil Service has adjusted more swiftly and genuinely to the management reforms of the 1980s and 1990s than I would have expected had I known what was about to happen at the end of the 1970s. The same applies to the great surge of judicial review (from 160 cases in England and Wales in 1974 to 2,886 in 1993[89]) and the ever-lapping tide of European business and practice. I am genuinely confident, too, that the Civil Service would, notwithstanding a dash of transient mutual unfamiliarity, adapt wholeheartedly and properly to a future Labour administration. (I'm sure the fruitful discourse between the Treasury and Civil Service Committee and the government will have helped reassure the Shadow Cabinet on this point.) I am confident, too, that, if they had to, officials would skilfully adapt to a transformed constitutional scene: proportional representation; devolution – the lot. They may be like British colonial officials of old, knowing how to concede gracefully at the fifty-ninth minute of the eleventh hour, but a profession does not survive in the way the 1870 marque British Civil Service has without streaks of genuine flexibility concealed behind that 'monstrous experience'.

SIX

Parliament

The Little Room

There is no statute or legal usage of this country which requires that the ministers of the Crown shall hold seats in one or other of the Houses of Parliament. It is perhaps on this account that, while most of my countrymen would as I suppose declare it to be a becoming and convenient custom, yet comparatively few are aware how near the seat of life the observance lies, how closely it is connected with the equipoise and unity of the social forces.

W. E. Gladstone, 1879[1]

Account should be taken of the extent and real character of the responsibility of ministers; the relations of members of the Cabinet to one another and to the Prime Minister; the development of the party system; and the diminished power of the House of Commons as compared with the ministry on the one hand and the electorate on the other.

Sir Sidney Low, 1904[2]

This little room is the shrine of the world's liberties.

Winston Churchill, 1917[3]

There is one particular condition which is necessary for the successful working of any form of democracy, but more particularly that of the Westminster Model, that is the willingness of the minority to accept the will of the majority in the hope that they too will in due course become the majority.

Clement Attlee, 1943[4]

There is no more striking illustration of the immobility of British institutions than the House of Commons.

H. H. Asquith, 1926[5]

In word-association terms, Parliament (the House of Commons in particular) summons up an immediate image on the visual display unit of memory, an image all the more vivid since the House was televised regularly in 1989 just in time for the hugely telegenic demise of the Thatcher premiership. Once more we are contemplating an institution as deeply familiar as it is bafflingly arcane.

Yet no two images of the legislative limb of the constitutional pentangle that is the subject of this volume are quite the same. Whenever the subject of Parliament activates my own grey cells I feel the urge, to borrow a parliamentary phrase, to declare an interest. For me, Parliament is, as the representative principle would have it be, a microcosm of the United Kingdom in the sense that I wish both of them to flourish, want to think well of them and feel pained when I cannot. With Sir Henry Campbell-Bannerman, I want the Palace of Westminster, the House of Commons especially, to act as the 'grand inquest of the nation'.[6] Like Bagehot I recognize that its functioning as 'a great and open council' should be its prime performance indicator.[7] I only wish that Sir Sidney Low, writing in 1904, had been committing to paper a description that held good for parliamentary life at any point in the twentieth century when he depicted the House of Commons 'as the visible centre, the working motor of our constitution'.[8] I fear that Low and A. V. Dicey were more accurate when, with the development of the Cabinet in mind, plus the growth of the electorate and the rise of the party machine in the second half of the nineteenth century, they saw power by the turn into the twentieth as having seeped away from Parliament *out* to the electorate (when it came to the making and unmaking of governments) and *up* to the Cabinet (in terms of the initiation of legislation).[9]

Part of me wants to be utterly romantic about Parliament in the style of Enoch Powell – remember his extraordinary argument: 'take Parliament out of the history of England and that history itself becomes meaningless' and its rider that 'the British nation could not imagine itself except with and through its Parliament'?[10] – though

I'm too aware of how much power remained with the Prime Minister and ministers in Whitehall to share his view that the greatest gift of the monarchy after 1688 was to give its absolute powers absolutely to Parliament.[11] But being crossed in love, as it were, by both the Whitehall and the Westminster reality has left me sceptical rather than cynical – two very different states of mind. I want Parliament to come closer to the Campbell-Bannerman/Low/Bagehot specifications; and, unlike a cynic, I think it can – perhaps even in time for the twenty-first century. Without doubt, the twentieth has belonged to the executive, not the legislature. Ours is very much the executive's Constitution.

Yet I find consolation for my ambiguity, almost my near-schizophrenia about Parliament in discovering quite frequently that I am not alone in suffering from it. Take the greatest romantic of all about British constitutional practice, Winston Churchill. To him, unsurprisingly perhaps, goes the palm for the most eloquent single twentieth-century evocation of the romance of the Commons. It is recorded in the diary of McCallum Scott, then a fellow Liberal MP. It is March 1917; a particularly fraught moment in the Great War. 'As we were leaving the House that night,' McCallum Scott recorded, he [Churchill]

> called me into the Chamber to take a last look round. All was darkness except a ring of faint light all around under the Gallery. We could dimly see the Table but walls and roof were invisible. 'Look at it,' he said. 'This little place is what makes the difference between us and Germany. It is in virtue of this that we shall muddle through to success and for lack of this Germany's brilliant efficiency leads her to final destruction. This little room is the shrine of the world's liberties.[12]

The same Churchill, admittedly fading and having recently suffered the stroke that almost terminated his premiership in June 1953,[13] dictated the following dismissively dyspeptic minute despatching early suggestions that Parliament should be televised:

> Although I am against televising or broadcasting Parliamentary Debates, except on special occasions in wartime, I see no objec-

tion to doing this for the State Opening of Parliament. This ceremony is spectacular and infrequent: Parliamentary debate is boring, commonplace and perpetual.[14]

Routine, of course, is the great enemy of romance in all its forms.

Harold Macmillan, another melancholy romantic in politics, suffered similarly when romance met reality. The man who in the late 1940s could declare, with impeccably parliamentarian spirit, that 'we have not overthrown the divine right of Kings to fall down before the divine right of experts'[15] (if ever that had been, or would be, a danger in our polity) reacted dismissively as Prime Minister in 1959 to a suggestion from the Speaker that Ministers could be more effective in imparting information to MPs if they kept their replies to parliamentary questions brief, enabling thereby more questions to be handled in the time allotted. The Cabinet Secretary, Sir Norman Brook, thought the Speaker's point a valid one and pressed it on his Prime Minister, only to be 'reminded' by Macmillan 'that when Mr Cross, in a difficulty, asked Mr Disraeli whether he should be short, Mr Disraeli's advice was "No, you should be prolix and obscure." '[16]

Yet romanticism in the pursuit of successful and effective parliamentary government is no vice, and cynicism in the face of the humdrum, often trivial daily reality is no virtue, because a vibrant legislature at the centre of a nation's political life is an indispensable precondition for the maintenance of an open and a civil society. It is a first-order question. The factors which diminish its vitality, centrality and relevance need serious attention; and as the twentieth century fades, those factors are abundant. The 'anonymous empire' (to borrow Sammy Finer's phrase[17]) of hidden financial interests at Westminster, a key trigger for the commissioning of the Nolan Inquiry, is but the latest and most prominent cause of public unease. I do not in any way diminish its importance, believing with Tony Benn that 'Members of Parliament are elected to act as consultants to the British people,'[18] not this company, that PR firm or those financial interests. The ecology of any legislature is seriously contaminated if the suspicion arises that a significant number of its legislators are up for sale.

The besetting problem of any attempted analysis of our parliamentary malaise is an overconcentration on detail (however revealing and significant in itself) at the expense of the bigger picture. Pondering this over the Christmas and New Year break in 1994–5 I was helped, as I so often am, by a bout of immersion in the newly released files at the Public Record Office. Another batch arrived from the engine room of the British state: the working papers of the Cabinet Office, preserved in the CAB 21 series which affords the richest and rarest glimpses of our mercurial Constitution, as we have seen in previous chapters.

The particular file that set me thinking on this occasion concerned the House of Commons Select Committee on Procedure, which sat from 1956 to 1959 under the chairmanship of James Stuart.[19] The initiative for it came not from the House but from the Lord Privy Seal and Leader of the House, R. A. Butler. He thought an inquiry would suit the government provided its terms of reference were carefully restricted to the possibility of using Standing Committees to take minor government Bills, the reorganization of the Scottish Grand Committee and the handling of Private Members' Bills that might involve public expenditure. The whole enterprise reeks of executive-mindedness – which is not surprising as the real running was made by a group of civil servants commissioned by the Cabinet's Home Affairs Committee. They even provided Rab with speaking notes for his appearance before the Procedure Committee itself, suggesting appealing phrases appropriate for delivery by a devoted parliamentarian. Parliament had two main features, they argued in their staccato note form:

(a) Natural coming together of MPs, mart of exchange of ideas.
(b) Place where human nature given full rein and applies its
     own restraints.
    Politics a struggle for power and rules of procedure must not
remove mainspring from human nature or flatten all opportunity
for controversy.

Rab, though a genuine believer in all the ancient institutions of state, was gratefully guided by his civil servants, so much so that he penned one of the celebrated thank-you notes which made him such a favourite inside Whitehall. To Michael Reed of the Cabinet Office he wrote: 'This is a line to thank you (and your Committee) for doing such hard work on the Procedure of Parliament. I gave evidence based on your hard labour and I think it was successful.'[20] It was, to put it crudely, an inside job from start to finish.

What of the Opposition? Did they make a spirited stand for back-bench power? They did not. As Rab told the Cabinet at the outset, 'From the Government's point of view, there is no . . . need for a comprehensive review of procedure . . . Nor is there any inclination, at least on the surface, that the Opposition wish for it.'[21] The reason is plain. The powerful executive bias within the British system of government suited Labour perfectly well. It had done so when they were in office and propelled by a big majority between 1945 and 1950, and they had every expectation that it would do so again.

Those inside files, which can be raided so fruitfully by those in search of the private thoughts of the mighty (especially in the period for which there was no fifty- let alone thirty-year rule for the disclosure of official papers), also throw a bright and revealing light on the 'we are the masters at the moment' period (to borrow the famous phrase of Hartley Shawcross[22]) of British Labour. At the very moment when Parliament needed to raise its game to match the extending reach of the British state, with the great postwar nationalizations and the construction of a Beveridge-style welfare system, the Labour government, very much influenced by the views of the new Leader of the House, Herbert Morrison, would have no truck with this idea, even when the reform blueprint came from so seasoned and respected a pair of hands as those of Sir Gilbert Campion, Clerk of the House of Commons.

Campion proposed a fusion of the Public Accounts and Estimates Committees to create a new Public Expenditure Committee which would break down into seven sub-committees to examine the accounts and estimates of all government departments. Ministers were appalled and produced 'strong objections' in the Cabinet group set up to deal with the Procedure Committee Report of 1946.[23] 'The history of the war-time Select Committee on National Expenditure shows that the proposed Committee would be likely to encroach on

policy and thus come into conflict with Ministers,'[24] declared the
minutes of the meeting; and that would never do. This was a government, too, which commandeered all Private Members' time until
1949 to enable it to ram its legislative programme through
Parliament.[25]

Mr Attlee spoke for virtually all the possessors of power in the
twentieth-century British state when he said: 'We have our debates
and opposition but at the end there is not left a little barren controversy, but a good fat volume of Acts of Parliament.'[26] For the central
feature of the parliamentary patch of the British Constitution since
Balfour consolidated the procedural reforms of the late nineteenth
century in 1902[27] is that the century has belonged to the executive.
Everything else is overshadowed by that fact. There have been exceptions when governments have possessed a slim majority or no majority at all. But our first-past-the-post system of voting, plus the
growing shadow of William Holmes (the first recognizably modern
and grand manipulator in the Whips' Office between 1812 and
1830[28]) has meant that in modern times the Westminster Parliament
has been the parade ground of the best-drilled brute votes in any
advanced Western democracy, notwithstanding the growing appetite
for backbench dissent over the past quarter of a century.[29] For most
of the postwar period on most issues our elected representatives
have been reduced, in Austin Mitchell's vivid phase, to 'heckling the
steamroller'.[30] Add to this the narrowing of the British political class
that has accompanied its growing professionalization, leaving 'politicians ... increasingly a caste apart' (as Peter Riddell has put it
in his marvellous study of the rise of the career politician, *Honest
Opportunism*[31]), and you have before you a House of Commons that
falls well short of Bagehot's 'great and open council'. Remind your-
self of the convention which restricts the choice of ministers to the
members of one or other of the Houses of Parliament (which, as
the century wore on, increasingly meant the Commons rather than
the Lords), and you find causes for real concern.

A note of caution should be sounded at this point. Beware of
incipient bufferdom on the part of those who, like Willie Whitelaw[32]
and Denis Healey,[33] tend to lament the differences between the

political generation fashioned by slump and war and that which had virtually completely succeeded it by the end of the 1980s. More seriously, it is time to call in the phantom management consultant and examine the functions of Parliament, the House of Commons especially, to establish some performance criteria before continuing this critique. In short, what is Parliament for?

Providing a brief and simple answer has never been easy for what, since 1707 at least, we can call the British Parliament, as it fuses 'legislative, judicial and executive functions in an exceptional constitutional mixture', as David Judge has put it,[34] deliberately blending powers where other nations have tended to separate them out. Like David Judge, I am convinced that it is necessary to restate the commonplace that our parliamentary practice is 'representative' rather than 'democratic' and has remained so ever since 1950, the first general election in which the British people polled on the basis of one person, one vote. As Judge puts it:

> The enduring features of the parliamentary tradition in England, and later in the United Kingdom, have stemmed from the practical requirements and consequences of the process of representation, not from popular participation. The parliamentary tradition has thus been one of the transmission of opinion between the 'political nation' – variously defined throughout history – and the executive. Through this simple process of transmission, governments have been controlled, executive actions have been consented to by the representatives of the 'political nation' and changes of governors legitimised.[35]

Absolutely right; and I am with Professor Judge, too, when he goes on to remind those who succumb too readily and too completely to the view that both power *and* influence (which are not the same things at all) have long since quit the Palace of Westminster, whether it be to Whitehall, to the European Union, to NATO or to the money markets, that Parliament still matters. For the functions he cites 'are the traditional hallmarks of the British State . . . the features that have persisted . . . in the institutional form of Parliament',[36] a view not that far removed from Bagehot's, in his 1867 list in *The*

English Constitution. Bagehot produced five functions, plus a possible sixth:

1 The provision and maintenance of the executive.
2 The expressive function, i.e. reflecting the mind of 'the English people in all matters that come before it'.
3 The teaching function (here's where the 'great and open council' comes in, teaching 'the nation what it does not know').
4 The informing function, expressing the grievances of the governed to the government.
5 The function of legislation.[37]

Bagehot was ambivalent about the sixth function – finance[38] – which is odd, as the granting of supply was one of the original purposes of Parliament.

Aided by Bagehot, David Judge and that skilled contemporary anatomist of parliamentary purposes, Professor Philip Norton, I would offer the following list for the mid-1990s British Parliament (by which I mean principally the House of Commons):

1 The ultimate determination of who gains, retains and loses power on the basis that the distribution of seats in the Commons reflects and transmits the wishes of the electorate.
2 Providing the ministerial cadre of government; testing the mettle of both ministers and would-be ministers; operating as a crude indicator of reputation (who's up and who's down). Television has enhanced this function, as was illustrated most dramatically by Sir Geoffrey Howe's resignation speech in November 1990 and its subsequent effect on Mrs Thatcher's position.
3 The granting of assent and legitimacy to some, though not all, of the policies, decisions and actions of the executive (remember the swathe of powers available to ministers under the Royal Prerogative) through the passage of legislation, debate and divisions of the House.
4 Scrutinizing and influencing the conduct and administration of government policy through parliamentary questions, Select

Committee hearings and correspondence between MPs, ministers and agency chief executives.

5 The voting of funds to finance those (and only those) activities approved by Parliament.

6 The scrutiny of European legislation and policy.

7 Transmitting the concerns, grievances and opinions of the governed to the government.

8 Representing the wider nation (in terms not just of constituencies and parties but also of interests, lobby groups and minorities) to facilitate the operation of democracy and democratic accountability between election days.

Apart from number 6, the European entry, which dates from 1 January 1973, there is a timelessness about this list (though I do accept that Tony Benn's general point about the parliamentary consequences of Britain's membership of the European Communities/Union has bite when he says of the period since accession: 'The link between the grievance, the ballot box and the remedy has been broken'[39]). The list has a core quality, too, for even if the notion of subsidiarity came to mean anything substantial, with powers siphoned from Westminster and Whitehall upwards to Brussels and Strasbourg or downwards to Edinburgh, Cardiff, some new regional tier of government in England or a revivified local government, those functions, albeit perhaps a little clipped or curtailed, would remain the purposes of the national Parliament – a view very much in line with both Powell's and Judge's notions of the centrality of Parliament to the history of the English, and later the British, nation-state.

It is all the more important, therefore, that these functions should be performed in good order and with something approaching general approval. In fact, it is very easy to point to under-performance in all of them. Let us scan some of the more commonplace reservations about each in turn.

1 On the retention of power, tight whipping usually saves the day for the government; and if it does not, deals can be struck (as with the Ulster Unionists since the Maastricht showdowns) with groups representing a tiny fraction of the

electorate who do not wish a government to fall for narrow reasons of their own.

2 The pool of talent contained by Parliament is artificially shallow and meagre compared to the needs of a trading nation locked in relative economic decline, and parliamentary reputations have little to do with real quality.

3 Too many MPs in the governing party are too supine to provide a real check on their ministers on most issues; oppositions are too indiscriminate in their opposition; and a mere glance at the Hansard Society's 1993 study of the legislative process should dispel any lingering illusions about quality in that core activity.[40]

4 The Select Committees, sometimes, apart, the Commons is too inexpert and too slovenly to stretch the executive seriously when calling its activities to account.

5 The bulk of the £250 billion plus of annual public expenditure goes through unexamined in detail. Even the Select Committees are remiss here.

6 The Commons and Lords Committees watching Europe try hard, but many issues come to them too late and they fail to sound the tocsins in time. Their work is almost completely unknown to the public and the press pays too little attention to them.

7 The transmission of grievances is flawed (again, with the occasional exception of the Select Committees) because MPs are partisans who get where they are and stay where they are by 'mobilizing prejudice', to use David Marquand's apt phrase.[41]

8 The same problem applies to the representation of wider interests, though the Select Committees are, once more, an exception, given their ability to summon the personnel of regulatory bodies, quangos, pressure groups, companies and academics to give evidence in person or on paper, thereby incorporating them, albeit to a limited degree, within the parliamentary process. They can and do do the same with officials of the European Commission.

One reaction to this syndrome of underachievement is to treat it as a systems failure and to argue that tinkering is hopeless. There is something in this. It would make sense to have an all-encompassing look at the representational working parts of the Constitution with subsidiarity especially in mind. It would be sensible to agree first on what is best done at which level, from parish council to Strasbourg, and to arrange functions, powers and relationships accordingly, not least checks and balances, bills of rights and ways of arbitrating disputes between all levels. And while about this, one might look at the voting systems at the various levels – the ways the parties choose their candidates for winnable seats, the conventions about who can and who cannot be a minister.

Nor should the House of Lords be forgotten. No grand new settlement could credibly leave important legislative functions in the hands of those who owe their position either to blood or to executive patronage. Though a believer in a second, revising chamber; fond as I am of many who adorn today's red leather benches; and purr with pleasure as I did when their lordships inflicted over a hundred defeats, albeit mainly temporary ones, on Mrs Thatcher's government in her first two Parliaments as Prime Minister – even now I sometimes curse Harold Macmillan for saving the Lords as a patronage House through the creation of life peerages in 1958. 'Bobbety' Salisbury was surely right when he told the Cabinet Committee on Lords Reform three years earlier that a 'surgical operation' was needed 'in the very near future if the patient's life was to be saved' or 'it would die through sheer lack of vitality'.[42]

Another way of reacting to the shortcomings, which the most astute parliamentarians themselves recognize (I have in mind MPs like John Garrett,[43] Graham Allen[44] and Austin Mitchell[45]), is to pretend that the proposed remedies are more damaging and dangerous than the ills they seek to cure. The law of unintended consequences is often invoked, as is an appeal to the bequest of history as giving us governing arrangements that are organic, logically indefensible but adaptable, tried and tested and sanctified by posterity and lauded by envious foreigners. The Prime Minister is currently the leading exponent of this school, the intensity of his appeals to the sanctity of 'the Union' varying in inverse relationship to his standing in the polls. Of the Labour leadership and their plans for devolution he said in December 1994: 'If ever they had their way, you wouldn't be able to recognize the Britain we have known for 300 years. It would not be a new Britain, but the beginning of the end of Britain.'[46] As *The Economist*'s 'Bagehot' rather cruelly observed of Mr Major: 'He has not had the benefit of a leisured education, of immersion in constitutional study. His own elevation – born at the bottom, now occupying the highest post in the land – had made him a fervent believer in the *status quo*.'[47]

That last point is a powerful one. Never underestimate the constitutional conservatism of those who have been propelled to the top under the existing rules of the game. They are the last people to see shortcomings in current arrangements; and yet, usually, they are the only ones in a position to initiate and engineer change: hence the constitutional paralysis which is Britain's normal condition. Add to this the folk memory of the 1960s and 1970s, of the failed attempt to reform the Lords in 1968–9 and those fruitless hours frittered away on devolution by the Labour government between 1976 and 1979 and you can see why the likes of Jim Callaghan and Denis Healey are sceptical of their successors' plans to reopen the constitutional question if power is regained.[48]

There is a third reaction to any audit of the human, procedural and constitutional shortcomings of Parliament which avoids both the 'all's well and even if it isn't don't tamper' school and the 'tear it all down' tendency, which is the 'let's make what we have work better' approach; what one might call the 'go guilefully with the grain' line. This is the one I favour, partly from a personal streak of traditionalism but chiefly because it is the only kind of reform with a real chance of taking relatively swiftly. Nor is it necessarily a counsel of despair. There have been developments in its last quarter that have begun to mitigate some of the worst effects of the executive century. Given my partial exemption of them from several of my strictures, it is plain that I have the post-1979 network of House of Commons Select Committees primarily in mind. And it is these same bodies that come to mind when pondering an incremental approach to reform, in view of my inability to wave the wand of subsidiarity over our hierarchy of representation, or to infiltrate the selection committees of the two major parties in their winnable seats, or to change the electoral system, or to design and build a new elected second chamber.

I rate the establishment of the so-called departmentally related Commons Select Committees in 1979 as not just the most significant parliamentary development of the postwar period, but the single most important clawback in terms of the relative influence of the legislature and the executive since the Balfour reforms of 1902. I use the work 'influence' deliberately. It is not the same as 'power'. Governments govern; Parliament does not, even though without the consent of Parliament no government can exercise power for long.

It was unfortunate for the new Select Committees that the Leader of the House who introduced them, Norman St John-Stevas, rather oversold them when presenting his plans to the Commons in June 1979. 'The proposals that the Government are placing before the House of Commons', he said, 'are intended to redress the balance of power to enable the House of Commons to do more effectively the job it has been elected to do.'[49] I am reluctant to criticize Lord St John of Fawsley (as he now is) in any way. He steered his proposals through the Cabinet skilfully (doing a deal with Lord Hailsham whereby the Law Officers' departments were exempted – an anomaly not put right till 1992[50]); and we now know from Geoffrey Howe's memoirs just how reluctant Mrs Thatcher, one of the most executive-minded Premiers of the century, was about the whole idea.[51] But that phrase about 'redressing the balance of power' inflated expectations. Given the adversarial, knock-down drag-out nature of the world of politics, unless governments were undone, or, at the least, the occasional Cabinet minister scalped, as a result of Select Committee grillings and reports, the new bodies were doomed to be deemed by some to have failed.

There is always a danger of this kind of lurking behind long-awaited constitutional change: the expected apocalypse fails to materialize. (Devolved assemblies and freedom of information, when and if they come, will, I predict, be subject to the same syndrome.)

And the departmental Select Committees *had* taken an age to come. They were foreshadowed in the great Haldane Report of 1918.[52] Campion's 1946 vision was more or less made flesh in the Expenditure Committee and its sub-groups in 1971 (though the Public Accounts Committee has continued magisterially and effectively as a solo performer). And, like all reforms, the St John-Stevas proposals could only create the possibility of change, not guarantee it: that would be up to the MPs who peopled the new committees. But in 1979, at last, the artificial and self-defeating neurosis about the distinction between policy and administration was ended once and for all. Though Herbert Morrison and Rab Butler would have been horrified, the constitutional roof failed to fall in upon the once forbidden garden of policy.

Within ten years it was difficult to see what the fuss had been about. When the Procedure Committee examined their performance in 1989–90, Geoffrey Howe, by this time Leader of the House, said the new Select Committees have become 'an indispensable part of the work of the House of Commons ... They have established themselves as important contributors to the parliamentary functions of scrutiny, investigation and influence over the work of the executive'[53] – which given the fusion of our executive and legislature in Parliament, is as much as could have been hoped for them in terms of power (a word that Howe, unlike St John-Stevas, omitted to use).

The Select Committees are now a huge enterprise, a new sub-estate (if not quite a full estate) of the realm and one which, unlike the Commons Chamber itself, usually proceeds on a consensual, all-party basis. They began as fourteen in 1979 and there are now seventeen of them (including, I am pleased to say, a Science and Technology Committee to restore the greatest single loss in the rejigging of fifteen years ago). For the 1992–3 session of Parliament, thanks to the researches of Philip Giddings, we can almost weigh the scrutiny function as now carried out by the Commons. In that year, the departmental Select Committees held 663 meetings and issued 129 reports totalling 16,456 pages after 57 sessions with Cabinet ministers, 55 with ministers below Cabinet rank, 427 civil servants and 215 officials from so-called 'associated public bodies'. To this one must add the Public Accounts Committee's 63 reports and 4,436 pages, the Select Committee on the Parliamentary Commissioner for Administration's four reports and 214 pages and the Select Committee on European Legislation's 41 reports and 1,232 pages. In all 300 MPs were involved in this business out of a total House of 651.[54] Big business by any standards.

I use the word 'weigh' deliberately. Measurement is another matter. Quality has varied, as has impact, over the past fifteen years. I am aware of the deficiencies; here is a list of the most important.

1 Of the 500 plus departmental Select Committee reports since 1979, only four have been debated *and* voted upon on the floor of the Commons.[55]

2 The committees have proved reluctant to examine the details of departmental expenditure, despite an improvement in the data available.

3 There have been very few instances of committees holding pre-legislative hearings.

4 Some committees have deliberately kept away from the most important, if politically controversial, subjects for fear of jeopardizing their consensuality: the Environment, Scotland, and Wales Committees' failure to tackle the poll tax question is the most glaring example.[56]

5 The committees generally have declined to have showdowns with the government on the floor of the House when Whitehall departments have proved reluctant to recognize in full the committees' right to 'send for persons papers and records'.[57] For example, the gap between the material available to the Select Committee on Trade and Industry during its inquiry into the Iraqi 'Supergun' affair and the papers available to the Matrix Churchill trial after Judge Smedley insisted on the 'discovery of documents' was painful to behold.

6 Successive serving Prime Ministers have not appeared before any Select Committee.

7 The influence of the Whips, though always difficult to
  measure precisely, has been too great in determining Select
  Committee membership and chairmanships, despite the
  existence of a Committee of Selection to do the job.

Notwithstanding these shortcomings, I would maintain that the
Select Committees have come the closest by far of any of the working
parts of today's House of Commons to Bagehot's 'great and open
council', not least in their success at bringing what Mr Gladstone
would have called 'out of doors' elements within the embrace of the
House of Commons. This was perhaps the most striking feature to
emerge from Derek Hawes' case study of the Environment Select
Committee.[58] Hawes constructed what he called 'a taxonomy of
influence'[59] which was impressive (even allowing for my earlier strictures about the Environment Committee and the poll tax) – especially if you accept, as I do, Leo Amery's view that 'the main task of
Parliament is still what it was when first summoned, not to legislate
or govern, but to secure full discussion and ventilation of all matters.'[60] Here, in summary, is the 'Hawes taxonomy' of Select Committee influence:

1 exposing loopholes in existing legislation;
2 bringing new concerns to the attention of the House;
3 exposing inadequacies of performance on the part of
  departments, agencies and quangos;
4 scrutinizing the quality of administrative decision-taking;
5 eliciting facts, forecasts and projections from departments,
  agencies and quangos;
6 exposing conflicts of policy between departments;
7 exposing unannounced policy change;
8 updating publicly available knowledge and supplying
  backbenchers with new, specialist knowledge;
9 providing a 'bridge to Europe' by inviting the European
  Commission and other governments to provide evidence;
10 incorporating quangos into Parliament's orbit by inquiring
  into their funding and operations;

11 exposing interest groups and lobbyists and accommodating them within the parliamentary process;

12 mediating between interests, creating the possibility of new 'policy coalitions' and influencing the 'policy community' generally;

13 raising the profile of issues and spurring departments, agencies and quangos to action.

I would add one important factor to the 'Hawes taxonomy' – the impact of television. Since 1989 Select Committee hearings have had a much greater chance of featuring on the main television bulletins, sometimes even of leading them if a Cabinet Minister or, occasionally, a Permanent Secretary or agency chief executive has found him- or herself pinned to the committee room panelling by a tough line of questioning. This gave the new Select Committees a whole new order of public visibility a decade after their creation.[61]

This, of course, is not the story of all committees and every inquiry. But the possibility of sustained scrutiny is there, and the information accumulated and disseminated since 1979 does leave the Select Committees unchallenged in-house as the thinking and analytical capacity of Parliament. If MPs wish to make use of committee products they are now in a position to be far more informed than any previous parliamentary generation. The same applies to the opposition; Select Committees are a way of reducing, though not eliminating, the briefing gap between the two front benches.

Developments since 1979 have, I think, created the possibility of the Select Committees becoming not, in Bagehot's imagery, the hyphen which joins (or buckle which fastens) the legislature to the executive, but rather something more subtle, though in its way potentially very effective. For what the Select Committees already are (and could become to a greater degree) is a sensitive membrane between the legislature and the executive, capable of transmitting swiftly and efficiently the knowledge, views and insights of each to the other – the whole process tautened by that touch of the adversarial which, quite rightly, spices the relationship (though the government of the day, if it has a parliamentary majority, will enjoy one too on each committee), despite the bias towards consensus inherent in the all-party format.

So, in the spirit of Bagehot, I would argue that the late 1990s should see an improvement in the best of the 'living reality' in Parliament. If a Labour government is elected in 1996 or 1997, its Leader of the House should suggest that the Procedure Committee does not wait until the turn of the century to examine the Select Committee system once more. If such a government were about to carry out its pledges to legislate for devolution to Scotland and Wales in its first year, while at the same time embracing the European Union, its institutions and its parliament more warmly, the Westminster Parliament really would need to raise its game in a climate of subsidiarity on every side.

This, I suggest, would be a sensible and achievable agenda for the next stage of reform.

1 The creation of an expectation, if not an obligation, that the Select Committees will undertake pre-legislative hearings on important Bills.

2 The arousal of a similar expectation that they will examine regularly the expenditure plans of the departments, agencies and quangos which come within their remits.

3 To assist the achievement of this, the National Audit Office (which currently serves the Public Accounts Committee alone) should be redesigned and extended to enable it to work for other Select Committees interested in examining the efficiency and effectiveness of current, not past, departmental activity.

4 An enhancement of the official information available to Select Committees. Already there are encouraging signs here. The 'new Osmotherly Rules', published in December 1994,[62] are a great improvement. They have been purged of the more absurdly restrictive and patronizing passages in the previous *Memorandum of Guidance for Officials Appearing Before Select Committees*.[63] They reflect the contents of the 1993 *Open Government* White Paper,[64] which itself creates the

possibility of a much richer flow of material on current policy to Select Committees.

5 Committees should follow the lead of the Treasury and Civil Service Committee in its 1993–4 inquiry into the role of the Civil Service[65] by interesting themselves in the constitutional and procedural aspects of state activity. (And the TCSC itself would do us all a great service if it prised out of the Cabinet Office as much as possible of Sir Robin Butler's 'Precedent Book'.) It is high time Parliament wrote itself back into the constitutional script as the scrutineer of the mysterious operations of British constitutional practice. The hidden wiring of the central state should be a matter of crucial interest to the House of Commons. For this reason a convention should be established that the committees, the TCSC in particular (because of its public service remit), should be able to summon and question both the Prime Minister and the Deputy Prime Minister.

6 Another look should be taken at Parliament's capacity to examine proposed European legislation effectively and in time.

7 Thought will need to be given to possible adjustments at Select Committee level if, in an era of devolution, Scottish and Welsh (and perhaps English regional) matters are to be handled and incorporated in a serious, sensible way within the national Parliament.

In short, this time Parliament must be ahead of the game rather than trapped in a time-lag, a prisoner of its own ancient structures (to adopt a phrase of Peter Jenkins's[66]), contributing in its own way to our domestic democratic deficit.

I finish this chapter where I began it, by reiterating the enduring centrality of the Westminster Parliament in our national life. If changes of any serious kind to the policies, the politics or the constitutional arrangements of our country are to take place, they will have to be discussed and shaped and legitimized through Parliament. There is no surrogate forum. And for those in pursuit of power, even if they ultimately wish to alter its distribution, command of a majority in the Commons is the indispensable prior requirement. As Graham Allen never tired of telling his Nottingham constituents in the mid-1990s: 'Even in Labour Nottinghamshire where we have won at District, County and European levels, it is still essential to win at Westminster level because only then can we make a real difference by breaking the command politics of the centre ... It is necessary to win the centre in order that it may be devolved.'[67] More on that centre and the burdens laid upon it in the next chapter.

SEVEN

Overload

Stress and the Opposition of Events

He was possessed of an imperious vitality, and what Burke called a 'quadrumanous activity' which penetrated into every office of the state ... It is always a new source of wonder to me to think of how inexhaustible Mr Gladstone's energies were.

Sir Algernon West, 1899[1]

MPs from both sides have commented on the immense workload that had led to a trail of 'broken marriages, ruined health and exhausted irrationality' ... and which means that 'outside bodies usually know far more about the impending legislation' than the people who are supposed to debate it.

Ashley Weinberg, 1993[2]

Those in élite positions very often succumb to the temptation to allow themselves to be told only what they want to hear, and this tendency may be encouraged by such personality traits as aggression or dogmatism, which have helped them to reach such positions.

Hugh Freeman, 1991[3]

There had been moments, even in democratic states, when the citizen body was so identified with the purposes of a government enjoying legitimacy and public trust that a sense of the common interest prevailed, as in Britain during the Second World War ... Governments had also, often enough, been able to rely on a consensus of peer judgement among their technical and scientific advisers, indispensable to administrations of laymen. When they spoke with the same voice, or, at any rate, their consensus overrode dissidents, policy controversy narrowed. It is when they do not, that lay decision-makers grope through darkness, like juries faced with rival psychologists called by prosecution and defence, neither of whom there is strong reason to believe.

Eric Hobsbawm, 1994[4]

Only after three months of rest did Jim Callaghan realise how tired he had been. The Queen had sympathetically commented to him on how relentless the Prime Minister's life had become.

John Cole, former BBC Political Editor, 1995[5]

In discussions of government, for much of the postwar period, the words 'system' and 'stress' have gone together: a malign reversal of the 'dignity' with 'efficiency' which Walter Bagehot saw as the key to stable and good government a century earlier.[6] This conjunction has affected both parties of government in equal measure, as two swift examples will illustrate.

Come with me first to Chequers in November 1974. The Labour government has just been returned with a majority of three. What Harold Wilson liked to describe as the most experienced Cabinet since Campbell-Bannerman's[7] has gathered to discuss strategy against a backdrop of a country gripped by stagflation and an economy tottering from a quadrupling of the oil price. Tony Crosland, Environment Secretary, Oxford-trained economist, philosopher of social democracy,[8] confronts the gathering gloom with this bleak and defeatist analysis. 'We did not know', he told the Cabinet, 'how our relative decline had taken place. "All we can do is to press every button we've got. We do not know which, if any of them, will have the desired results." '[9] Earlier, Jim Callaghan had confessed: 'When I am shaving in the morning I say to myself that if I were a young man I would emigrate. By the time I am sitting down to breakfast I ask myself "Where would I go?" '[10] Though he has insisted to me more than once since that he was joking, that is not exactly how others there at the time remember it.[11]

Come with me next to No. 10 Downing Street in the spring of 1981. Wilson has gone. Callaghan has come and gone, too, though mercifully not to Australia or Canada. (The 1970s were a decade that ate Prime Ministers.) Mrs Thatcher is now installed and preparing a punitively deflationary budget in the pit of a depression, this time against the backdrop of a divided Cabinet and an intensely polarized domestic politics. The former Chancellor and now party chairman, the seasoned and usually irrepressibly cheerful Peter Thorneycroft, comes into Mrs Thatcher's Policy Unit en route to a meeting with her and declares: 'Nothing works any more.'[12]

Power, of course, brings frustration as much as satisfaction, especially in a nation in relative economic decline. Asquith spoke for every twentieth-century Premier when, asked by a lady if he 'enjoyed having so much power?' he replied: 'Power, power? You may think you are going to get it but you never do.'[13] Churchill spoke for every Chancellor of the Exchequer since 1914 when he admitted in 1930 after his spell at the Treasury: 'It is no longer a case of one party fighting another, nor of one set of politicians scoring off another. It is the case of successive governments facing economic problems and being judged by their success or failure in the duel . . . The compass has been damaged. The charts are out of date.'[14]

Those who have worked closely with Premiers especially have noticed this paradox of weakness within strength at the top, from Douglas Jay in No. 10 in 1945–6 (likening even the highly efficient Attlee to 'more . . . of a cornered animal, or a climber on a rockface unable to go up or down, than that of a general ordering his troops wherever he wished around the landscape'[15]) to Bernard Donoughue in the Downing Street of the mid to late 1970s ('I was less aware of the Prime Minister's power than the constraints upon his power. When you are in there, you don't feel you can do anything'[16]). As I write I am sure that Mr Major, if he were able to look over my shoulder at the manuscript, would agree with Douglas Jay's conclusion that ' "power" tends to be something believed in mainly by those who have never worked near the putative centre of it.'[17] If he had a moment for reflection, it is the kind of thought that might occur to today's Premier during the frantic two-hour sessions that precede Prime Minister's Questions every Tuesday and Thursday when the House of Commons is sitting, during which Mr Major in the early to mid-1990s had to absorb 'around fifty bits of briefing'[18] to prepare for that unstructured and, in information terms, highly unproductive fifteen minutes of brouhaha which is so much a part of what John Birt accurately calls the 'feeding frenzy'[19] pattern into which much of our political discourse now falls.

Yet, as a senior civil servant put it, this twice-weekly Downing Street frenzy is 'a very important part of the PM's intelligence service'[20] as it channels information from departments into No. 10. And, as Lord Donoughue noted recently, a crisis gives a Premier the oppor-

tunity to intervene in departmental policy, and (though Lord Donoughue does not subscribe, and never has subscribed, to the prime
ministerial government thesis[21]) his experience tells him that in
governmental terms, 'the hidden wires don't come alive until they are
plugged in to the Prime Minister who is the generator.'[22]

In this chapter I want to look at 'overload' at the top, a problem
tackled by many if not all postwar Premiers with scant success.
Twenty years ago, Tony King expressed it in 'Sorcerer's Apprentice'
terms that still fit today: 'The waters rise. The apprentice rushes
around with his bucket. And none of us knows when, or whether,
the magician will come home.'[23] I shall examine it not just in terms
of workload, but in the context of recent medical and psychological
work on the health of the political class generally. I shall treat it,
too, in terms of systems as well as people, ground rules as well as
behaviour, including the perhaps partly avoidable price we pay for
living under what my sage friend Vernon Bogdanor described in
early 1995 as 'a very peculiar constitution which no one intended
. . . whereby the government of the day decides what the constitution
is'.[24] By way of conclusion I shall suggest possible remedies, of which
I believe there are some even when one has given full weight to my
opening theme – the crushing difficulty of managing the affairs of
a nation still, in Joe Chamberlain's words about the 'weary titan' of
late Victorian times, 'staggering under the too vast orb of its fate';[25]
and always bearing in mind Harold Macmillan's splendid line about
the force of punishing happenings unforeseen by any election manifesto, 'the opposition of events'[26] – a phrase John Major was heard
to quote to comfort himself after his own special events of 'Black
Wednesday' in September 1992.[27]

I am not a 'doomsday' man by either temperament or conviction.
But I have a growing belief that 'overload' is becoming ever more
serious as a problem (not least because successive efforts to roll back
the state since 1979 seem to have had little or no effect upon it);
that the special conditions which produced that tolerance on which
the British political system could rest, according to Mr Attlee in a
paper delivered to the War Cabinet in 1943,[28] can no longer be
presumed upon; and that the decencies of our Civil Service tradition

cannot be assumed to be secure for the next century, despite the reassurances of two successive White Papers.[29] Nor, sadly, do I see any real sign that A. J. Balfour's 1928 verdict on the ideological cohesion of our polity and politics is any more a vibrant reality – and only partly because his precondition of 'alternating Cabinets' has been absent for so long. 'Our whole political machinery', he observed so perceptively during the life of the second Labour government, 'presupposes a people so fundamentally at one that they can safely afford to bicker; and so sure of their own moderation that they are not dangerously disturbed by the never-ending din of political conflict.'[30] He added: 'May it always be so'[31] (conveniently forgetting, of course, the fundamental threats to party tolerance and even to the constitution posed by the Irish question a mere fifteen years earlier). It was so for an extended period after 1945. It is so no more; and gone with this climate is the trust once invested in the political class, as those ICM poll results quoted in chapter 1 show.[32]

However, I do believe there are some remedies (though no panaceas) within our grasp, provided we shed the smug habit, as Lord Hailsham once put it, 'of acquiring [our] institutions by chance or inadvertence, and shedding them in a fit of absent-mindedness'.[33] I am convinced that it is possible to work with the grain of experience and tradition while making matters better.

Lord Hailsham himself, as we know from a batch of No. 10 files declassified in January 1995, reckoned 'the present system [was] breaking down' as long ago as October 1962 and told the Prime Minister, Harold Macmillan, so in a paper on 'The Machinery of Government'.[34] Macmillan found Hailsham's analysis 'very impressive'[35] and the following January began to ponder ways of easing the burden on senior ministers to allow them collectively the time and space in Cabinet to examine policy across the board rather than piecemeal.[36] This became part of the 'modernization' theme with which he hoped to win the coming election; but the 'opposition of events' and his poor health swept him away before such a strategy could be put to the test.

Three days after his initial reply to Hailsham, Macmillan placed the problem of a wider systems failure before the full Cabinet. '*The Prime Minister* said', the minutes record,

> that discussion in Cabinet had shown that great changes would be taking place in the next two decades in the patterns of population and industry. He would like to present them to his colleagues in the wider context of the modernisation of Britain. This had many aspects. First, there was the question whether the present machinery of Ministerial Government was suitable for the conditions of to-day and the coming years. The burden on Ministers was becoming almost intolerably heavy, not merely in meeting the responsibility of the Cabinet, but also in taking the growing volume of decisions which their Departments and the public expected them to take personally, and in facing the daily barrage of the Press, radio and television. Members of Parliament generally were under similar pressures in meeting the demands of their constituencies. At the same time, the procedures of Parliament were designed for a less busy age. There were many Bills which had to come before Parliament, which were important and difficult in themselves, and absorbed a great deal of Parliamentary time, but were not concerned with matters of general policy or national interest. An abortive attempt had been made under the Labour Administration immediately after the last war to modernise Parliamentary procedure. It might be time for a new attempt. The Government should perhaps work out a plan to modernise their own machinery and that of Parliament, and seize the initiative in demonstrating that changes must be made to help the country to operate successfully in modern conditions.[37]

Macmillan's case is worth lingering over, because as one of his first acts as Prime Minister in 1957 he had commissioned a special inquiry into 'The Burden on Ministers' from a committee of Privy Counsellors under Lord Attlee; and yet no real purchase on the problem had been gained by the time of his resignation over six years later. Attlee's own attempt as Prime Minister to tackle 'overload' had, apart from one or two changes stemming from the Commons Procedure Committee Report of 1946,[38] concentrated on a more efficient use of the Cabinet committee system.[39] Churchill's revival of 'overlords' in peacetime was a graft that did not take, as we saw in chapter 4.[40] But until Ted Heath's 1970 White Paper, *The Reorganisation of Central Government*,[41] Macmillan's 1957 review was the most serious attempt to grapple with governmental overstretch since the break-up of the wartime coalition.

The idea for it was Sir Norman Brook's.[42] As Cabinet Secretary since 1947 he had, as his suggested draft Cabinet Paper told Macmillan, watched and witnessed the development of 'a strain which represents a real threat to efficiency and, in the long run, to health. There is no prospect that this will be lessened ... by a relaxation of the pressure of public business. We cannot, therefore, look for any automatic relief. If we are to have relief, we must secure it by adjusting our own methods of work.'[43]

Attlee's all-party committee of Privy Counsellors reported at the end of July 1957 and concentrated, with one dissenting voice to which I shall come shortly, on a better use of Cabinet committees, i.e. a streamlined status quo. 'We consider', they declared,

> that the Cabinet Committee system is the best means of co-ordinating policy, resolving disputes and giving effect to the collective responsibility of the Government. Our own experience and that of others whom we have consulted has, however, impressed on us the heavy burden of work which Committees throw on Ministers, particularly the most senior ones, unless they are organised and run with great efficiency. We therefore attach importance to the following measures for maintaining the efficiency of Committees and preventing them from adding unnecessarily to the pressures on ministers:
>
> 1 The number of Cabinet Committees and their membership should be regularly and critically reviewed.
> 2 Ministers should be instructed to settle as much as possible of their inter-departmental business direct with the other Ministers immediately concerned. Overburdening of Committees with unnecessary business often arises from lack of guidance to Ministers on the kind of question which needs to be referred to Committee or to the Cabinet.
> 3 Greater use should be made of Committees as instruments of decision to avoid repeated discussion of the same

question and overburdening of the Cabinet.
4 Chairmen of Committees should authorise senior
   Ministers with only a peripheral interest in the business
   under discussion to be represented by a Ministerial
   assistant. (We do not advise that this should be extended
   to Cabinet save, as hitherto, in exceptional circumstances.)
5 Constant vigilance is required to enforce brevity in Cabinet
   and Cabinet Committee memoranda. This is first and
   foremost the duty of the Ministers circulating papers. If
   their efforts are ineffective the Prime Minister and the
   Chairmen of the principal Committees should intervene.
6 Senior Ministers with heavy co-ordinating responsibilities
   as Chairmen of Committees need assistance in the form of
   precis and briefs on Committee memoranda. This
   should be provided by strengthening their Private Offices
   rather than by appointing officials specially for the
   purpose.[44]

Precious little happened as a result of this. A special Cabinet Committee on the Burden on Ministers, GEN 616, met but once in
October 1957 to consider the Attlee Report. Ministers, it decided,
might with benefit attend fewer public functions, unless they were
to speak, and 'attendance to welcome foreign visitors at airports
should be reduced to the unavoidable minimum.'[45]

A certain Edward Heath, present at both the GEN 616 meeting
and the Cabinet which considered stress on the system five years
later, did, however, make a spirited attempt as Prime Minister after
1970 to tackle these problems, and some of his solutions – notably
a smaller Cabinet with a strategic input from a Central Policy Review
Staff – could and should be revived with benefit all round. As mentioned in chapter 4, a new-style 'inner cabinet' could be linked to
such a rediscovery of old insights.

But each time I pick up Macmillan's 'The Burden on Ministers'
file from 1957 I am more and more convinced that the analysis of
the lone dissenter must be absorbed if the problem is ever to be
addressed seriously. That dissenter was Clement Davies, the former
Leader of the Liberal Party. In a separate letter to Macmillan he

argued that the recommendation of his colleagues, especially the proposal to make better use of junior ministers, 'will, to some extent, relieve the burden upon Ministers ... nevertheless the changes so made will not really affect the present position to the extent that is required.'[46] The lot of Parliament and Whitehall would be eased, Davies continued, only when they were 'relieved of duties which could be undertaken and better performed by Regional Sub-Parliaments or Councils'. He proposed 'a complete review of our forms of Local Government'. 'I believe', he concluded,

> that with the creation of the Regional Bodies working effectively, the Parliament of Westminster could complete its work in a three-day week. If that be so, one result would be to attract to the House of Commons men and women who, today, find themselves by reason of the importance of their calling, their work, or position, incapable of devoting any time to Parliament.[47]

There would, he added, be a concomitant reduction in the burden on Ministers.[48]

For his pains, Davies' views were casually dismissed by Macmillan's Principal Private Secretary, Freddie Bishop. In a brief for Macmillan he referred to 'a rather off-the-point minority suggestion by Mr Clement Davies'.[49] GEN 616 did not consider any of Davies' points.[50] Yet I am ever more convinced that unless the workload of Whitehall and Westminster is dispersed by some means, the problem will return again and again to haunt future Premiers as it has the last ten. I am a devolutionist for Scotland and Wales and by no means averse to regionalism for England (though I recognize the difficulties, which go way beyond the boundary-drawing problem). The single absurdity in the recent White Paper *The Civil Service: Taking Forward Continuity and Change* is its blank refusal to contemplate any examination of 'the effectiveness and efficiency of the work of Ministers and support for Ministers'.[51] Mr Major would do well to send for those old 'Burden on Ministers' files and think again.

He might send, too, for the 'Study of Future Policy' files from 1959–60 to see just what Whitehall at its best could manage when commissioned by Macmillan to take a no-holds-barred look at

Britain's place in the world by 1970.[52] A senior figure engaged in the Chequers briefing on an identical theme in January 1995[53] said that there was no comparison between the two:

> It was the first time for ages that there had been a gathering of this kind – you can never get ministers to *think* in London. There are always meetings to go to, people to see. And a great deal of their time is spent reacting to breaking stories in the news. The degree to which the media now drives policy is extraordinary and regrettable.
>
> But the machine, I'm sad to say, is no longer geared to producing the kind of work Macmillan received in 1960, partly because of current fixations about management when our core business should be policy advice. I wish it was.[54]

The depressing message contained in this heartfelt aside from a very seasoned official was that ministers and senior civil servants had over thirty-five years seen a decline in the capacity of British central government to think in depth about the long term. 'Day-to-day matters are so much easier,' he added. 'They are frightened of the really difficult subjects.'[55] Mr Major should ponder seriously this loss of capacity at the heart of his machine. Better still, he could consider commissioning a modern version of the Attlee Inquiry, with the brief of examining the processes of government as a systems question rather than a suitable case for tinkering. If he cannot be so persuaded, perhaps the Commons Treasury and Civil Service Select Committee, building on its own enhanced reputation for the serious treatment of matters governmental,[56] could be persuaded to do the job itself, in the interests not just of Mr Major but of the country as a whole.

If nothing is done, it is not only the efficiency of government that will continue to suffer; so, too, as Norman Brook warned nearly forty years ago, will the health of its leading practitioners, to the detriment of both them and us. For the burden is even greater now than it was in 1957. In fact, just through the famous door which separates No. 10 from the Cabinet Office, Mr Major will find a gem of an item prepared by one of his officials, David Laughrin, for businessmen who are members of the excellent Whitehall and Industry Group. It contains a very precise summation of the modern burden on ministers, known to my students as the 'Laughrin List'. Those whom Mr Laughrin calls the 'most senior ministers' with 'immensely crowded diaries' must:

- head a department and set the main policy agenda;
- make key decisions on the operation and organization of their departments;
- defend their policy and their departments in parliamentary scrutiny, at Question Time and before Select Committees, and in debates, against assaults from a 'rival firm' mounting every day a hostile 'takeover bid' (Her Majesty's Opposition);
- be the advocates of legislation in Parliament;
- take a leading role in public relations in front of an often hostile media;
- take a leading role in international negotiations;
- deal with pressure groups, companies and the public who wish to lobby for or against change;
- play a part for their party in making speeches and staying up late at night to vote on government legislation;
- play their full role as constituency MPs;
- play a role as husband/wife/father/mother in what remains of their private lives.[57]

To that list I would add 'play a full part in Cabinet and Cabinet committees, not just on items affecting his or her department but in shaping the collective line of the government as a whole'.

That, without doubt, is a physically and mentally health-sapping regime. As they say in the social services world, these people need help; and, as so often in life, they are the last ones to realize it. The wife of a very senior 1980s Cabinet minister once said of the constant decision-making under pressure 'Oh, they love it,'[58] and Peter Shore explained why. Being a Cabinet minister, he said, is 'endlessly stimulating . . . there is a kind of flow of energy that all Cabinet ministers have to have in order to deal with the workload which is truly enormous.'[59] Some, as Roy Jenkins once opined of Barbara Castle, make 'exhaustion into a political virility symbol'.[60]

I am sure this contributes to a twofold delusion among ministers

– first about their own competence and fitness to take decisions, and secondly about the power of the British Cabinet to influence events even within these shores. On the first point, I have never forgotten that every minister he asked refused to take the test dreamed up by Victor Rothschild in the early 1970s when head of the Central Policy Review Staff, which he called 'Are You Fit to Make Decisions After a Long Air Flight and Two Extra Gins?'[61] On the second I shall always remember David Howell, himself relatively fresh from the Cabinet, admitting: 'The history of postwar British Cabinets has been a continuous story of people trying to do too much, believing that they had power over events which in fact they lacked, treating national circumstances as entirely within their control and twirling the wheel on the bridge as though every move would produce an instant response in some well-oiled engine room below.'[62]

Of course, politics as a profession is immensely risky and tends to appeal to chancers who live on a diet of adrenalin and are engaged in a constant search for 'boredom avoidance'. The psychologist Professor Norman Dixon has painted a truly alarming picture of this *genus* which, to make matters worse, has an inclination to think that rules, moral or financial, apply to others rather than to them.[63] As a result, he says, self-interest is put before the common good. Their wants 'include the need for adulation and approval, the urge to bolster self-esteem, the compulsion to act out some private prejudice or delusion, to avenge some personally experienced slight, to redress an ancient grievance, to dispel doubts about one's virility, and of course sheer unadulterated megalomania – the seeking of power over others'.[64] Not quite how Sir Norman Brook would have put it.

But the health matters of the mighty should preoccupy us. For, as the psychiatrist Dr Hugh Freeman has put it, 'like anyone else, statesmen are fallible human beings,'[65] and, given the phenomenon Michael Foley has diagnosed as 'leadership stretch',[66] ever more attention and expectation fall upon the most prominent of our political players, Premiers especially. Of 'statesmen' generally, Freeman adds:

> the tendency both of political processes and of the mass media
> to project them as having superhuman wisdom or abilities can

only result in disillusionment, if not worse. Also, like other
people, political leaders may experience an infinite variety of disorders, mental or physical, which could harm their capacity for
decision-making ... The much more complex nature of modern
societies, and particularly their hugely increased flow of information, results in the cognitive and executive abilities of
these individuals being subject to unprecedented long-term
stress.

Compared with earlier periods, the scale of such issues in the
present political agenda as unchecked population growth, climatic
degradation, and the dangers of nuclear accidents means that the
stakes for success or failure have risen beyond any previously
known. Although leaders are only human, some of them control
superhuman power, in a way that uncomfortably recalls the sorcerer's apprentice.[67]

Dr Freeman, naturally, is keen for extra work to be done on the
'cerebral functioning' of political leaders,[68] though co-operative vol-
unteers will be hard to find. It would be very interesting, in the
unlikely event that collaboration was forthcoming, to have a series
of very private bilateral discussions with serving Cabinet ministers,
starting with a showing of Norman Dixon's latest stress-and-
decision-making slides (reproduced as figures 1 and 2[69]), with a view

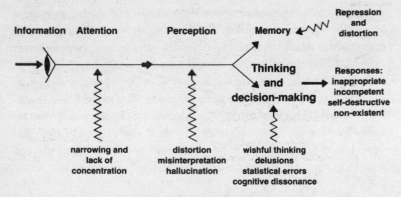

Fig 1   Effects of stress on cognitive processes
Copyright © Norman Dixon

to seeing how much of their contents our overloaded Secretaries of State recognized as reflecting reality.

Nor is it just politicians of Cabinet rank who are buckling under the strain. Ashley Weinberg has recently completed a study of 'Workload, Stress and Family Life in Britain's MPs'. His findings, though less vividly expressed than Norman Dixon's, were far from reassuring. Noting an increase in Parliament's workload in the 1980s (the development of Select Committees, more constituency work, the efflorescence of lobby groups and so on), Dr Weinberg found that:

- four out of five MPs put in fifty-five hours of work a week and 40 per cent worked more than seventy hours;
- one in six showed 'quite poor psychological health';
- 80 per cent were pessimistic about their control over their lives.[70]

The pressure on ministers, especially those of Cabinet rank, will be even greater. Dr Hugh L'Etang, an occupational health expert, has devoted his life to chronicling the physical and mental disorders

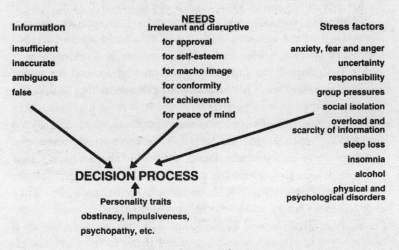

Fig 2   Sources of error
Copyright © Norman Dixon

of the mighty. In his *The Pathology of Leadership*[71] and *Fit to Lead?*[72] he goes way beyond the best-known cases of ailment at the top (Roosevelt at Yalta or Churchill as a walking off-licence-cum-pharmacy after 1953 in particular[73]); and his latest study, *Ailing Leaders in Power 1914–1994*[74] brings naught for our comfort. Though I think it unlikely that his idea of an obligatory retiring age of sixty for British Prime Ministers would find acceptance here,[75] the case for greater transparency about the health of our political leaders is a strong one. For they do, to adopt Abraham Maslow's phrase, have 'a hierarchy of needs',[76] and a real attack on institutional overload and its Siamese twin, personal overstretch, is a priority.

John Major should be only too aware of this, given the personal and political buffeting he has received since the currency melted on 'Black Wednesday' in September 1992; and, of course, on one level he is. As he put it rather poignantly to the 150th Anniversary Dinner of the Surrey County Cricket Club: 'The game is uncertain. The career is chancy. But they both have their own charm. Politics is often about nightmares. Cricket mainly is about dreams,'[77] or 'about the management of illusions', if one of his disillusioned MPs, the former diplomat George Walden, is to be believed.[78]

Nightmares, naturally, cannot be managed completely satisfactorily, even in the best-run state served by throbbing and flexible systems of analysis, advice and implementation. But reform here is within the grasp of the Downing Street incumbent and his senior ministerial colleagues. They should not need persuading of this, but they do. That process of persuasion could start now, precisely where they are sitting. In front of each minister is a small white card slotted into a wooden holder. It is changed daily by their private secretaries and lists every appointment facing them during the twenty-four hours in which their lives are now engaged – meetings, Cabinet committees, questions in the House, official functions, constituency engagements. These cards represent 'overload' writ small. Every Secretary of State, as well as the Prime Minister, should gaze upon his or her card sceptically and ask: 'Do I really have to do that, go there, see him? Can I use the time to greater effect? Where is the space in this schedule for thought about tomorrow, next week, next

month, next year, the next millennium?' The first enemy to be slain
lies there. They should put an end to the tyranny of the White Card.
It is not in their interest – or ours – that ministers should 'burn
themselves out for Britain', as Lord Tonypandy claimed Harold Wilson
had done[79] (a remark which reminded me of Mrs Thatcher's
reaction in the summer of 1979 when, a few months into her
Premiership, a Downing Street official suggested she might take a
holiday – 'But I must govern!' came the reply).[80]

If any minister doubts the gnawing durability of the 'overload'
problem in the postwar period they should consult the farewell interview
given by that seasoned Whitehall veteran, Douglas Hurd, on
his departure from the Foreign and Commonwealth Office in July
1995. 'The difficulty about being a politician in this country', he
said,

> is the sheer piling up of things to do. You come back from a
> dinner at 11 o'clock and you have two or three hours of work –
> some of it quite difficult – and only a small proportion of which
> you can postpone. Or you can get home from a fairly gruelling
> week and there are four boxes waiting for you, each containing
> an hour or an hour and a half's work, that's six hours out of your
> weekend. You plan a holiday in August, something happens and
> it's aborted. And this goes on and on.[81]

It shouldn't. And Douglas Hurd, with his Diplomatic Service as well
as his ministerial experience (not to mention his days as Ted Heath's
Political Secretary in the afterglow of the 1970 reforms[82]), would be
the ideal person to revisit the scene examined by Attlee and the
Privy Counsellors nearly forty years ago, an idea which prompted
an admiring Cabinet minister to say: 'Douglas would be the ideal
man to do that. He handled overload better than anyone else thanks
to his extraordinary powers of organisation'.[83]

EIGHT

Standards of Conduct in Public Life

The Nolan Inquiry as Ethical Workshop

Certainly, politics is not an ethical business. But there does nevertheless exist a certain minimum of shame and obligation to behave decently which cannot be violated with impunity, even in politics.

Max Weber, 1917[1]

The [Nolan] inquiry has evolved into a study of the constitution, or rather of the practices which have developed over nearly sixteen years of one-party rule. That was not what the Government had in mind when the committee was set up.

Peter Riddell, 1995[2]

A degree of austerity, a respect for the traditions of upright behaviour in British public life is not only desirable but essential. We recommend procedures and institutions that will deter and detect wrong-doing. We seek to restore respect for the ethical values inherent in the idea of public service.

First Report from the Nolan Committee on Standards in Public Life, 1995[3]

A very major constitutional innovation.

Lord Nolan, launching the proposals for a Parliamentary Commissioner for Standards and a Public Appointments Commissioner, 1994[4]

The Report is a way of codifying what has previously been done on a nod and a wink. It was all right for those who were in the game but you need it spelled out these days.

Official close to the Nolan Committee, 1995[5]

The British Constitution is a curious box of tricks. For years nothing happens and then you accidentally hit the magic button and it biffs you in the face. John Major and Sir Robin Butler thought they were smart in coming up with Lord Nolan . . . Yet after just three months, [he] has blithely begun to rewrite the British Constitution.

Simon Jenkins, 1995[6]

When the Prime Minister established the Nolan Committee in October 1994 he declared he wished it to become 'an ethical workshop' to provide 'running repairs on standards in public life'.[7] Mr Major did not anticipate or welcome the Committee's metamorphosis into a miniature, if informal, constitutional convention. Lord Nolan and his colleagues 'quite deliberately'[8] went beyond their terms of reference, which were:

> To examine current concerns about standards of conduct of all holders of public office, including arrangements relating to financial and commercial activities, and make recommendations as to any changes in present arrangements which might be required to ensure the highest standards of propriety in public life.
>
> For these purposes, public life should include Ministers, civil servants and advisers, Members of Parliament and UK Members of the European Parliament, members and senior officers of all non-departmental public bodies and of National Health Service bodies, non-ministerial office holders, members and other senior officers of other bodies discharging publicly-funded functions, and elected members and senior officers of local authorities.[9]

Like most terms of reference, they appeared dry, specific and self-contained – except that, in this case, Lord Nolan was given a three-year rolling brief which meant, among other things, that his Committee would be in a position to monitor the fate of their earlier recommendations.

The absence of a follow-up capacity had long been seen as a weakness in standard 'Great and Good'[10] inquiries over the postwar period.[11] But, in the grand tradition of the best high-minded and path-breaking 'Great and Good' operations such as the Beveridge Inquiry of 1941–2 into social insurance and allied services,[12] Lord Nolan picked up his terms of reference and ran with them way beyond the expected touchline.[13] And his was the first report since Beveridge's (with its 'five giants on the road of reconstruction' – 'Want, Disease, Ignorance, Squalor and Idleness'[14]) to summon up what the future Lady Beveridge called 'a Cromwellian spirit'[15] by enunciating 'The Seven Principles of Public Life':

Selflessness

Holders of public office should take decisions solely in terms of the public interest. They should not do so in order to gain financial or other material benefits for themselves, their family, or their friends.

Integrity

Holders of public office should not place themselves under any financial or other obligation to outside individuals or organisations that might influence them in the performance of their official duties.

Objectivity

In carrying out public business, including making public appointments, awarding contracts, or recommending individuals for rewards and benefits, holders of public office should make choices on merit.

Accountability

Holders of public office are accountable for their decisions and actions to the public and must submit themselves to whatever scrutiny is appropriate to their office.

Openness

Holders of public office should be as open as possible about all the decisions and actions that they take. They should give reasons for their decisions and restrict information only when the wider public interest clearly demands.

Honesty

Holders of public office have a duty to declare any private interests relating to their public duties and to take steps to resolve any conflicts arising in a way that protects the public interest.

Leadership

Holders of public office should promote and support these principles by leadership and example.

Above Sir Kenneth Stowe (at rear behind Tom McNally, Political Adviser to the Prime Minister): Stowe's 'interlocking circles' paved Jim Callaghan's constitutional path into No.10.

Below Lord Charteris in conversation with the author in the Royal Library at Windsor Castle: 'I suspect . . . that politics which are very polarized are very uncomfortable to the Sovereign.'

Above Sir John Hunt, gardener and technocrat-of-state: Cabinet as 'a democratic and accountable shambles'.

Right Tony Benn: avid recorder of the constitution in action.

Above Edmund Dell: time to end the 'dangerous myth' of collective responsibility.

Below A unique picture of a Cabinet in session at Chequers taken on 22 June 1977 by Tony Benn. Left to right: James Callaghan, Tom McNally, Michael Foot, Peter Shore

Harold Wilson's weekly treat at the Palace: an audience with the Queen at the height of the *In Place of Strife* crisis, June 1969.

The author in discussion with two constitutional artefacts. Enoch Powell: 'The British nation could not imagine itself except with and through its Parliament.' Tony Benn: 'To understand how we're governed, and hence the power of the Prime Minister, you have to understand the power of the Crown.'

Lord Bancroft contemplating the 'hardware and software of state' at the Gresham College seminar.

Michael Heseltine, a 'Heineken amongst deputy prime ministers', lionized by his colleagues in the garden of No.10 after his first Cabinet meeting as First Secretary. From left to right: John Gummer, Heseltine, Gillian Shephard, John Major, Michael Portillo.

A Walter Bagehot triptych by Riddell of the *Economist*: *above* Bagehot contemplating the Monarch's reserve powers; *right* adding clarity and refinement to the secret garden of the British Constitution; *below* absorbing the anticipated contents of Queen Elizabeth II's diary.

Above Sir Robin Butler in the Old Treasury Board Room (where the Cabinet used to meet with the king in attendance), about to shift a constitutional understanding in response to a student's question.
Below Nicholas Garland's view of Lord Nolan as a Frankenstein's monster starting out on a three-year march through the British constitution.

'I am a coalition government on my own': John Major at the Cabinet
Table (complete with stiff white appointments card).

These principles apply to all aspects of public life. The Committee has set them out here for the benefit of all who serve the public in any way.[16]

In its own Cromwellian way, the Nolan Committee was, in effect, recommending the application of a set of gold standards of comparable lustre and rigour for the wide swathe of public life and activities laid out in its terms of reference, beginning with the three areas on which it concentrated initially – Parliament (MPs' financial interests in particular); central government (standards of personal conduct when in office; relations with the Civil Service; procedures for transferring their post-office energies to the private sector without taint or suspicion); and ministerial appointments to 'quangoland'. In so doing, the Nolan Committee was urging that Sidney Low's 'tacit understandings'[17] be replaced by something both more precise and more capable of being monitored by those charged with oversight of their application and adherence.

In a word, Nolan was saying that our 'great ghost of a constitution' *should* be reduced to the 'flesh' (though the far from 'corruptible' flesh) of a code.[18] This was generally overlooked in the mêlée which greeted the Committee's first report in May 1995, driven as that was by some truly 'narrow' and possibly 'corruptible' behaviour on the part of some MPs in the House of Commons in the debate which followed[19] – even though Lord Nolan himself made plain that he did not see his report as marking a step on the road to a written constitution. 'The feel of our recommendations', he said, 'tends if anything towards informality. We've tried to avoid anything that requires legislation: partly because we want it to move quickly, but also because legislation produces inflexibility.'[20]

In saying this Lord Nolan was reflecting a widespread belief in the United Kingdom that, for it to be perceived as such, a written British Constitution would have to be labelled as exactly that, cover just about every aspect of state, parliamentary and judicial activity, and be stoneclad in entrenched legislation and policed by some kind of constitutional court. This amounts to the Tommy Cooper school of analysis: one minute all is traditional vagueness and informality; the next – just like that – all is precision and formality. Lord Nolan is right to imply that the legislative route, even on a narrow front, could be an invitation to delay and inflexibility.

But when changes have come about in the British Constitution, all-encompassing precision backed by statute has not been the British way. As another member of the Nolan Committee put it: 'The British like to live in a series of half-way houses,'[21] which is exactly what Nolan's codes, if adopted, will build for them. Constitutions, after all, are about rules of conduct, proper procedure and predictability of application – again, central Nolan territory. And the government swiftly accepted the Nolan recommendations in general for those parts of the Report where the decision to implement was its alone, even for the rules affecting its most sensitive inner garden, *Questions of Procedure for Ministers*.[22]

The nature of the Westminster reaction to the Nolan Report was especially revealing in the context of the suggestion that there should be a new code of conduct for MPs on extra-parliamentary remuneration and potential conflicts of interest, monitored by an outside figure, a Parliamentary Commissioner for Standards, who would advise a Select Committee established for the purpose of examining breaches of the new code.[23] For the principled, as opposed to the self-serving dissent from the Nolan philosophy (virtually all of which was confined to Conservative MPs), concentrated upon the constitutional implications of what Lord Nolan acknowledged at his press conference would be 'a very major constitutional innovation'.

The similarity of approach between Sir Edward Heath (still an MP) and Enoch Powell (a former Conservative Member who had finished his Commons life as an Ulster Unionist) was particularly striking, given the nature of their relationship at least since Powell's 1968 speech on immigration policy.[24] Father of the House of Commons since 1992, Sir Edward told the Carlton Club:

> I don't believe that outsiders should run Parliament. Members know far more about what is happening in the House than any bureaucrat from outside could ever learn. A line must be drawn. If we cannot run our own affairs, how can we run other people's affairs?[25]

Mr Powell, for his part, told the readers of *The Times*:

I do not know in what manner it may be proposed to implement the Nolan Committee's recommendations; but I very much fear that the easy way out will be taken and that they will be implemented by resolution [of the House of Commons] which would expose to disciplinary proceedings in the House any Member who contravened them. But there is an extremely serious point here which goes to the right [*sic*] and liberties of the individual citizen.

The conditions and requirements for being a Member of Parliament are laid down by statute. They cannot therefore, in form or in substance, be altered by resolution of either House. In fact, they are the nearest thing we possess to an 'entrenched' part of the constitution.[26]

I checked with Mr Powell that 'by statute' he meant by the accumulated Representation of the People Acts.[27] He confirmed that this was so – 'The electoral acts, the rules governing election, the Representation of the People Acts,'[28] he explained.

In his *Times* article he went on:

The trouble about the Nolan Committee is that it was established to define the indefinable and reduce to a set of rules that which cannot be so treated. The House of Commons expects its members to behave as a gentleman would behave; but to sit down and draw up a schedule of how a gentleman will behave is in the nature of the case not possible. If it were, we could do without gentlemen.[29]

This is the finest exposition of the 'Great-Ghost'-cum-Code-of-the-Woosters school of British constitutional thought that I have encountered for a very long time. And, as is Mr Powell's special trade mark, the whole argument was rounded off by an appeal to the sanction of the past, Bagehot's great 'cake of custom':[30] 'Impulse and ignorant clamour are ill counsellors in the matter of such an institution as the House of Commons with which history and habit have endowed the British nation,'[31] he declared.

Nicholas Budgen took a similar line to Mr Powell (for whose old seat of Wolverhampton South-West he now sits) in the Commons debate on Nolan when he asked David Hunt, Chancellor of the Duchy of Lancaster: 'Surely if our terms of employment are to be restricted in some way, that ought to be set out in statute. Is that not quite different from the old custom of our unwritten Constitution, that the procedures of the House and the way in which we behave here are ordered within the House, with no statutory backing?'[32] Mr Hunt was non-committal in his reply.[33]

Plainly, for the likes of Heath, Powell and Budgen, Nolan *is* a constitutional issue. It is, too, for ministers; the Nolan 'Frankenstein', to borrow Nicholas Garland's cartoon image,[34] has marched not just through the Chamber of the House of Commons but across Parliament Square and into 10 Downing Street as well. There are profound Cabinet Room implications in his recommendations, for he had much of significance to say about *Questions of Procedure for Ministers* and the Prime Minister's role as its guardian.

The Nolan Committee pondered the queasiness of *QPM*'s constitutional status and sensed accurately the haphazard nature of its development and the accretion of conduct, as opposed to procedural, clauses as time has passed since Mr Attlee promulgated the first modern version:

> What guidance there is for Ministers on standards of conduct, as well as on procedural matters, is contained in *Questions of Procedure for Ministers*. In the context of the British constitution, *QPM* is a youthful document, dating from 1945 (although elements within it are older). For many years, *Questions of Procedure* was a confidential document. It was only in 1992 that the present Prime Minister took the decision to publish it.
>
> *QPM* has no particular constitutional status, but because it is issued by each Prime Minister to ministerial colleagues at the start of an administration or on their appointment to office, and any changes can only be authorised by the Prime Minister, it is in practice binding on all members of a Government. The records show that *QPM* has grown organically over the years, beginning as a document that was not much more than what Lord Trend described as 'tips on etiquette for beginners' but with fresh sections being added to deal with new circumstances. Over the years,

the growth in *QPM* has largely been in the area of conduct and not procedure.

> We do not believe that the explanation for this is a decline in ministerial standards of conduct. We think that the addition of ethical material to *QPM* has resulted from a combination of responses to specific incidents and a general trend, not confined to Government, towards codification of what might once have been assumed to be common ground.[35]

In other words, the 'good chap' theory of government could no longer serve alone as the guarantor of proper behaviour at the heart of government.[36]

Lord Nolan saw straight through the permissiveness that has infected the opening paragraph of *QPM* since 1987 – aptly and unforgettably described by one of my undergraduates, Zai Bennett, as 'ministers' get-out-of-jail-free clause'.[37] The Nolan Committee had no truck with it:

> *QPM* begins by setting out some fundamental principles:

>> *It will be for individual Ministers to judge how best to act in order to uphold the highest standards. Ministers will want to see that no conflict arises or appears to arise between their private interests and their public duties. They will wish to be as open as possible with Parliament and the public. These notes should be read against the background of these general obligations.*[38]

> Ministers themselves are individually and separately responsible for upholding the standards of conduct applicable to their office. Everyone in public life has a personal responsibility for judging a course of action – the acceptance of hospitality, for example – weighing up its ethical implications using their own judgement. In the case of Ministers, their need to account to Parliament for their actions reinforces that responsibility.

> Yet Ministers do not make their ethical judgements in isolation. To remain in office they must retain the confidence of the Prime Minister and, in a question of conduct, that will involve the Prime Minister's own judgement of the ethics of the case. This is axiomatic and should be reflected in *QPM*.

> **We recommend that the first paragraph of *Questions of***

Procedure for Ministers should be amended to say: 'It will be for the individual Ministers to judge how best to act in order to uphold the highest standards. *It will be for the Prime Minister to determine whether or not they have done so in any particular circumstance.*'[39]

At this point Lord Nolan engineered yet another 'major constitutional innovation' by suggesting improvements in the detailed contents of a revised *QPM*, something that had formerly been the sole prerogative of those ultimate insiders, the postwar Cabinet Secretaries and the Premiers they served:

We believe that there are general principles of conduct which are applicable to Ministers; that it is possible to set these out in a clear and comprehensible form that will be of assistance to the Prime Minister, to Ministers themselves and to members of the public; and that this can indicate unacceptable aspects of ministerial behaviour. This approach will not, of course, stop misconduct. But it will do much to counter present public uncertainty about what is and is not acceptable.

QPM does not offer a coherent series of principles which can be applied by Ministers who are in doubt about possible courses of action. The document is a miscellany: 'a mix of immutable principles with housekeeping practicalities', as Professor Peter Hennessy described it to us.

We recommend that the Prime Minister puts in hand the production of a document drawing out from *QPM* the ethical principles and rules which it contains to form a free-standing code of conduct or a separate section within a new *QPM*. If *QPM* is to remain the home for this guidance, we recommend that it is retitled *Conduct and Procedure for Ministers* to reflect its scope.

The precise wording of the new guidance will be a matter for the Prime Minister. We believe, however, that the following essential principles should be spelt out, supported where necessary by detailed rules, some of which already exist in *QPM*:

Ministers of the Crown are expected to behave according to the highest standards of constitutional and personal conduct. In particular they must observe the following principles of ministerial conduct:

> (i) *Ministers must ensure that no conflict arises, or appears to arise, between their public duties and their private interests;*
>
> (ii) *Ministers must not mislead Parliament. They must be as open as possible with Parliament and the public;*
>
> (iii) *Ministers are accountable to Parliament for the policies and operations of their departments and agencies;*
>
> (iv) *Ministers should avoid accepting any gift or hospitality which might, or might appear to, compromise their judgement or place them under an improper obligation;*
>
> (v) *Ministers in the House of Commons must keep separate their roles as Minister and constituency Member;*
>
> (vi) *Ministers must keep their party and ministerial roles separate. They must not ask civil servants to carry out party political duties or to act in any other way that would conflict with the Civil Service Code.*

Setting out these principles for Ministers might seem unnecessary or obvious. We do not share that view. The Government has accepted the proposition that there should be a code of conduct for civil servants. It is difficult to see why the same approach should not apply to Ministers. The advantages of a code can be seen by considering the number of Ministers who have had to resign since the war because of avoidable errors of judgement. We do not, though, believe that express sanctions need to be set out to prevent Ministers from doing wrong. Public and media scrutiny of ministerial conduct in the light of the principles we have listed above is likely to be far more effective. Ministers themselves will be able to judge possible courses of action against these principles, supported by the useful rules-of-thumb recommended to us by Lord Howe: 'Would you ... feel happy to see all the relevant facts of any transaction or relationship fully and fairly reported on the front page of your favourite newspaper,' and 'If in doubt, cut it out.'[40]

The government accepted this recommendation *in toto*.[41] Lord Nolan's 'Frankenstein' had marched right through the Cabinet Secretary's office, too; and once the revised *QPM* is in existence he will stride up and down Whitehall through the private offices of each and every minister of the Crown.

Nolan's positive statement of what a revised *QPM* should contain was significant. The document, once past its prototypical August 1945 version, has tended to accrue retrospectively in response to things that have gone wrong rather than in anticipation of new problems that need dealing with in a foresightful fashion. As one of my students, Vicky Barrett, put it, *QPM* 'is a book of hindsight'.[42] By implication Nolan wishes that to change too; and the government, implicitly once more, has concurred. When it does, will it alter the constitutional status of *QPM*? Will it remain 'discretionary' in Sir Robin Butler's sense?[43] Will it at last amount to an unarguable convention? I think the latter. It will not have the force of law any more than its precursors had. A new Prime Minister could alter it; but, in practice, no government is likely to be able to change it in the sense of loosening it. It will, therefore, be a velcro code that sticks, a new and, in effect, permanent adhesion to the constitutional fabric. With the Prime Minister as its specified enforcer, the new-style *QPM* would be both more precise and more binding – a force to be reckoned with rather than finessed, bypassed or overlooked. The 'get out of jail free' days would be gone.

What a difference three years can make in the life of a document! The rise of *QPM* is a perfect illustration of the Simon Jenkins principle of the Constitution coming from nowhere and 'biffing you in the face'.[44] Before May 1992 it was classified, little discussed and very much part of the private preserve of the executive. In May 1992 it goes public. In May 1995 it becomes the crucial and acknowledged instrument of decency and proper procedure at the apex of the political and governmental system.

Mr Attlee would have been horrified if he had thought intruders would break into his secret procedural garden fifty years after he had nurtured its early blooms. Nor would this most moral of men (who memorably told his biographer, Kenneth Harris, in his customary staccato way: 'Believe in the ethics of Christianity. Can't believe in the mumbo-jumbo'[45]) have found it easy to accept that, two generations on, the decencies of political life would need to be spelt out to the extent of applying rules to ex-ministers whose dash for the private-sector boardroom began the moment they left Buckingham Palace after handing in their seals of office.

In an interesting example of ethics transfer, Nolan recommended that the rules applying to senior civil servants taking up business appointments should in future be applied to ministers. The government, at first dismissive of the idea when Nolan took evidence,[46] concurred once the report was published.[47] In future such moves will be vetted by the Advisory Committee on Business Appointments, which will be able to go public if ministers forgo the obligatory three-month period of post-office purdah or ignore the Advisory Committee's recommendations on which jobs they should and should not take up during the first twenty-one months thereafter.

Ministerial behaviour while still in office, *vis-à-vis* the Civil Service, is placed still more firmly and urgently on the political agenda by the Nolan Report. *Questions of Procedure for Ministers* is not the only Nolan-related quasi-constitutional artefact to have moved quickly from the arcane to the central; the arrival of the Civil Service Code on the centre stage of the Constitution was similarly swift, impressive and important. As we have seen, the House of Commons Treasury and Civil Service Committee brokered it with an initially sceptical government; but Nolan recommended a significant extension of its scope and gave it a mighty shove in the direction of accelerated implementation.

After endorsing the ringing declarations in both *Continuity and Change* and the Treasury and Civil Service Committee's Report on the indispensability of permanence and neutrality for the career Civil Service,[48] Nolan went on to express concern that the new pay and appraisal regime for the senior Civil Service might cut against that all-important grain and that outsiders brought in to lead Next Steps executive agencies may well need special help to absorb the crucial public service ethic:

> We welcome the establishment of a new senior civil service as a symbol of the importance of shared values throughout the whole civil service. We agree, however, with the view of some of our witnesses that caution should be exercised in the introduction of performance pay and appraisal arrangements for this group. Many, though not all, of the senior civil service will be in contact with Ministers and will handle sensitive policy matters. A percep-

tion that reward and promotion may depend in any way on commitment to Ministerial ideology inconsistent with the impartiality required of a civil servant would of course be wholly unacceptable.

We recommend that the new performance pay arrangements for the senior civil service should be structured so as not to undermine political impartiality.

A guide for Agency Chief Executives on core values and standards properly responds, in our view, to the pressures which may occur when traditional public sector values are applied in an organisation with a sharper commercial focus, such as some executive agencies.[49]

Nolan recognized the value of a code as a kind of public service bonding agent within an otherwise fragmenting Civil Service, but wanted it to be toughened substantially:

(a) to enable civil servants to make known examples of 'wrongdoing or maladministration' even if not personally involved in it;[50]

(b) to lay a requirement upon them to ensure 'the proper, effective and efficient use of public money', even if that expenditure is not within their direct control;[51]

(c) by authorizing each department to appoint a senior official 'outside the line management structure' to investigate staff concerns and complaints;[52]

(d) by ensuring that *all* complaints upheld by the Civil Service Commissioners be reported to Parliament;[53]

(e) by introducing the code 'with immediate effect, without waiting for legislation'.[54]

Nolan went on to suggest that: 'The code should not itself appear in primary legislation, which would make it difficult to amend in the light of changing circumstances. Instead it should be contained in secondary legislation subject to the affirmative resolution of both Houses, ensuring that flexibility is joined with scrutiny.'[55]

During the Commons debate on Nolan, David Hunt stressed the 'great value' of a Civil Service code and declared: 'The Government will look constructively at the further points that the Nolan committee has raised and will take them all into account' in the consultation exercise with Civil Service staff and trade unions, as well as the opposition parties, should they respond to the government's invitation to submit their views.[56]

The two-month period following the publication of the first Nolan Report turned into an extraordinary example of semi-public constitution-brokering of a kind unprecedented since Parliament completed its long agony in turning Britain into a one person/one vote nation. Most of the attention focused on the specially created Select Committee on Standards in Public Life which met fourteen times between 15 June and 6 July 1995 in the rush to complete its interim report before the Commons rose for its summer recess.[57] Its terms of reference suggested that the question before it was not whether to implement Nolan's recommendations on the standards appropriate to MPs but how.[58] Even so, it swiftly became plain that for some of the Conservative members of the Select Committee nothing was taken for granted; at one stage, it even looked as if the idea of a Parliamentary Commissioner for Standards might not get their endorsement.[59] But, in the end, it did.

The Select Committee, however, could not bring itself to make recommendations which reflected in full that 'degree of austerity'[60] urged on Parliament by Nolan, let alone the 1947 resolution of the House of Commons itself (by which Nolan set such store) which declared, 'that it is inconsistent with the dignity of the House, with the duty of a Member to his constituency, and with the maintenance of the privilege of freedom of speech, for any member of the House to enter into any contractual agreement with an outside body, controlling or limiting the Member's complete independence and freedom of action in Parliament or stipulating that he shall act in any way as the representative of such an outside body in regard to any matters to be transacted in Parliament'.[61]

Instead, the select committee sought,[62] and was given,[63] more time by the Commons to produce proposals on disclosure of consultancies and fees. It was a considerable step forward to have reached agreement on the need for a code of conduct for MPs, a Select Committee to monitor it and a Standards Commissioner to advise that committee, but, as Peter Riddell observed, the Standards Select Committee confused principle and implementation:

> The former is straightforward. Either MPs should disclose their earnings from 'the provision of services in their capacity as members' or they should not. Equally, MPs should either be banned from entering into agreements with multiple-consultancies or they should not. The committee could have said that it accepted the principle of disclosure and the ban on multi-client consultancies and would come up with detailed resolutions in the autumn.[64]

Mercifully, the consultancy industry itself was by midsummer 1995 behaving as if MPs had already accepted both. As one experienced public affairs consultant put it:

> Nolan finally exposed how ridiculous it is to be paid as an MP to give advice on how Parliament works on a multi-client basis. In future consultancies won't work like that. Nolan has made everybody nervous. Leading companies have said 'We don't want to use MPs.' Nolan has underlined the fact that you are going to come under scrutiny if you retain MPs. Boardrooms have been asking 'Do we have to be associated with these kind of consultants that bring the risk of embarrassment for us?' And they have been increasingly asking 'What do you really get out of retaining an MP?' You now have a more discerning marketplace where serious people have more nous about how political lobbying works. Nolan caught a tide that was on the turn.[65]

Compared to its response on recommendations affecting the legislature, the government's reply to Nolan in respect of recommendations directed towards the executive was relatively enthusiastic and unambiguous, though a good deal of tweaking was done in the White Paper, *The Government's Response to the First Report from the Committee on Standards in Public Life*,[66] to bend it slightly to suit executive convenience.

Its proposed amendments to Nolan's draft Civil Service Code were mainly of a language-tautening nature. Most importantly, the Cabinet accepted the extra dimension of probity recommended by Nolan whereby, in the White Paper's draft: 'A civil servant should also report to the appropriate authorities evidence of criminal or unlawful activity by others and may also report in accordance with departmental procedures if he or she becomes aware of other breaches of this Code or is otherwise required to act in a way which, for him or her, raises a fundamental issue of conscience.'[67] After consultations within the Civil Service, the government rephrased the section of the code designed to protect the public service from political contamination. Referring to the requirements laid upon ministers by *QPM*, the new section declared that ministers have 'the duty not to use public resources for party political purposes, to uphold the political impartiality of the Civil Service, and not to ask civil servants to act in any other way which would conflict with the Civil Service Code'.[68]

However, the most important outbreak of executive tweaking took place around the government's proposals for the new wording of *QPM* which, once it had been redrafted, was to become known as *Conduct and Procedure for Ministers*. (The idea for a free-standing code separate from *QPM* was not taken up.) Suspicion was aroused by the rewording of the old paragraph 27 in the White Paper's draft, which was now to read as follows:

> Ministers must not *knowingly* mislead Parliament *and the public and should correct any inadvertent errors at the earliest opportunity*. They must be seen as open as possible with Parliament and the public, *withholding information only when disclosures would not be in the public interest*. [emphasis added where the White Paper redrafted Nolan][69]

I have no objection to the use of the word 'knowingly' or the reference to 'inadvertent errors'. Governments, like every other institution, often have to act on imperfect information. It was the old Whitehall appetite for vague catch-all phrases such as 'the public interest' that concerned me. It would have been far better for the government to have harmonized that paragraph with its existing Open Government Code by referring in its response to Nolan to those areas that are exempted from disclosure under the latter.[70] Indeed, Roger Freeman, the new minister for the public service, rightly pointed out during the Commons debate on the government's response to Nolan that the suggestions for a revised *QPM* corresponded to exemptions to the Open Government provisions 'which include defence, security, international relations, communications with the royal household, law enforcement and legal proceedings, and operations of the public service such as setting bank rates'.[71]

The significant weakness in the government's reply, however, was its unwillingness to make the Prime Minister the firm and unequivocal arbiter of the new *Conduct and Procedure for Ministers*. The get-out-of-jail-free card was still there, supplemented by a feeble section on the need for ministers to retain the Prime Minister's confidence. The new *QPM* will, therefore, read as follows: 'It will be for individual Ministers to judge how best to act in order to uphold the highest standards. They are responsible for justifying their conduct to Parliament. And they can only remain in office for as long as they retain the Prime Minister's confidence.'[72] This is much weaker than the Nolan version which, as we have seen, consisted of two sentences: 'It will be for individual Ministers to judge how best to act in order to uphold the highest standards. *It will be for the Prime Minister to determine whether or not they have done so in any particular circumstances.* [Nolan's emphasis]'[73]

That said, by the end of 1995, barring unforeseen developments, codes will be in place for ministers, MPs and civil servants.[74] What is more, the government wished to proceed on a consensual basis in respect of the Civil Service Code. 'I am happy to consult the Opposition Front Bench team', Mr Freeman told Ann Taylor, Shadow Leader of the House, 'on the way forward in terms of placing in statute [the] new Civil Service code which we intend to implement by the end of the year. I cannot promise to give the timetable of any legislation, but if the Hon. Lady will join me on further discussions on that subject, it would be appreciated.'[75]

Achieving such a consensus was hugely important to the permanent secretaries in Whitehall. As Sir Robin Butler had told a Policy Studies Institute seminar shortly before the government replied to Nolan:

As far as I and my colleagues in the Civil Service are concerned, we have a duty to do whatever the Government wants us to do. I think we can give a much clearer lead to the Civil Service where we know that what we're doing has bi-partisan support because clearly in those circumstances we know there is agreement across the political spectrum and we're not prejudicing our own position if there is a change of government.[76]

It has to be said that the executive behaved far better than the legislature in implementing Nolan Mark I. Robert Maclennan, the Liberal Democrat member of the Select Committee on Standards in Public Life, recognized this when he told the Commons: 'The good name of the House, and its keystone place in our democracy, must be in the mind of every one of us. The House validates Government. If that process were to be corrupted by the self-interested action of Members, it would diminish our claim to speak for the country.'[77]

Quite so. And the tone and quality of the first two post-Nolan debates in the Commons did just that. By the summer of 1995 its attitude to Nolan, especially to those recommendations which, to quote a former Conservative Cabinet Minister, 'hit our side where it hurts – in their pockets',[78] had become a talisman of Parliament's good intentions and the capacity of the House of Commons to reform itself. Some MPs behaved as if they had no conception of how their behaviour appeared to outsiders – as so many shop stewards operating the rules in their own interest, almost wilfully trading personal enrichment for public esteem. For all the need to refine the detail of some of Nolan's recommendations, the principle at stake was shiningly obvious – that the brains and lips and votes of MPs should not be available for purchase on the open market.

Yet for all the demeaning caveats entered by some MPs when confronted by the Nolan proposals, the codes for the Cabinet Room, Whitehall and the House of Commons were of an importance that should not be lost sight of amid the bluster and the detail. For, taken together, they were hugely significant advances in constitutional terms for a nation which, in Owen Hickey's words displays

a wide absence of the mechanisms political science proposes for constraining political power. No entrenchments, no constitutional court, no formal separation of powers, no Bill of rights, not much written down ... [though] ... Rules embedded in precedent may possess a more serviceable strength and flexibility than rules inscribed on yellowing paper.[79]

It took practical issues such as the cash-for-questions affair involving two Conservative MPs, worries about the growth of a new patronage state alongside the spread of 'quangoland', concern about the alleged politicization of the Civil Service, dismay about the clinging qualities of some ministers who seemed to treat office as a freehold rather than a leasehold when allegations about their personal or financial behaviour began to affect their capacity to fulfil their duties, to prod the Prime Minister into sending for Lord Nolan. And out of these practicalities has come the beginnings of a significant constitutional change.

We should not be surprised by this. It has been very much the British way of altering its constitutional arrangements in the past. R. H. Tawney, writing shortly after the Great War and changes in the franchise which transformed the British electorate, declared:

> It is a commonplace that the characteristic virtue of Englishmen is their power of sustained practical activity, and their character-istic vice a reluctance to test the quality of that activity by refer-ence to principles. They are incurious as to theory, take fundamentals for granted, and are more interested in the state of the roads than in their place on the map ... Most generations ... walk in a path which they neither make nor discover, but accept ...
>
> The blinkers worn by Englishmen enable them to trot all the more steadily along the beaten road, without being disturbed by curiosity as to their destination. But if the medicine of the constitution ought not to be made its daily food, neither can its daily food be made medicine. There are times which are not ordinary, and in such times it is not enough to follow the road.[80]

The words with which Tawney opened his classic work on *The Acquisitive Society* fit late twentieth-century Britain. It is as if the soothing blinkers that have for so long concealed changes in the nature of the political class, the coarsening of our political discourse and, to some extent, the self-cleansing capacity of our governing systems have suddenly been removed. As a result, the work of the Nolan Committee has had a real bite and its suggested codifications have had a real impact on those constitutional practices which for so long had been taken for granted – if, indeed, they had been thought about at all.

How can one best judge the significance of such constitution-making by stealth? By applying the Bagehot test and asking: Will the cluster of codes, the mechanics of their implementation and the methods of their oversight change the 'living reality' in Whitehall and Westminster?

As the scholar, journalist and constitutionalist Andrew Adonis put it shortly after the publication of the first Nolan Report, 'If we'd had twenty years of this kind of thing there wouldn't be much to worry about now.'[81] There will be an element of loss as Nolan turns several (though not all) of the spectral limbs of the 'great ghost' of a constitution into his fleshly codes. Ghosts are more magical entities than prosaic blood and bone. As a senior civil servant on the constitutional side of Whitehall put it to me in the days following Nolan Mark I: 'It's good to find that you still think the Constitution is so exciting. It could cease to be so glamorous. By the time you've had it all written down it won't be quite so nice.'[82]

Perhaps so. Nor will codification by itself improve the quality of public and political life. The constitutional hardware will be toughened – an improvement in itself – but the software cannot be so easily engineered into a higher state. The shades of Mr Gladstone's men and women of 'good sense' and 'good faith' and Enoch Powell's 'gentleman' are relevant here. As that great Victorian value, Lord Radcliffe,[83] put it: 'Constitutional forms and legal systems are very well in their way, but they are the costumes for the men who wear them. Their sober shapes can be seen performing the strangest antics unless the people inside them have a real grasp of the civil ideas which they are designed to express.'[84]

Exactly so. Rules and procedures have to be absorbed almost organically if they are to become second nature, and an almost automatic motivator of public life. Does this suggest, therefore, that reforms with the greatest chance of taking will be those grafted with care and a necessary understanding of its past on to our singular body politic?

NINE

A Very Discreditable Chapter?

Government, Parliament and the Scott Inquiry

Paragraph 27 of *Questions of Procedure for Ministers* identifies as one of the facets of Ministerial accountability to Parliament 'the duty to give Parliament, including its Select Committees, and the public as full information as possible about the policies, decisions and actions of the Government, and not to deceive or mislead Parliament and the public.' In the course of the Inquiry example after example has come to light of an apparent failure by Ministers to discharge that obligation.

The Scott Report, February 1996[1]

The key words are 'so far as possible'. Those responsible for the conduct of foreign, diplomatic and economic policy have always been obliged to safeguard a wide range of information: from many hostile or competing nations, institutions and individuals around the world.

Geoffrey Howe in the House of Lords debate on Scott[2]

You cannot conduct a successful foreign policy on the basis of moral outrage or perpetual public scrutiny. You have to have realism and you have to have confidentiality.

Sir Percy Cradock, former Chairman of the Joint
Intelligence Committee, on the day the Scott Report was
published[3]

It is . . . a tragedy that Scott does not set out any general principles in the short section of his report (eight pages out of 1800) dealing with ministerial accountability . . . The real issues raised by his report are . . . to what extent Parliament can hold the executive to account and how the national interest is established.

Lord Hunt of Tanworth, former Cabinet Secretary,
February 1996[4]

In my view there have been better reports; there have probably been greater deceptions of Parliament; but never in my experience has there been a more cynical handling of a major report produced at their own request by a British Government . . . It is a very discreditable chapter.

Lord Jenkins of Hillhead, former Home Secretary and
Chancellor of the Exchequer, February 1996[5]

The Scott Report suffered from a variety of drawbacks: prolixity, delay, an absence of stark conclusions stirringly written and a split remit. Not all of these were the fault of Sir Richard Scott and his team. For example, it took an age to circulate drafts to all those affected and to amend them in the light of comments. The absence of a sharp conclusion, too, reflects Sir Richard's sensitivity to those involved who argued that his findings on them should be set (and read) in the wider context of their actions and not reduced to staccato paragraphs that lent themselves to crude, I-name-the-guilty-men-style interpretations.[6]

In the event, this enabled ministers to cherry-pick those findings that suited them, as it did the media and party machines. More seriously, it opened up the possibility, quickly fulfilled, that the sheer width and scarcely absorbable density of the report would allow it to sink very swiftly from parliamentary, public and press attention as seasoned commentators like Peter Riddell predicted would happen once the search for 'Sir Richard's smoking paragraph' had passed and attention had lapsed from the question of whether or not the Attorney-General, Sir Nicholas Lyell, and the Chief Secretary to the Treasury, William Waldegrave, would be forced into resignation.[7] The Scott Report simply did not have the impact it deserved.

Sir Frank Cooper, a former Permanent Secretary at the Ministry of Defence (and no slouch when it comes to the sensitivity surrounding arms deals or the fissile possibilities where oil meets sand and warfare meets diplomacy in the context of Middle East politics at their most raw, as they did in the case of arms to Iraq) seemed as regretful as he was dismissive of Scott in the doldrum weeks which followed the Report's publication as all mention of it slipped from public prints that became obsessed in turn by the Dunblane massacre and the possible transmission of 'mad cow' disease into the food chain. 'Scott', he said,

> blew the whole thing. That's the trouble with getting lawyers in. It should have been the length of the Franks Report on the

Falklands [339 paragraphs over 90 pages, completed in six months and published in January 1983[8]]. Scott has mixed up whether he was writing a tract about political life in this country, the way politics is conducted, with what was essentially a factual investigation. He slipped absolutely into the crack between the two.[9]

Hence the problems which sprang from the inquiry's split remit. Sir Frank continued:

Take the famous Paragraph 27 of *Questions of Procedure for Ministers* – a splendid statement capable of many interpretations and complications and famous mostly for nobody taking the slightest bit of notice of it, not least in parliamentary institutions. Scott says the denial of information means the public cannot reach informed judgements and that withholding information should not rest on avoiding political embarrassment. That seems to be the heart of Scott because it is the heart of the way we are governed. And we are governed very badly in the democratic sense. The great sadness of Scott sinking beneath its own weight is that people have lost sight of this.[10]

The cynical may be surprised by the degree to which ex-Whitehall insiders like Cooper and Hunt (who were the toughest of operators in their time[11]) emphasize the key linkage in Scott between informing Parliament and the quality of overall governance in Britain. But, in stressing the paramountcy of the accountability theme, they went to the heart of the Scott Report as well as to its enduring and wider significance. And the one area where the Major administration's response to the Report did not deserve Roy Jenkins' strictures was in its invitation, extended by Ian Lang, Secretary of State for Trade and Industry, to the all-party House of Commons Public Service Committee, to examine further questions of accountability and responsibility to Parliament[12] (an invitation they promptly took up[13]).

What were Sir Richard Scott's key findings on ministerial accountability, the subject of the eighth and most important chapter in his recommendations section?[14] First and foremost, the judge gave seven specific instances where the 'obligation' (his word) to answer parliamentary questions in the manner required by paragraph 27 of *QPM* was not discharged ('an apparent failure', as he perhaps too gently expressed it[15]). 'The obligation of Ministers', the judge declared, 'to give information about the activities of their departments and to give information and explanations for the actions and omissions of their civil servants, lies at the heart of Ministerial accountability.'[16]

What were the seven holes at the heart of government accountability Sir Richard anatomized during his examination of the arms-to-Iraq affair?

(i) The [Sir Geoffrey] Howe Guidelines were agreed upon in December 1984 but when in April and May 1985 Parliamentary Questions asking about Government policy on defence sales to Iran and Iraq came to be answered the existence of the Guidelines was deliberately not disclosed.

(ii) From 1983 until the ceasefire in August 1988, arrangements were in place for defence sales to Iraq to be facilitated by the provision of medium term ECGD [Export Credit Guarantee Department] credit cover. This defence allocation represented an agreed proportion of the credit facilities for Iraq which had been agreed between the United Kingdom and Iraq. Yet when in 1990 Parliamentary Questions sought details of the Protocols, no mention was made of the defence allocation.

(iii) A written answer given to a Parliamentary Question in January 1990 seeking the 'total capital project cost cover offered under the export credit guarantee system' to a number of specified countries refused to supply the information. The ground given for the refusal was 'commercial confidentiality'.

(iv) Government statements made in 1989 and 1990, both in answers to Parliamentary Questions and in letters intended for members of the public, consistently failed to disclose either the terms of the adjustment to the Guidelines that had followed the ceasefire or the decision to adopt a more liberal policy on defence sales to Iraq.

(v) The answer given in February 1991 to Mr Tony Banks' question asking whether any MOD [Ministry of Defence] officials attended the Baghdad Military Exhibition of April/May 1989 represented a deliberate concealment from Parliament of the circumstances under which Mr David Hastie [a British Aerospace employee seconded to the Civil Service who the MOD claimed had travelled to Iraq in his private-sector, not his official, capacity] had attended the Exhibition.

(vi) The answer given in December 1990 to Mr Caborn's question asking what action the DTI [Department of Trade and Industry] took 'when it was first made aware of the pipeline equipment built in the UK for Iraq having possible military implications' did not constitute an adequate response to the question.

(vii) The refusal to authorise or facilitate the giving of evidence to TISC [Trade and Industry Select Committee inquiry into the 'Supergun'] by Mr Harding and Mr Primrose had the effect of depriving TISC of the first hand evidence that TISC had sought and that the two retired officials were in a position to have given.[17]

Scott was unequivocal and uncompromising on the implications of these seven evasions. In perhaps the most important single paragraph of his enormous report, Sir Richard declared:

it may be concluded that if, and to the extent that, the account given by a Minister to Parliament, whether in answering Parliamentary Questions, or in a debate, or in evidence to a Select Committee, withholds information on the matter under review, it is not a full account and the obligation of Ministerial accountability has, *prima facie*, not been discharged. Without the provision of full information it is not possible for Parliament, or for that matter the public, to assess what consequences, in the form of attribution of responsibility or blame, ought to follow. A denial of information to the public denies the public the ability to make an informed judgement on the Government's record. A failure by Ministers to meet the obligations of Ministerial accountability by providing information about the activities of their departments undermines, in my opinion, the democratic process.[18]

As the Secretary of Sir Richard's inquiry put it: 'The problem arises when Parliament doesn't even know that there is something not to know about.'[19] And in his attempt to confront this 'problem', Scott lifted his report firmly above the particular into the general with very significant and wide resonances for the British Constitution as a whole.

In fact, when confronting the Whitehall versions of accountability, Scott sensed opacity enveloping him all round in everything he saw and heard. He had, for example, some difficulty with the distinction drawn by the Cabinet Secretary, Sir Robin Butler, 'between Ministerial "accountability" and Ministerial "responsibility"'.[20] Continuing to paraphrase Sir Robin's evidence to him, Scott went on:

> Ministerial 'accountability' is a constitutional burden that rests on the shoulders of Ministers and cannot be set aside. It does not necessarily, however, require blame to be accepted by a Minister in whose department some blameworthy error or failure has occurred. A Minister should not be held to blame or required to accept personal criticism unless he has some personal responsibility for or some personal involvement in what has occurred.[21]

Scott found it 'difficult to disagree' that the complexities of modern government had made this so.[22]

But here the judge failed to bite the bullet. He offered, as Lord Hunt noticed and regretted,[23] no guidance of his own on how these fuzzy distinctions would be interpreted or by whom. Instead he suggested that 'any re-examination of the practices and conventions relied on by Government in declining to answer, or to answer fully, certain Parliamentary Questions should take account of the implications of the distinction drawn by Sir Robin . . .'[24] As a *quid pro quo* for his, Scott's, acceptance of such a distinction, ministers should be obliged to be forthcoming with such information as would enable such distinction between accountability and responsibility to be drawn.[25] Ministers conveniently kicked this recommendation into touch by asking the all-party Select Committee on Public Service to examine it.[26]

It was, however, on the central constitutional terrain charted by *Questions of Procedure for Ministers* that Scott had the most specific and, in terms of his personal constitutional contribution, the most significant things to say. As Peter Riddell put it: 'The lasting importance of the Scott Report will turn on "Questions of Procedure for Ministers."'[27] For Sir Richard Scott, as for Lord Nolan, *QPM* crept up on his inquiry as it progressed and finished up as a – perhaps the –

central vehicle for his recommendations. The weight their respective reports placed on that document confirmed the judgement of Peter Madgwick and Diana Woodhouse that '*Questions of Procedure* may now be taken as the defining constitutional document on Prime Minister and Cabinet.'[28]

Departmental guidance to officials on the preparation of answers to parliamentary questions, whose genesis lies in *QPM*, had been an issue from the early days of the inquiry. But the Scott team's interest in it escalated when they were preparing to receive Lady Thatcher's evidence. 'It became increasingly obvious to us that we had a real treasure trove in *QPM*, especially paragraph 27,' Sir Richard's Secretary explained, adding that it was in the inquiry's view 'the litmus test for the conduct of Ministers ... Sir Richard regarded it as the basis on which Ministers were expected to conduct themselves in relation to Parliament; not merely as something that could be discarded at the whim of the executive.'[29]

But, in keeping a close eye on *QPM* as his inquiry progressed, Sir Richard Scott was examining a moving picture. He was particularly exercised by the post-Nolan refinement of the document as it ultimately appeared when Roger Freeman, the Lord Privy Seal, unveiled the final version of the redrafted front-end of *QPM* in the House of Commons on 2 November 1995. As expected, it was a declaration of high principle surrounded by a wall of caveats; and it failed to materialize, as Nolan wished, as 'a separate section within a new *QPM*'.[30]

Sir Richard Scott picked carefully over paragraph (iii), the new nose of *QPM*, which read as follows:

> Ministers must not knowingly mislead Parliament and the public and should correct any inadvertent errors at the earliest opportunity. They must be as open as possible with Parliament and the public, withholding information only when disclosure would not be in the public interest, which should be decided in accordance with established Parliamentary convention, the law and any relevant Government Code of Practice.[31]

The difficulties arose, as Scott divined, over the words 'knowingly mislead', 'public interest' and 'established Parliamentary convention'. Sir Richard did service, too, in establishing, after consultations with the Cabinet Office, that 'Insofar as any inconsistency between the amendments and paragraph 27 of *QPM* arises, the amendments will, it is understood, take precedence.'[32]

Scott found no difficulty with the addition of the word 'knowingly' to the word 'mislead' (and I agree with him). He was concerned, however, about the phrase 'the public interest' (where I, too, have worries). It is simply too slippery a phrase for comfort. Like the phrase 'national interest', it reeks of executive convenience. Shortly after Scott reported, Sir Frank Cooper addressed my MA students in these candid and (given his ex-insider status) worrying terms: 'For me the real red rag to the bull is in the phrase "It's in the national interest." I have never ever discovered who is the guardian of the national interest. It's very rarely got anything to do with the national interest. It has to do with the people advocating a particular interest.'[33] For Scott, this reflected 'and rightly so, that there always have been and always will be some subjects in respect of which full information, or sometimes any information, cannot be given'.[34] That said, he acknowledged that this 'involves a dilution . . . of the obligations imposed by Ministerial accountability'[35] and, as corollary, 'it follows that the withholding of information by an accountable Minister should never be based on reasons of convenience or for the avoidance of political embarrassment, but should always require special and carefully considered justification. The interpretation of "in the public interest" in the new formulation should, in my opinion, adopt that approach.' I could not agree more. But this is akin to asking ministers not to think or behave like politicians.

Sir Richard showed bite and penetration, however, when he noticed just how powerful a buttress of executive convenience the concept of parliamentary conventions (escape clause number three in the new opening of *QPM*) could be. This was an important aspect of his findings whose significance I had failed to appreciate until Peter Riddell, the commentator most sensitively attuned to the parliamentary implications of both Scott and Nolan,[36] drew it to my attention.[37] In terms of conventions, however, it was as significant as it was rare for the executive to invite the legislature not just to visit the once secret garden of the Constitution but to suggest changes, too, both to the layout of the flowerbeds and to the blooms planted in them. The new Public Service Committee, and Parliament as a whole, gained thereby an unprecedented opportunity. Their initial preoccupation, rightly, was with the wording of *QPM*, and with the penumbra of similarly procedural documents which, in many respects, take their cue from its central themes and obligations (the Civil Service Code and the 'Osmotherly Rules' in particular).

At their first post-Scott hearing I suggested to the Public Service Committee that they should invite Sir Richard Scott to draft for them the kind of front-end to *QPM* that would reflect the key strictures on accountability in chapter eight of his report.[38] The Committee's chairman, Giles Radice, asked me to furnish the committee with a draft of my own.[39] My first concern was to make sure that the onus for making *QPM* work should be placed firmly on the shoulders of the Prime Minister, as Lord Nolan had wished, for this purpose; and Lord Nolan's suggested words ('It will be for the individual Ministers to judge how best to act in order to uphold the highest standards. It will be for the Prime Minister to determine whether or not they have done so in any particular circumstances'[40]) could not be improved upon. The next requirement was to tackle that most weaselly duo of words, the 'public interest'.

In response, then, to the Public Service Committee's request, I refashioned the nose of *QPM*, retaining where possible the government's own November 1995 wording, grafting on the Nolan requirements and adding some stiffening of my own. I presented a draft to my 'Hidden Wiring' MA seminar which, turning itself one spring afternoon into a mini-constitutional convention, suggested still further stiffening, some extensions and several embellishments.[41] This was the result:

QUESTIONS OF PROCEDURE FOR MINISTERS
THE PRINCIPLES AND OBLIGATIONS OF MINISTERIAL CONDUCT

1. Ministers of the Crown must behave according to the highest standards of constitutional and personal conduct. In particular

they must at all times and in all circumstances observe the following principles of ministerial conduct which, though they have no legal basis, represent the paramount obligations of ministerial duty and public service.

2. Ministers are ultimately accountable and responsible to Parliament for all the policies, decisions, actions and omissions of their departments and agencies.

3. Ministers must not knowingly mislead Parliament and the public and should correct any inadvertent errors at the earliest opportunity. Statements and Parliamentary answers must be based on the fullest and best information available to the government at the time. Ministers must be as open as possible with Parliament and the public. Withholding information must be restricted to those matters and such occasions where demonstrable harm might occur to especially sensitive state actions, activities and relationships to a degree that would clearly override the obligation to disclose. It is the duty of the Prime Minister to ensure that in all the government's dealings with Parliament and the public, the onus will normally be on full and timely disclosure. On matters in which Parliament has shown an interest where full disclosure might incur serious harm, Ministers should make the case for confidentiality privately either to the leaders of the opposition parties on a privy counsellor basis or to the chair of the relevant House of Commons or House of Lords Select Committee. It will be for the Prime Minister to ensure that Ministers live up to their responsibilities in this area and to set an example himself/herself. It will be for officials to follow the lead of their Ministers.

4. Ministers must ensure that no conflict arises, or appears to arise, between their public duties and their private interests.

5. Ministers should avoid accepting any gift or hospitality which might, or might reasonably appear to, compromise their judgement or place them under an improper obligation.

6. Ministers in the House of Commons must keep separate their roles as Minister and constituency member.

7. Ministers must not use public resources for party political purposes. They must uphold the political impartiality of the Civil Service and not ask civil servants to act in any way which would conflict with the Civil Service Code.

8. Ministers and officials must at all times act in accordance with the law. In cases where the courts have overturned a government decision, Ministers and officials must treat this as precedent in future instances unless specific legislation is passed by Parliament to restore or change the position.

9. These principles and the obligations that derive from them represent the pillars of ministerial life and public service. It will be for individual Ministers to judge how best to act in order to uphold the highest standards. It will be for the Prime Minister to determine whether or not they have done so in any particular circumstance. Any adverse findings about the conduct of his/her colleagues on the part of the Prime Minister must be reported to Parliament.[42]

Plainly, any post-Scott rejigging of the rule books and procedural guidelines must start with *QPM*, which is the master document of British central government. Other documents such as the Civil Service Code or the 'Osmotherly Rules' would take their cue from it.

Quite apart from its salience for the fundamental accountability of the state, the Scott Report provided a dazzling illumination of another intractable feature of the British way of government – overload. The picture it painted was of an overstretched system in which the left hand had little idea what the right was doing. Whitehall's fabled gifts for co-ordination and interdepartmental consultation were lacking both when it came to the interpretation and application of arms export policy and when it came to the preparation of material for the Matrix Churchill trial – indeed even from the procedures which led to the prosecution of the case in the first instance. Equally striking were the levels at which matters rested. Very rarely did they impinge on a Cabinet committee, let alone the full Cabinet or the Prime Minister, or even the Joint Intelligence Committee.

Sir Percy Cradock, former Chairman of the JIC, was quite explicit about such factors during the BBC Radio 4 *Analysis Special* discussion on the evening of the Scott Report's publication. 'The intelligence services', he explained,

> are tasked services. They are given certain jobs to do, certain areas of priority. They're given that by the Joint Intelligence Committee. But their actual operations are for the agencies themselves. The intelligence services in this matter were told that we wanted information about Iraq's weapons of mass destruction – the big things, the nuclear weapons, the chemical, the biological, the Supergun – and they got that. They did the job extremely well. They were not given any such priority orders for the sort of thing [dual-use machine tools] that came up in the Matrix Churchill case.[43]

Sir Percy went on to explain the left hand/right hand phenomenon from the perspective of a JIC official who, as he liked to put it, sat at the 'high table of British intelligence'.[44]

> You have here a case where the activities of a particular firm ran into the official machine at two very separate points. First of all, Mr Henderson [Managing Director of Matrix Churchill] provided some intelligence about Iraq. He was used. He was then let go. Later, as an entirely separate episode, his firm were charged with falsifying, or attempting to falsify, export licence applications and action was taken by the Customs [and Excise] who operate very independently. And no one would suggest that we should not bring an action in a case of illegality like this simply because particular firms have helped intelligence at an earlier part of their career.[45]

But it was on the question of overload that Sir Percy's judgements have a near-ubiquitous relevance. 'It is all done at breakneck speed,' he said. 'There's a certain artificiality about the Scott Report in that you have one considerable legal mind applied to one facet of foreign policy. The clock has been stopped for the benefit of Sir Richard Scott.[46] Here the parallels with the Franks Report on the Falklands were very striking.[47]

On similar lines to Sir Percy Cradock, the former Foreign and Commonwealth Secretary, Lord Howe, voiced many complaints about the conduct and procedure of the Scott Inquiry before and after Sir Richard had presented his findings.[48] Several of them struck me as a refined version of special pleading on the part of a life-long executive man. But on overload, Lord Howe was convincing, especially on 'the extent to which a judge sitting alone, however distinguished, can sometimes take insufficient account of the pressures of day-to-day ministerial and official life'.[49] (Though Sir Richard, it must be said, if one reads his report carefully, is plainly aware of pressure at the top.) Lord Howe recalled telling his inquisitor when he appeared before the Scott Inquiry 'that I calculated that during my six years as Foreign Secretary, taking home an average three boxes a night five to six nights a week forty weeks a year for six years, the weight of paper that crossed my midnight desk was twenty-four tons. It is no wonder that my colleague in the United States, George Shultz, said that being Secretary of State was "like trying to get a drink out of a fire hose".'[50]

The Scott Report, taken as a whole, provided an intensely revealing chapter about British government in the 1980s and early 1990s. But was it a discreditable one? It was in two senses. First, because the government's response to the Scott Report was driven above all else by the need, as ministers saw it, to protect two of their own. The No. 10 press pack accompanying the Report contained items such as a Treasury brief entitled 'Scott Clears Waldegrave of Intent to Mislead',[51] with similar material provided by the Attorney-General's chambers.[52] Ministers sang along identical lines to a pre-orchestrated refrain in Parliament and in public in the days after the Report's publication. Putting matters right sounded to them entirely secondary. Like Roy Jenkins, I'm not a great believer in capital punishment for ministers.[53] But William Waldegrave and Sir Nicholas Lyell should have 'walked' like Test cricketers of old. By all means, they could have said they continued to believe they had done nothing wrong, citing Sir Richard's belief that they were without 'duplicitous intentions'[54] when, as Scott saw it, they transgressed paragraph 27 of *QPM*. Had they recognized, however, that a large measure of parliamentary and public opinion did not agree with them (or Sir Richard on this), and that a period on the back benches might be a suitable recognition of that, there would not have been a dry eye in the House. Instead, the less than heroic sight of their clinging on to office distracted the press, enraged the opposition and, if the opinion polls are a guide, disgusted the public for days to come.[55]

But it only was for days. The caravanserai of press, public and political attention soon moved on to a mad youth club organizer and to mad cows, leaving Parliament as the last, best hope for keeping sight of the essentials and for ensuring matters were put right. The initial signs were not encouraging. When giving evidence before the Public Service Committee on 20 March 1996, I suggested that ministers should be reminded about the requirement contained in the post-Nolan front end of *QPM* that they 'should correct any inadvertent errors at the earliest opportunity'. 'It would be very helpful', I continued, 'if ministers went back over all the years from 1984 to 1990 and put right all the misleading answers they had given to people like you.'[56] Within a few days, Lord Jenkins of Putney (the former Labour minister, Hugh Jenkins) tried to extract just such a pledge, citing the 'recast first paragraph of *Questions of Procedure for Ministers*'.[57] For the government, Earl Howe, junior defence minister (not to be confused with the former Foreign Secretary, Lord Howe), replied simply by reiterating that, unlike Sir Richard Scott,[58] 'the government take the view that the Howe guidelines were not changed and do not consider that a statement on replies to questions on exports to Iraq is necessary.'[59] This reply, though largely unnoticed, was as shameless as any other aspect of the government's post-Scott strategy, which was simply to brazen it out.

The main task of post-Scott scrutiny, however, fell not to individual parliamentarians like Lord Jenkins of Putney but to two committees in particular – Giles Radice's Public Service Committee and Tom King's Committee on Intelligence and Security. On the 'No End of a Lesson?' *Analysis Special*, Mr King, a former Defence Secretary, when asked if his committee would follow up the failures in intelligence distribution identified by Scott,[60] replied: 'We shall say some things about the need for coordination ... and ... maybe ... we'll do a bit of work on structure.'[61] The Scott Inquiry initially served as a test for the executive. Once published, the Report became a challenge for the legislature. The top civil servants' union, the First Division Association, was right to claim that Scott had left a 'chasm' in notions of responsibility and accountability,[62] and John Hunt was equally right to declare that, post-Scott, the House of Commons should 'concentrate' on this.[63] Parliament's initial efforts to do so were met with scepticism. As a seasoned press observer said of the opening session of the Public Service Committee's hearing into ministerial and parliamentary accountability and responsibility, 'they [the MPs] were utterly defeatist.'[64] And as a veteran Whitehall figure, steeped in the imperatives of the secret state, put it: 'Senior mandarins think Parliament is just a waste of time. The select committees are hopeless. They have got to raise their game and the aftermath of the Scott Report is their great opportunity. They should go to the very top on this.'[65] By this he meant summoning the Prime Minister to give evidence to the select committee. (The convention that premiers do not appear before the post-1979 committees was, as a senior Whitehall figure put it, 'invented by Mrs Thatcher in 1986'[66] when she did not wish to appear before the Commons Defence Committee in the aftermath of the Westland affair.)

The Whitehall 'veteran' is absolutely right. The Prime Minister alone is the quality controller of that mercurial but crucial patch of the Constitution which deals with the swathe of concerns embraced by *QPM*. So, as the Scott team prepared to disband and arrange the preservation of their enormous archive, attention, rightly, shifted to Churchill's 'little room', or the miniaturized versions of it along the committee corridor of the Palace of Westminster overlooking the Thames. For only there, given the paucity of shame on the part of the Major administration and the lack of sustained attention from the press, could a rather discreditable chapter in the history of British government be turned into something of enduring benefit to the nation's constitutional well-being.

CONCLUSION

Reforming with the Grain

Thoughts on Walking Down Constitution Hill

When you get to No. 10, you've climbed there on a little ladder called 'the status quo'. And, when you're there, the status quo looks very good.

Tony Benn, 1995[1]

Beware of telling the people that the things which are most valuable to them are not endangered if their representatives in Parliament do not function efficiently.

Enoch Powell, 1989[2]

Our constitution is not based upon any fixed or immutable laws, nor do we require any special procedure to change it. This so-called flexibility is our greatest asset, it should enable the constitution to adapt itself momentarily to the desires and wishes of the people.

G. D. H. Cole, 1932[3]

Only those institutions are loved which touch the imagination.

R. H. Tawney, 1917[4]

[Lord Esher] began by saying he never believed in hara-kiri. Many people after 1911 thought the House of Lords was doomed and gave up the struggle, whereas it still survives. He believes it fulfils today another but no less necessary function than it did in 1910. The same could be said of the Monarchy, now that it is constitutional. This is why he believes the National Trust will survive.

Viscount Esher to James Lees-Milne, 1946[5]

There is more than a touch of heritage about the British Constitution and the institutions that embody it. And, strangely enough, it can sometimes best be sensed while accumulating what Simon Schama has called 'the archive of the feet'.[6] For example, we may live under the peculiar shadow of the most evanescent constitution in the advanced world, but take a walk down the entirely tangible Constitution Hill in London SW1 and you will discover what I mean. On your right is Buckingham Palace; to your left Green Park; ahead the towers of the Palace of Westminster and, the luxuriance of the leaves in St James's Park permitting, a vista of what Sir Neville Cardus, that great connoisseur of grass and Englishness, once described as the 'accumulated nobility of dome and turret vanishing like white ghosts in the sky' above Whitehall.[7] Such a perambulation has an almost timeless air. Modernity is represented only by the roar of the traffic on tarmac, the scream above of jet engines being 'feathered' for the approach to Heathrow and the extra barbed wire and new electronic protection above the wall separating the walker from the back garden of Her Majesty the Queen.

Lord Esher, as chairman of the National Trust after the Second World War, may have been describing the stone-and-sward side of what Angus Calder has called 'deep England',[8] but his words would have fitted our constitutional artefacts equally well. Bernard Crick sensed this when contributing to a *New Statesman* symposium on 'England, Whose England?' nearly half a century after Esher's disquisition on constitutional durability when he wrote: ' "British" seems to me a political and legal concept bound up with a broad acceptance of the laws, parliament and, historically, the crown. It's not a catch-all cultural term.'[9] And it was Esher's father, Reginald Brett, that great Royal confidant of the early twentieth century, who linked the procedural and the human when he wrote at the height of the crisis over the power of the House of Lords in 1910 that 'an unwritten Constitution rests upon precedent and reasonableness.'[10]

A scattering of Labour governments over seven decades and two world wars inside twenty-one years did nothing to disturb this tranquillity, apart from a dash of high explosive on both Buckingham Palace and the Palace of Westminster in 1940–1. Indeed, the 'deep play'[11] of Britain's political and administrative systems was so profound that when the one-person, one-vote franchise was completed with the passage of the Representation of the People Act 1948 three years after Labour took office for the first time with a majority, the country still lived under what was essentially a late seventeenth-century Constitution with votes bolted on to it. So naturally did Attlee's personal behaviour and attitudes go with the grain of this deep past (he was given to such statements as 'a conscientious constitutional monarch is a strong element of stability and continuity in our constitution',[12] and he wept when news of George VI's death was brought to him[13]) that a Conservative MP said of him at the height of Labour's 'high tide',[14] that if he had got up in the House of Commons to announce 'The Revolution' he would have made it sound like a change in a regional railway timetable.[15]

There is every reason to believe that the bulk of the British people, certainly those below what John Major likes to call 'the upper one thousand of politics',[16] were quite content with our peculiar constitutional arrangements, in so far as they thought about them at all, until the past twenty, perhaps only the past ten years. As late as 1973 nearly half those polled thought the British system of government worked well.[17] Twenty-two years later, three-quarters think that system should be improved.[18] There may well have been a crude relationship between the postwar consensus and general satisfaction with the institutional instruments of that post-1945 settlement.

Seepage of faith in the efficacy of Parliament is especially worrying, and in the early 1990s it turned into a steady flow. In 1991, 58 per cent of those polled believed Parliament worked 'fairly well'. By the spring of 1995 that figure had fallen to 43 per cent.[19] But what was particularly striking about the MORI data accumulated for the Joseph Rowntree Reform Trust in the spring of 1995 was not just the degree of dissatisfaction with Britain's governing processes and institutions but the level of support for their radical refashioning. As Patrick Dunleavy and Stuart Weir put it:

> Four out of five voters (79 per cent) agree that Britain needs a
> written constitution, 'providing clear legal rules which govern-
> ment ministers are forced to operate' ... This is a consensus
> which goes far beyond popular distaste for sleaze. The public
> is rejecting established practice across the existing constitution.
> Important canons of faith at Westminster and Whitehall have
> effectively lost all legitimacy.[20]

'All legitimacy lost' strikes me as an exaggeration. It could be that
a fusion of factors – lingering unease from a decade of 'command
premiership' under Mrs Thatcher, another half-decade and more of
Conservative government on top of that, a sense increasingly of
Westminster–Whitehall irrelevance beneath the European shadow,
all boosted by sleaze, Nolan and the anticipation of Scott, could
mean that spring 1995 opinion is somewhat unrepresentative as it
was measured at an unusual moment. It may not have been the best
time to gauge the 'deep play' of the collective British mind on matters
constitutional.

What Churchill called 'the long continuity of our institutions' in
his 'Finest Hour' speech in May 1940[21] really is part of 'deep England', if not 'deep Britain', and should never be underestimated as
the kind of latent, small 'c' conservative ballast that represents a real
and continuous force for sustaining the status quo. But the search
for a better status quo, as an improved 'half-way house' towards
some future grand constitutional settlement which may or may not
come about, is certainly worth close and immediate attention. The
suggestions made in this volume have all been framed with such a
relatively modest but practically achievable philosophy in mind, and
coloured also by Tawney's point about love and imagination. The
familiar can continue to inspire affection even when a slippage of
standards or sustained institutional underachievement stimulates out-
breaks of rattiness or recrimination – rather like Orwell's image of
England as a family with the wrong members in charge.[22]

The philosophy of reforming-with-the-grain can also be applied
to efficiency questions that impinge upon the mechanics of state; on
overload and even the 'opposition of events'. A refashioning of the
traditional Cabinet structure with a new Strategic Policy Committee

assisted by a revived 'think tank' would, I am convinced, help the full Cabinet (not just its inner core) fulfil its traditional remit of acting as 'the ultimate arbiter of all Government policy'.[23] Similarly, the sensible ideas for a more thoughtful, less yah-booish Prime Minister's Questions (once a week at least) put forward by the House of Commons Select Committee on Procedure in July 1995 are a classic example of how best to rescue an important instrument of accountability from the excesses which set in scarcely a decade after it became a twice-weekly fixture (when Parliament was sitting) in July 1961.[24] As the political philosopher Michael Oakeshott put it: 'the seamanship [in political activity] consists in using the resources of a traditional manner of behaviour in order to make a friend of every inimical occasion.'[25]

Even so radical a reformer as Will Hutton, whose *The State We're In* is premissed on the belief that ancient constitutional practices shackle the forces of economic modernity in the United Kingdom, recognizes the value of new ways clothed in old forms and that 'after the great exception of the Civil War, the hallmark of English life has been the capacity to organise ... transformations peacefully – forming an historical memory of reformist change that passes subliminally from generation to generation and which may still exist today.'[26] Mr Hutton would, for example, countenance the retention of 'the monarch as titular head of state' because 'too many generations of Britains [sic] have fought and died for King and Country for this unifying symbol to be thrown aside lightly.'[27] Harold Nicolson, with a dash of enthusiastic grandiloquence, had, over forty years earlier, lauded the capacity of a nation 'cemented together by the gigantic pressures of history' for achieving what he called a 'wonderful fusion of tradition and invention' at a time when the so-called 'postwar settlement' had seemed to do just that in social and economic terms.[28]

The first Nolan Report is written in exactly this kind of modern-within-the-ancient reformist spirit and promises to be all the more effective for that. For the proliferation of codes represents constitution-making by stealth disguised in a typically British fashion as something practical and informal and organically inseparable from the compost of tradition. Peter Riddell put this very bluntly in *The Times* four years after the declassification of *Questions of Procedure for Ministers* when he wrote: 'Britain no longer has an unwritten constitution. The framework of a written constitution is being created' as the country's 'political culture' was moving 'away from informal understandings and precedents to a more formal system of rules'.[29] Lord Nolan, whom Mr Riddell had very much in mind, acknowledged this two days after the article appeared. Addressing a seminar at the Institute of Historical Research to mark the first anniversary of the publication of his report, he said that I had summed up what his committee had tried to do when I wrote that 'Nolan was saying that our "great ghost" of a constitution *should* be reduced to the flesh of a code,' though Lord Nolan went on to remind the seminar that 'codes are not laws'.[30]

The importance of such an advance – from the back of the envelope to the back of a code – should not be underestimated in so profoundly inert a polity as the United Kingdom's, where, as Tony Benn observed, the status quo has a shining allure for those who have risen by converting its traditional usages into their own ladder of personal and political advancement. Arriving in No. 10 or the Cabinet Room is enough of an achievement to assuage the itch to change – the human equivalent of Herbert Morrison saying smugly that 'socialism is what the Labour Government does'[31] or John Griffith's regretful observation that 'the constitution is what happens.'[32] There is, however, an urgent requirement even for those who recoil from the 'big bang' approach to constitutional change: that of recognizing the continuing validity of another Morrisonian remark, of 'making the irrational work' better.[33] It may sound unheroic, even prosaic. But with powerful forces and factors still ranged against it as the executive century draws to a close, it will be a prize worth seriously striving for as ancient polity meets new millennium.

NOTES

Preface

1 Peter Hennessy and Simon Coates, *The Back of the Envelope: Hung Parliaments, the Queen and the Constitution*, Strathclyde *Analysis* Paper no. 5 (Department of Government, University of Strathclyde, 1991), p. 18.

2 Quoted in Ross Terrill, *R. H. Tawney and His Times: Socialism as Fellowship* (Harvard University Press, 1973), p. 173.

3 Quoted in Peter Hennessy, *Whitehall* (Secker & Warburg, 1989), p. 306.

4 It was the celebrated 1963 Fontana reissue of this classic work, with its oft-quoted 'Introduction by R. H. S. Crossman'.

5 John Young, *Britain and Europe, 1945–92* (Macmillan, 1993), pp. 167–8.

6 L. S. Amery, 'The Nature of British Parliamentary Government', in Lord Campion et al., *Parliament: A Survey* (Allen & Unwin, 1952), pp. 37–8.

7 Hennessy and Coates, *The Back of the Envelope*, p. 8.

8 Noel Coward, 'The Stately Homes of England' (1938), *More Compact Coward*, CDP 7971572 (EMI, 1991).

9 Andrew Marr, *Ruling Britannia: The Failure and Future of British Democracy* (Michael Joseph, 1995), p. 2.

10 Conversation with Tony Benn, 20 July 1995.

11 It was published as Peter Hennessy, *The Hidden Wiring: Power, Politics and the Constitution*, Fabian Society Discussion Paper No. 2 (Fabian Society, 1990).

Prologue

1 Simon Jenkins, 'The Nasty Party: John Major Needs Heseltine and Portillo to Fight in an Open Contest', *The Times*, 28 June 1995.

2 Enoch Powell, 'Body Blow to the Constitution', *Daily Mail*, 27 June 1995.

3 Private information.

4 Letter to *The Times*, 30 June 1995.

5 'Major's Statement: "Every Leader is Leader Only with the Support of his Party"', *Guardian*, 23 June 1995.

6 Donald Macintyre, 'Major's Big Gamble Pays Off', *Independent*, 5 July 1995.

7 Powell, 'Body Blow to the Constitution'.

8 Private information.

9 'Major's Statement'.

10 The former private secretary was Ronald Fraser, who served the Cabinet Secretary, Sir Norman Brook, in the late 1940s, quoted in Peter Hennessy, 'Harvesting the Cupboards: Why Britain has Produced no Administrative Theory or Ideology in the Twentieth Century', *Transactions of the Royal Historical Society*, 6th ser., vol. 4 (1994), p. 216. It was another private secretary, a Downing Street one in this case, Derek Mitchell, who began his hastily compiled brief for Sir Alec Douglas-Home in the small hours of 16 October 1964, when it looked as if the previous day's election might produce a hung result, with the words 'Deadlock. The Queen's Government must be carried on': Public Record Office (PRO), PREM 11/4756 (see below pp. 63–4).

11 Conversation with Sir Kenneth Stowe, 11 April 1994.

12 Ibid.

13 The phrase is Enoch Powell's, in 'Body Blow to the Constitution.'

14 Jenkins, 'The Nasty Party'.

15 Philip Webster, 'Major Swings Cabinet to Left; Heseltine Rewarded with Overlord Role', *The Times*, 6 July 1995.

16 Conversation with Enoch Powell, 5 July 1995.

17 Anthony Howard, 'History Offers Scant Hope to Bearer of Title', *The Times*, 6 July 1995; Alan Watkins, 'Mr Major Astonishes the Right with his Ingratitude', *Independent on Sunday*, 9 July 1995; *Who's Who 1995* (A. & C. Black, 1995), Lord Howe entry p. 945, Lord Whitelaw entry, p. 2041.

18 See p. 79 below.

19 See Robert Blake, *The Office of Prime Minister* (British Academy/Oxford University Press, 1975), pp. 70–3.

20 John W. Wheeler-Bennett, *King George VI: His Life and Reign* (Macmillan, 1958), p. 797.

21 Ibid.

22 Ibid.

23 For the debate about the modern scope and force of these personal prerogatives see pp. 53–67 below.

24 PRO, PREM 5/431, 'Ministerial Appointments 1940–45', Bridges to Churchill, 'Precedence of War Cabinet Ministers', 2 October 1940.

25 Ibid., Bridges to Churchill, 3 October 1940.

26 Ibid.

27 PRO, PREM 5/211, 'Ministerial Appointments 1942–43'.

28 Ibid.
29 Michael White, 'Deputy Moves In at Once to Show he Means Business', *Guardian*, 7 July 1995.
30 'The office of Prime Minister is what its holder chooses and is able to make of it.' The Earl of Oxford and Asquith, *Fifty Years of Parliament*, vol. 2 (Cassell, 1926), p. 185.
31 Peter Hennessy, *Whitehall* (Fontana, 1990), p. 708. The day before Mr Heseltine briefed lobby correspondents on the purposes and parameters of his new job, I anticipated he would take a maximalist approach to it, as 'he's an interventionist by nature and will be able to do what Willie Whitelaw did without any fuss. He's unsackable and he loves great sweeps – because he's interested in *everything*.' Quoted in White, 'Deputy Moves in at Once to Show he Means Business'.
32 Conversation with Tony Bevins, 8 July 1995.
33 Anthony Bevins, 'Major Cedes an Empire to Heseltine', *Observer*, 9 July 1995.
34 Ibid., and Patrick Wintour, 'Tension and Tetchiness over Voting Fair Play as MPs Filed through the Corridor of Power', *Guardian*, 5 July 1995.
35 For Heseltine and Westland see Peter Hennessy, 'Helicopter Crashes into Cabinet: Prime Minister and Constitution Hurt', *Journal of Law and Society*, vol. 13, no. 3 (Winter 1986), pp. 423–32.
36 Private information.
37 Bevins, 'Major Cedes an Empire to Heseltine'.
38 Ibid. The day Tony Bevins' story ran in the *Observer*, Mr Heseltine sought to reassure his Cabinet colleagues still further by declaring: 'Cabinet ministers are responsible for their own departments and nothing must be seen to blur that clear line of acceptability and responsibility'. Michael White, 'Heseltine Woos Colleagues', *Guardian*, 10 July 1995.
39 See Hennessy, *Whitehall*, pp. 607–8.
40 Bevins, 'Major Cedes an Empire to Heseltine'.
41 Ibid.
42 Private information and '10 Downing Street Press Notice: Department for Education and Employment', 5 July 1995, 'Notes for Editors' (which stated: 'As First Secretary of State and Deputy Prime Minister, Mr Heseltine will assist the Prime Minister generally and will have specific responsibility for the competitiveness agenda, the working of Government and the presentation of its policies. He will chair a number of Cabinet Committees and will be an ex officio member of Cabinet Committees generally').
43 Conversation with Tony Bevins, 8 July 1995.
44 Bevins, 'Major Cedes an Empire to Heseltine'.
45 Private information.

46 The Privy Council meeting at which Mr Heseltine was sworn in was held on 10 July 1995.

47 *Ministerial Committees of the Cabinet: Membership and Terms of Reference*, Cabinet Office, 18 July 1995.

48 Peter Riddell, 'Heseltine to Oversee Policy on Industry', *The Times*, 19 July 1995.

49 Ibid. Michael Heseltine, *Where There's a Will* (Hutchinson, 1987).

50 Private information. For Mr Waldegrave's phrase see William Waldegrave, 'The Future of Parliamentary Government', *The Journal of Legislative Studies*, vol. 1, summer 1995, no. 2, p. 176.

51 Quoted in Sir Ivor Jennings, *Cabinet Government* (Cambridge University Press, 1936), p. 12.

Introduction

1 Lord Bancroft, speaking at the Gresham College Seminar, 'In the Steps of Walter Bagehot: A Constitutional Health-Check', 13 March 1995.

2 Vernon Bogdanor, answering questions after delivering his paper, 'The Monarchy and the Constitution: A Historical Approach', to the Twentieth Century British History Seminar, Institute of Historical Research, 1 February 1995.

3 Peter Clarke, 'The Edwardians and the Constitution', in Donald Read (ed.), *Edwardian England* (Croom Helm for the Historical Association, 1985), p. 46.

4 Lord Hailsham, 'The Future of Cabinet Government', The Granada Guildhall Lecture 1987, delivered at the Guildhall, City of London, 10 November 1987.

5 House of Commons Debates, *Official Report*, 8 February 1960, col. 70.

6 W. E. Gladstone, *Gleanings of Past Years*, vol. 1 (John Murray, 1879), p. 245.

7 D. Lindsay Keir, *The Constitutional History of Modern Britain, 1485–1937* (Adam and Charles Black, 1946), p. 491.

8 L. S. Amery, 'The Nature of British Parliamentary Government', in Lord Campion et al., *Parliament: A Survey* (Allen & Unwin, 1952), p. 37.

9 Peter Hennessy, unpublished diary entry for 24 July 1990. The conversation took place the day before. I have Sir Robin's permission to attribute his remarks.

10 Private information.

11 Gilbert Campion, 'Parliamentary Procedure, Old and New', in Campion et al., *Parliament: A Survey*, p. 141.

Chapter 1

1 George Dangerfield, *The Strange Death of Liberal England* (Constable, 1936), pp. 34–5.

2 Public Record Office (PRO), CAB 129/119, CP (64) 1, 19 October 1964, 'Questions of Procedure for Ministers: Note by the Prime Minister'.

3 Tony Benn MP, briefing for 'Cabinet and Premiership' course and 'Hidden Wiring' option of MA in Contemporary British History since 1939, Department of History, Queen Mary and Westfield College, held at House of Commons, 1 March 1995.

4 R. H. S. Crossman, 'Introduction', in Walter Bagehot, *The English Constitution* (Fontana, 1963), p. 2.

5 Private information.

6 *The Best Future for Britain* (Conservative Party, March 1992).

7 Peter Hennessy, *Cabinet* (Blackwell, 1986), pp. 8–13.

8 Cf. Peter Hennessy, 'Whitehall Watch: Thatcher Declines to Disclose Rules of the Ministerial Game', *Independent*, 1 May 1989, and Peter Hennessy, 'Whitehall Watch: Major Considers Revealing Hidden Cabinet Workings', *Independent*, 25 November 1991.

9 House of Commons Debates, *Official Report*, 8 February 1960, col. 70.

10 My memory of this is especially sharp, as I was the commentator called upon to flaunt *QPM* before the cameras and intone it into the microphones. The descent of the electronic media on the home of my friends, Peter and Elizabeth Freeman, in Cambridge, where our two families were supposed to be having a quiet get-together, is still the cause of occasional pangs of conscience on my part.

11 Patricia Wynn Davies, 'Roll-Call of Tories who Departed under a Cloud', *Independent*, 10 April 1995.

12 Sarah Hogg, 'Policy-making in Government', *The Sunday Times* Lecture, 7 March 1995.

13 Conversation with Lord Trend, 1 October 1986.

14 Trend to Wilson, 16 October 1964. The file containing this exchange has yet to reach the Public Record Office, but its internal Cabinet Office title and number are as follows: 'Cabinet, Questions of Procedure for Ministers', Part 4, 4/1/6/2. I am grateful to Sir Robin Butler for allowing access to it and to Pat Andrews and Richard Ponman of the Cabinet Office for their hospitality when I consulted it.

15 Conversation with Lord Trend, 1 October 1986.

16 See their fourteenth session on 15 February 1995, during which I presented evidence: *Standards in Public Life: First Report of the Committee on Standards in Public Life*, vol. 2: *Transcripts of Oral Evidence*, Cm 2850-II (HMSO, 1995), pp. 363–70.

17 These were PRO, CAB 21/1624, 'Cabinet Procedure: Consolidated
    Version of the Prime Minister's Directives', 1946–9; PRO, CAB 21/2778,
    'Cabinet Procedure: Consolidated Version of the Prime Minister's
    Directives', 1949–52, plus assorted later versions of the document.
18 Martin Le Jeune to Peter Hennessy, undated (late February 1995).
19 A. V. Dicey, *Introduction to the Study of the Law of the Constitution*
    (Macmillan, 1948 edn), p. 418.
20 G. H. L. Le May, *The Victorian Constitution* (Duckworth, 1979), p. 1.
21 House of Commons Treasury and Civil Service Committee, *The Role of
    the Civil Service*, Minutes of Evidence, 23 November 1993, 27-I (HMSO,
    1994), pp. 66–70.
22 Private information.
23 Sir Robin Butler, briefing for 'Cabinet and Premiership' course,
    Department of History, Queen Mary and Westfield College, held at the
    Cabinet Office, 4 December 1992.
24 Dicey, *Introduction to the Study of the Law of the Constitution*, pp. 422–3.
25 PRO, CAB 129/119, CP (64) 1.
26 Conversation with Sir Robin Butler, 18 January 1994.
27 *Questions of Procedure for Ministers* (Cabinet Office, May 1992), para. 27.
28 House of Commons Select Committee on Procedure, *Report*, HC92,
    1958–9.
29 House of Commons Debates, *Official Report*, 8 February 1960, col. 70.
30 Lord Hailsham, 'The Elective Dictatorship', The Dimbleby Lecture,
    1976, broadcast on BBC1, 19 October 1976.
31 House of Commons Treasury and Civil Service Sub-Committee, session
    1994–95, *The Dual Role of Secretary to the Cabinet and Head of the Home
    Civil Service*, Minutes of Evidence, 8 March 1995, Sir Robin Butler, HC
    300-i (HMSO, 1995), p. 7.
32 It was circulated on 27 June 1982 as C(P)(83)5 and acquired privately.
33 *Questions of Procedure for Ministers*, 1992 edn.
34 *Standards in Public Life*, vol. 2, *Transcripts of Oral Evidence*, p. 364. See also
    below pp. 187–80.
35 There have been many editions of this fabled work. I shall use the one
    which first brought Bagehot to my attention as an undergraduate newly
    arrived at St John's College, Cambridge, in the autumn of 1966: Walter
    Bagehot, *The English Constitution*, with an introduction by R. H. S.
    Crossman (Fontana, 1963).
36 The First Earl of Balfour, 'Introduction', in Walter Bagehot, *The English
    Constitution*, 'World's Classics' edn (Oxford University Press, 1928), pp.
    vi–vii.
37 Bagehot, *The English Constitution* (1963 edn), pp. 161–3.
38 For an absorbing short life of Bagehot see Alastair Buchan, *The Spare
    Chancellor: The Life of Walter Bagehot* (Chatto & Windus, 1959).

39 I am very grateful to my Queen Mary and Westfield colleague, Dr John Ramsden, for this 'Rabism', which he discovered in the Butler Papers at Trinity College, Cambridge: untitled note dated 28 April 1963, file G40.

40 Harold Macmillan, 'Walter Bagehot', *The Economist*, 30 December 1978.

41 Harold Wilson, 'Walter Bagehot', *The Economist*, 29 July 1967.

42 Walter Bagehot, *The English Constitution*, with an introduction by R. H. S. Crossman (Fontana, 1993).

43 K. C. Wheare, 'Walter Bagehot: Lecture on a Master Mind', *Proceedings of the British Academy*, vol. 60 (Oxford University Press, 1974), p. 25.

44 A MORI poll conducted for *The Times* between 18 and 22 August; Peter Riddell, ' "Blair Effect" Undermines Major and Lifts Labour to Record High', *The Times*, 26 August 1994. Professor Ivor Crewe regards the 'Gallup 9000' as the 'most reliable' opinion poll. Mr Major's all-time low here was reached in December 1994, when his satisfaction rating fell to 18.1 per cent. Conversation with Professor Ivor Crewe, 3 June 1995.

45 Martin Linton, 'One in Three Voters Say Ministers "Abuse Power" ', *Guardian*, 17 March 1994.

46 She used it on the occasion of my inaugural lecture as Professor of Contemporary British History at Queen Mary and Westfield College, University of London, 1 February 1994.

47 Bagehot, *The English Constitution* (1963 edn), p. 59.

48 See PRO CAB 21/1638, 'Function of the Prime Minister and His Staff', and PRO CAB 21/3720, 'Consultation with Leaders of the Parliamentary Opposition (Policy)'.

49 'Bittersweet' (1930), in Noel Coward, *Collected Sketches and Lyrics* (Hutchinson, undated).

50 Letter from Sir Robin Butler to Peter Hennessy, 27 June 1994.

51 Peter Hennessy and Simon Coates, *The Back of the Envelope: Hung Parliaments, the Queen and the Constitution*, Strathclyde *Analysis* Paper no. 5 (Department of Government, University of Strathclyde, 1991), p. 17.

Chapter 2

1 Philip Ziegler addressing the 'Hidden Wiring' seminar, MA in Contemporary British History since 1939, Department of History, Queen Mary and Westfield College, 8 February 1995. For Mr Benn and the controversy over the Queen's head on stamps see Tony Benn, *Out of the Wilderness: Diaries 1963–67* (Hutchinson, 1987), pp. 218–300.

2 Lord Charteris, interviewed for Channel 4 Television/Wide Vision Productions, *What Has Become of Us?*, 6 June 1994.

3 *Elizabeth R*, BBC video, BBC V 4710 (1992).

4 Tony Benn, briefing for 'Cabinet and Premiership' course, Department of History, Queen Mary and Westfield College, 26 April 1994.

5 Sir Perry was speaking at a meeting of officers of the Political Studies Association and Fleet Street political correspondents at the Royal Commonwealth Society, 5 December 1984.

6 Lord Blake, 'The Monarchy', lecture delivered for Gresham College at the Guildhall, City of London, 3 July 1984.

7 Her Majesty received a petition from Mrs Ann Scargill on behalf of 'Women Against Pit Closures' on 11 August 1984: Buckingham Palace Press Office, 1 May 1995.

8 For a good account of such personal misfortunes see Piers Brendon and Phillip Whitehead, *The Windsors: A Dynasty Revealed* (Hodder, 1994), esp. ch. 11, pp. 217–38.

9 I took a note as the film of it was run on the BBC Television *Nine O'Clock News* that evening.

10 Peter Riddell, 'Reason is not Treason in Monarchy Debate', *The Times*, 7 September 1994.

11 Walter Bagehot, *The English Constitution* (Fontana, 1963), p. 100.

12 Harold Nicolson, *King George V: His Life and Reign* (Constable, 1952), p. 61.

13 'Notes on Bagehot's *English Constitution*', undated, Royal Archives, Windsor, RA Z143.

14 Bagehot, *The English Constitution*, p. 111.

15 'Notes on Bagehot's *English Constitution*'. Also quoted in Nicolson, *King George V*, p. 62.

16 K. C. Wheare, 'Walter Bagehot: Lecture on a Master Mind', *Proceedings of the British Academy*, vol. 60 (Oxford University Press, 1974), p. 26.

17 Sir John Wheeler-Bennett, *King George VI: His Life and Reign* (Macmillan, 1958), p. 131.

18 Bagehot, *The English Constitution*, p. 96.

19 Wheeler-Bennett, *King George VI*, p. 132.

20 The occasion was a lecture and reception at the Guildhall in the City of London to mark the seventy-fifth anniversary of the Historical Association. Private information.

21 Kenneth Harris, *The Queen* (Weidenfeld & Nicolson, 1994), p. 14.

22 Bagehot, *The English Constitution*, pp. 93–4.

23 Ibid., p. 69.

24 Ibid., p. 66.

25 Lord Hailsham, *Values: Collapse and Cure* (HarperCollins, 1994), p. 18.

26 Sir William Heseltine, letter to *The Times*, 27 July 1986.

27 Douglas Hurd, *Vote to Kill* (Collins, 1975), p. 12.

28 Sir Robert Rhodes James, 'The British Monarchy: Its Changing Constitutional Role', *RSA Journal*, vol. 143, no. 5448 (April 1994), p. 25.

29 Ibid.

30 Private information.

31 I can recall seeing the clip on the television news.

32 Paul Addison, *Churchill on the Home Front 1900–1955* (Cape, 1992), p. 359.

33 Bagehot, *The English Constitution*, p. 61.

34 Ibid., p. 99.

35 Public Record Office (PRO), CAB 21/1638, 'Function of the Prime Minister and his Staff', 1947–9.

36 See Sir Alan Lascelles, letter under the pseudonym 'Scncx' ('wise old man'), *The Times*, 2 May 1960.

37 See John Colville, *The Fringes of Power: Downing Street Diaries 1939–1955* (Hodder, 1985), pp. 670–1.

38 See Alistair Horne, *Harold Macmillan*, vol. 1: *1894–1956* (Macmillan, 1988), pp. 459–60; Lord Butler, *The Art of the Possible* (Hamish Hamilton, 1971), pp. 195–6. On this occasion Her Majesty consulted Churchill, who advised her to send for Macmillan. She gave Eden a chance to express an opinion on his successor. He told her that his 'debt to Mr Butler is very real': Keith Kyle, *Suez* (Weidenfeld & Nicolson, 1991), p. 663.

39 See Alistair Horne, *Harold Macmillan*, vol. 2: *1957–1988* (Macmillan, 1988), pp. 556–66. On this occasion Macmillan offered the Queen a memorandum (a deeply controversial one, as it turned out) that he had prepared on the succession. She accepted his advice and sent for Home, but only first to offer him the chance of forming an administration. There was no time for her staff to consult the Royal Archives for precedents, but they checked their memory of George V giving Bonar Law time to try from back copies of *The Times* from October 1922. Interview with Sir Edward Ford for Channel 4 Television/Wide Vision Productions, *What Has Become of Us?*, 7 March 1994.

40 PRO, PREM 11/4756, 'Top Secret and Personal. Deadlock. The Queen's Government Must be Carried on. DJM [Derek Mitchell, Principal Private Secretary]', 16 October 1964.

41 For accounts of the ins and outs of what one participant called this 'very dicey . . . rather agonising weekend' see John Campbell, *Edward Heath* (Cape, 1993), pp. 615–18; Peter Hennessy and Simon Coates, *The Back of the Envelope: Hung Parliaments, the Queen and the Constitution*, Strathclyde *Analysis* Paper no. 5 (Department of Government, University of Strathclyde, 1991).

42 Robert Shepherd, *Iain Macleod* (Hutchinson, 1994), ch. 12, pp. 310–49.

43 The 'golden triangle' phrase is Philip Ziegler's: conversation with Philip

Ziegler, 13 June 1991. For the Cabinet Office's most recently declassified assessment of the monarch's personal power of dissolution see PRO CAB 21/3682, 'Parliament, Government Defeat in the House of Commons, the Constitutional Position', prepared in the spring of 1950.

44 Sidney Low, *The Governance of England* (Fisher Unwin, 1904), p. 12.
45 Private information.
46 Private information.
47 PRO, PREM 8/1262, 'Parliament Procedure', Brook to Rickett, 15 March 1950.
48 It is preserved in PRO, PREM 8/1262.
49 Ibid.
50 PRO, CAB 21/3682, 'Parliament, Government Defeat in the House of Commons, the Constitutional Position'.
51 See PRO, CAB 21/3682, Gibbs to Bavin, 28 April 1950.
52 Private information. For the Lascelles brief to the King see Wheeler-Bennett, *King George VI*, pp. 773–4. It reads as follows:

> If Mr. Attlee is beaten, two courses are open to him:
>
> (1) He can ask The King to accept his resignation and (if asked) advise His Majesty to send for Mr. Churchill. There could not be much doubt about what to do then, and The King's problem is simple. (I am told, however, on good authority that Mr. Attlee would *not* adopt this course, though the temptation to try and put the other side in on a very sticky wicket would obviously be strong.)
>
> (2) He can ask The King to dissolve Parliament. The King would be perfectly entitled to refuse this request if he were convinced that the present Parliament had not exhausted its present usefulness and that the country's interests demanded that the holding of another general election should be postponed as long as possible. It is doubtful whether the argument is valid in present circumstances; could anybody else form a Government capable of doing anything but exist precariously on a tiny majority – or even a minority? And would withholding a dissolution now do more than postpone the inevitable general election for more than a few weeks? So there does not seem to be sufficient reason here for the Sovereign to break the precedent followed by his predecessors for more than a century by refusing his Prime Minister a dissolution. In Canada, of course, Lord Byng did, on a famous occasion, refuse a dissolution; but, though he acted from the very best motives, it is questionable if this refusal did anybody any good in the long run, and it undoubtedly left in certain quarters in Canada a

considerable legacy of bitterness against the Crown. (I am aware that Mr. Churchill might argue in a directly contrary sense, but I do not believe that more than a small minority of his party would do so.)

But even if The King decided to grant a dissolution, he should certainly not do so save on the condition that it should not become operative until Parliament has done its duty of making at least a minimum provision for the national finance; no Prime Minister should ever be allowed to close the national legislative premises – particularly at this time of year – unless he can leave them in good financial order. Consequently The King would be bound to insist that the dissolution asked for by Mr. Attlee should not take effect until Parliament had dealt with a Minimal Finance Act, and an Appropriation Act, as explained in the attached copy of a Treasury paper given me this evening by Sir E. Bridges [21 April 1950]. As the Prime Minister himself called for this paper, it may fairly be presumed that, if he should ask The King for a dissolution, he would himself stipulate that Parliament should be made to sit until this minimal business were completed – a period, I understand, of at least ten days or even a fortnight. So, in the event of Mr. Attlee asking His Majesty for a dissolution on Thursday, April 27th, it could not take place until about May 10th.

To sum up, then: it does not seem probable that the Government will be faced with resignation during the next few weeks, but even if this should happen the only difficult problem which The King might be called on to solve is the decision to grant or to withhold a dissolution; in present circumstances the arguments in favour of granting it seem to outweigh those against it.

53 *The Times*, 24 April 1950.
54 *The Times*, 26 April 1950.
55 *The Times*, 2 May 1950.
56 PRO, CAB 21/3682. This final report is undated.
57 *The Times*, 2 May 1950.
58 BBC Radio 4, *Analysis*, 20 June 1991. Hennessy and Coates, *The Back of the Envelope*, contains the transcript of the programme. Sir Robin Butler confirmed its accuracy when chairing my inaugural lecture as Professor of Contemporary History at Queen Mary and Westfield College, 1 February 1994.
59 Lord Armstrong, quoted in Hennessy and Coates, *The Back of the Envelope*, p. 10.

60 The words are taken from Lascelles' 'Senex' letter in *The Times*, 2 May 1950.
61 Private information.
62 Private information.
63 PRO, PREM 11/4756.
64 Ibid., untitled longhand note, 16 October 1964.
65 I am indebted to my research student, David Welsh, for its discovery. He found it in a slightly surprising place in Macmillan's 'Ministerial Appointments' file for 1958–9. PRO, PREM 5/232.
66 Ibid. 'Deadlock. The Queen's Government must be carried on'. Bligh to Macmillan, 'Top Secret and Personal', 5 October 1959.
67 Ibid. The summary of events entitled 'General Election December 1923' is unsigned and undated. But the typeface and its appearance suggest that it was drawn up shortly after the events it describes.
68 Conversation with Sir Derek Mitchell, 4 February 1995.
69 Conversation with Sir Kenneth Stowe, 5 January 1995.
70 Ibid.
71 Pamela Baxter, 'The Hidden Wiring' MA seminar, Department of History, Queen Mary and Westfield College, 8 February 1995.
72 The whole of point 5 is based upon private information.
73 A student of mine at Queen Mary and Westfield College, Julie Quist-Johansen, compiled a table of the subject-matter discussed by Attlee and King George VI, based on PRO, CAB 21/2263, 'Prime Minister's Notes for Weekly Visits to the King, 1947–50'. The result was as follows:

Topic	No. of occurrences
Empire/Commonwealth	31
Foreign affairs (general)	30
Europe/postwar co-operation	22
General economy/trade	16
Current domestic affairs	14
NATO	11
Parliamentary matters	7
Ireland	7
United Nations	5
Visitors	5
USSR	2

Julie Quist-Johansen, 'The Most Special Relationship: The Constitutional Nexus between the Prime Minister and the Monarch since 1945', unpublished undergraduate research project, Queen Mary and Westfield College, 1994, p. 17.
74 Private information.
75 *Open Government*, Cm 2290 (HMSO, 1993), p. 68.

76 The phrase belongs to a senior Crown servant. See Peter Hennessy, 'The Pleasures and Pains of Contemporary History', *History Today*, vol. 44, no. 3 (March 1994), p. 16.

77 Colville, *Fringes of Power*, p. 611; conversation with Lord Jay for *What Has Become of Us?*, 12 August 1993.

78 See Wheeler-Bennett, *King George VI*, p. 662; conversation with Sir Edward Ford, 7 March 1994.

79 Conversation with Sir Edward Ford, 7 March 1994.

80 Philip Williams (ed.), *The Diary of Hugh Gaitskell, 1945–55* (Cape, 1983), p. 239, entry for 30 April 1951.

81 Letter from Ernest Bevin to the King, 8 March 1949, Royal Archives, Windsor, RA, George VI, 341/10; conversation with Sir Edward Ford, 7 March 1994.

82 Conversation with Sir Edward Ford, 7 March 1994.

83 Robert Rhodes James, *Anthony Eden* (Weidenfeld & Nicolson, 1986), p. 620.

84 James Callaghan, *Times and Chance* (Collins, 1987), p. 380.

85 He was speaking on Channel 4 Television/Brook Productions, *The Windsors*, 15 June 1994. Mr Hawke's actual words were: 'I think it is fair to say that the Queen didn't have a great affection for Mrs Thatcher ... She had the odd expression about it which I found rather fascinating. I think there was a sense in that she was not at ease with some of the attitudes and policies of Mrs Thatcher and she, I think, saw Mrs Thatcher as somewhat dangerous to the cohesiveness of the British structure.'

86 PRO, PREM 11/746, 'Letter to H.M. The Queen from Prime Minister concerning UK Manufacture of a Hydrogen Bomb', 16 July 1954.

87 Private information.

88 *Elizabeth R*, BBC video.

89 Nigel Lawson, *The View from No. 11: Memoirs of a Tory Radical* (Bantam, 1992), p. 799.

90 Graham Turner, 'The Very Private Woman Behind the Public Face', *The Daily Telegraph*, 19 March 1996.

91 Ibid.

92 Ibid.

93 Private information.

94 PRO, PREM 13/553, 'Possible Visit by Lord Mountbatten to Rhodesia', 'Note For the Record', 18 November 1965.

95 Ibid.

96 Private information.

97 Ibid.

98 Private information.

99 For a rich array of examples of regal assertiveness and bloody-mindedness

see G. H. L. Le May, *The Victorian Constitution* (Duckworth, 1979), ch. 3, 'Queen Victoria and Her Ministers'.

100 Private information.

101 Private information.

102 Private information.

103 Norman Macrae invented this brilliant phrase to illustrate the similarity of economic policy under Hugh Gaitskell and R. A. Butler in the early 1950s and placed it in *The Economist* of 13 February 1954 under the headline 'Mr Butskell's Dilemma'.

104 Lord Charteris, interviewed for *What Has Become of Us?*, 6 June 1994.

105 Michael Ratcliffe, 'The Other Alan Bennett Stands Up', *Observer*, 4 September 1994.

106 For an excellent summary of this see Dennis Kavanagh and Peter Morris, *Consensus Politics from Attlee to Thatcher* (Blackwell, 1989).

107 Letter from Tony Benn to Tony Newton, 27 June 1994. I am very grateful to Tony Benn for giving me access to this correspondence.

108 Ibid.

109 Letter from Tony Newton to Tony Benn, 19 July 1994.

110 Letter from Tony Benn to Peter Hennessy, 22 August 1994.

Chapter 3

1 C. R. Attlee, 'The Office of Prime Minister', *Municipal Review*, March 1965.

2 G. M. Young, 'The Future of British Parliamentary Government', in Lord Campion et al., *Parliament: A Survey* (Allen & Unwin, 1952), p. 273.

3 John Cole, *As It Seemed to Me: Political Memoirs* (Weidenfeld & Nicolson, 1995), p. 78.

4 Interview with Kenneth Harris, *Observer*, 25 February 1979.

5 David Dilks, *The Office of Prime Minister in Twentieth Century Britain* (University of Hull Press, 1992), p. 25.

6 Quoted in Peter Hennessy and Simon Coates, *The Back of the Envelope: Hung Parliaments, the Queen and the Constitution*, Strathclyde *Analysis* Paper no. 5 (Department of Government, University of Strathclyde, 1991, p. 12.

7 Private information.

8 As the office of 'Prime Minister' did not exist (no official piece of paper mentions it before December 1905), Walpole knew that he could only live in No. 10 at the state's expense as First Lord. Occasionally subsequent Premiers, including Churchill, have suggested that the brass plaque bearing

the inscription 'First Lord of the Treasury' be removed from the famous front door. They have been told that if it were, they would have to pay rent for the privilege of living there. Sir Robin Butler, 'Cabinet and Premiership' course briefing, Department of History, Queen Mary and Westfield College, 4 December 1992.

9 See Michael Cockerell, *Live from Number 10: The Inside Story of Prime Ministers and Television* (Faber, 1988), pp. 11–16, 66–8.

10 See his edited reader, Anthony King (ed.), *The British Prime Minister*, 2nd edn (Macmillan, 1986) and his chapter on 'The British Prime Ministership in the Age of the Career Politician', in G. W. Jones (ed.), *West European Prime Ministers* (Cass, 1991), pp. 25–47.

11 King (ed.), *The British Prime Minister*, p. 2.

12 Lady Thatcher was speaking on the BBC1 programme *The Thatcher Years* on 21 October 1993 which accompanied the publication of the first volume of her memoirs, *The Downing Street Years* (HarperCollins, 1993).

13 Mr Rifkind was speaking on the BBC2 programme *Maggie's Minister* on 11 September 1993 which accompanied the publication of Kenneth Baker's memoirs, *The Turbulent Years: My Life in Politics* (Faber, 1993).

14 Harold Wilson, *The Governance of Britain* (Weidenfeld/Michael Joseph, 1976), p. x.

15 King, 'The Prime Ministership in the Age of the Career Politician', p. 31.

16 Nicholas Henderson, *Mandarin: The Diaries of Nicholas Henderson* (Weidenfeld & Nicolson, 1994), p. 99; Robert Blake, *The Office of Prime Minister* (British Academy/Oxford University Press, 1975).

17 James Callaghan, *Time and Chance* (Collins, 1987), p. 386.

18 Henderson, *Mandarin*, p. 99.

19 Walter Bagehot, 'The Character of Sir Robert Peel', in Norman St John-Stevas (ed.), *The Collected Works of Walter Bagehot*, vol. 3 (*The Economist*, 1968), pp. 241–71.

20 Ibid., p. 242.

21 Martin Wiener, *English Culture and the Decline of the Industrial Spirit, 1850–1980* (Cambridge University Press, 1981).

22 R. A. Butler Papers, Trinity College, Cambridge, file G38. I am very grateful to my colleague at Queen Mary and Westfield College, Dr John Ramsden, for bringing this gem to my attention.

23 John Morley, *The Life of William Ewart Gladstone*, vol. 1 (Macmillan, 1903), p. 297.

24 Sidney Low, *The Governance of England* (Fisher Unwin, 1904), p. 155.

25 Ibid., p. 155n.

26 E. C. S. Wade and G. Godfrey Phillips, *Constitutional and Administrative Law*, 9th edn, ed. A. W. Bradley (Longman, 1977), p. 244.

27 W. E. Gladstone, *Gleanings of Past Years*, vol. 1 (John Murray, 1879), p. 244.

28 *Report of the House of Commons Select Committee on Official Salaries*, 1850, pp. 40–1.

29 Bagehot, 'The Character of Sir Robert Peel', pp. 255–6.

30 Anthony King, 'Overload: Problems of Governing in the 1970s', *Political Studies*, vol. 22, nos 2–3 (June–September 1975), p. 164. For Peel's *cri de coeur* see Low, *The Governance of England*, pp. 162–3.

31 *Report of the House of Commons Select Committee on Official Salaries*, 1850.

32 Walter Bagehot, 'The Premiership', in Norman St John-Stevas (ed.), *The Collected Works of Walter Bagehot*, vol. 6 (*The Economist*, 1974), p. 67.

33 Ibid., pp. 66–7.

34 Ministry of Reconstruction, *Report of the Machinery of Government Committee*, Cd 9230 (HMSO, 1918).

35 *The Reorganisation of Central Government*, Cmnd 4506 (HMSO, 1970).

36 Bagehot, 'The Premiership', p. 67.

37 Public Record Office (PRO) T 273/74, 'Cabinet Office Appointment of Mr E. E. Bridges as Permanent Secretary and Transfer of Sir Norman Brook to HM Treasury', Churchill to Bridges, October 1951 (no day given).

38 Bagehot, 'The Premiership', p. 67.

39 The article appeared in *North American Review*, September 1978. It was reprinted in Gladstone, *Gleanings of Past Years*, vol. 1, pp. 203–48.

40 John P. Mackintosh, *The British Cabinet*, 2nd edn (University Paperbacks, 1968), p. 265.

41 Gladstone, *Gleanings of Past Years*, vol. 1, pp. 242–3.

42 Quoted in Peter Hennessy and Caroline Anstey, *Diminished Responsibility: The Essence of Cabinet Government*, Strathclyde *Analysis* Papers no. 2 (Department of Government, University of Strathclyde, 1991), p. 6.

43 Gladstone, *Gleanings of Past Years*, vol. 1, p. 243.

44 Ibid.

45 Ibid.

46 For Walpole as first Premier see Blake, *The Office of Prime Minister*, pp. 5–7. For the Gladstonian implications of Morley's treatment see Low, *The Governance of England*, p. 22n. For Morley's admission in 1919 that 'the chapter in my book upon the Cabinet was in truth the work of WEG' see Earl of Oxford and Asquith, *Fifty Years in Parliament*, vol. 2 (Cassell, 1926), p. 183n.

47 John Morley, *Walpole* (Macmillan, 1889), p. 157.

48 Ibid., p. 158.

49 Low, *The Governance of England*, p. 37.

50 Lord Rosebery, *Sir Robert Peel* (Cassell, 1930), p. 193.

51 Mackintosh, *The British Cabinet*, p. 315.
52 A. J. Balfour, *Chapters of Autobiography* (Cassell, 1930), p. 193.
53 Ibid., p. 113.
54 Kenneth Young, *Arthur J. Balfour* (Bell, 1963), pp. 223–8.
55 Blake, *The Office of Prime Minister*, pp. 37–8.
56 Geoffrey Marshall, *Constitutional Conventions: The Rules and Forms of Political Accountability* (Clarendon Press, 1984), pp. 48–51.
57 Wilson, *The Governance of Britain*, p. 1. For the original see Asquith, *Fifty Years of Parliament*, vol. 2, p. 185.
58 Ibid., pp. 185–6.
59 Rosebery, *Sir Robert Peel*.
60 Lord Callaghan, *Premiership*, broadcast on BBC Radio 3, 18 October 1989.
61 Rosebery, *Sir Robert Peel*, p. 33.
62 Ibid.
63 Morley, *Walpole*, p. 158.
64 Rosebery, *Sir Robert Peel*, pp. 33–4.
65 Ibid., p. 35.
66 *The Thatcher Years*, BBC1, 20 October 1993.
67 Anthony Bevins, 'Decision to Quit Followed Loss of Faith among Friends', *Independent*, 29 June 1991.
68 Anthony King (ed.), *The British Prime Minister* (Macmillan, 1975), p. 233.
69 Conversation with Philip Ziegler, 13 June 1991.
70 PRO, CAB 21/1638, 'Function of the Prime Minister and his Staff'.
71 Lord Home, *Premiership*, broadcast on BBC Radio 3, 4 October 1989; Callaghan, *Premiership*.
72 King, 'The British Prime Ministership in the Age of the Career Politician', p. 43.
73 Tony Benn, *The Case for a Constitutional Premiership*, Institute for Workers' Control Pamphlet no. 67, 1979, p. 5.
74 Quoted in Peter Hennessy, *Whitehall* (Secker & Warburg, 1989), p. 6.
75 Private information.
76 'Bagehot', 'Mr World', *The Economist*, 10 September 1994, p. 34.
77 Ibid.
78 Mr Major's 'sticking-to-basics' approach to 'power dining' (insisting on steak and chips whenever and wherever possible) has caused nostrils to flare in the more cuisine-conscious chancelleries abroad. Private information.
79 Harvey Elliott, 'Major's Down-to-Earth Concorde Fare', *The Times*, 3 March 1995.
80 He used it at an Institute of Historical Research seminar on 20 October 1993.

Chapter 4

1 L. S. Amery, *Thoughts on the Constitution* (Oxford University Press, 1947), p. 70.

2 Earl of Oxford and Asquith, *Fifty Years of Parliament*, vol. 2 (Cassell, 1926), p. 183.

3 Lord Attlee, 'Premier and His Team: Advantages over Presidential System', *Daily Telegraph*, 9 August 1960.

4 John Cole, *As It Seemed to Me: Political Memoirs* (Weidenfeld & Nicolson, 1995), p. 206.

5 Ibid., p. 396.

6 Ben Pimlott originally delivered this observation as part of a Channel 4 Television lecture on 'The Myth of Consensus' in 1988. It is reproduced in his *Frustrate Their Knavish Tricks: Writings on Biography, History and Politics* (HarperCollins, 1994), pp. 237–8.

7 Quoted in G. H. L. Le May, *The Victorian Constitution* (Duckworth, 1979), p. 9.

8 Mr Hurd was speaking on London Weekend Television, *Weekend World*, 26 January 1986. Mr Gladstone is quoted in a brief for Lord Addison, the Lord Privy Seal, for a House of Lords debate on Cabinet government in May 1950. Public Record Office (PRO) CAB 21/1625, 'Machinery of Government: House of Lords Debate on the Power of the Cabinet'.

9 See Peter Hennessy, 'Helicopter Crashes into Cabinet: Prime Minister and Constitution Hurt', *Journal of Laws and Society*, vol. 13, no. 3 (Winter 1986), pp. 423–32.

10 Interview with Kenneth Harris, *Observer*, 25 February 1979.

11 Walter Bagehot, *The English Constitution* (Fontana, 1963), p. 65.

12 Ibid., p. 61.

13 Ibid., pp. 65–6, 68.

14 Lord Lawson, 'Cabinet Government in the Thatcher Years: Some Reflections and Wider Lessons', paper delivered to Twentieth Century British History seminar, Institute of Historical Research, 9 March 1994. An edited transcript of the seminar proceedings was published as Lord Lawson and Lord Armstrong of Ilminster, 'Cabinet Government in the Thatcher Years', *Contemporary Record*, vol. 8, no. 3 (Winter 1994), pp. 440–52.

15 Lord Wakeham, 'Cabinet Government', paper delivered at Brunel University, 10 November 1993. Reproduced in *Contemporary Record*, vol. 8, no. 3 (Winter 1994), pp. 473–83.

16 Ibid.

17 The First Earl of Balfour, 'Introduction', in Walter Bagehot, *The English*

Constitution, 'World's Classics' edn (Oxford University Press, 1928), p. xii; Lord Hailsham, 'The Future of Cabinet Government', Granada Guildhall Lecture, 10 November 1987.

18 Letter from Sir Robin Butler to Peter Hennessy, 27 June 1994; see chapter 1 in this volume.

19 W. Ivor Jennings, *Cabinet Government* (Cambridge University Press, 1936), p. 1.

20 Ibid.

21 Balfour, 'Introduction', in Bagehot, *The English Constitution*, p. xii.

22 See Stephen Roskill, *Hankey, Man of Secrets*, vol. 1: *1877–1918* (Collins, 1970), pp. 320–1, 337–8; John Grigg, *Lloyd George from Peace to War, 1912–1916* (Methuen, 1985), p. 488.

23 PRO, LCO 2/3215, 'Principles of Cabinet System and the Work of the Cabinet Secretariat', Hankey to Napier, 26 March 1946.

24 G. M. Trevelyan, *History of England* (Longmans Green, 1942), p. 510.

25 PRO, LCO 2/3215, 'The Cabinet: Draft of a Broadcast by Lord Hankey'. Hankey's final version was also transmitted on the BBC Home Service and printed under the heading 'The Cabinet System' in *The Listener*, 31 October 1946.

26 PRO, LCO 2/3215.

27 Colin Seymour-Ure, 'The "Disintegration" of the Cabinet and the Neglected Question of Cabinet Reform', *Parliamentary Affairs*, vol. 24, no. 3 (1971), p. 196.

28 See below, p. 109.

29 Seymour-Ure, 'The "Disintegration" of the Cabinet', p. 196.

30 Ibid.

31 Sir Frank Cooper, interviewed for Brook Productions/Channel 4 Television, *All The Prime Minister's Men*, 8 April 1986.

32 Lord Hunt, 'Cabinet Strategy and Management', paper delivered to CIPFA/RIPA Conference, Eastbourne, 9 June 1983.

33 Quoted in Olive Anderson, 'Cabinet Government and the Crimean War', *English Historical Review*, vol. 79 (1964), p. 549.

34 Lord Hunt, discussant on 'The Failings of Cabinet Government in the mid- to late 1970s', paper delivered by Edmund Dell to the Twentieth Century British History Seminar, Institute of Historical Research, 20 October 1993. An edited transcript of the seminar proceedings was published as Edmund Dell and Lord Hunt of Tanworth, 'The Failings of Cabinet Government in the mid- to late 1970s', *Contemporary Record*, vol. 8, no. 3 (Winter 1994), pp. 453–72.

35 Ibid.

36 *Ministerial Committees of the Cabinet: Membership and Terms of Reference* (Cabinet Office, May 1992).

37 *The Central Intelligence Machinery* (HMSO, 1993).

38 Quoted in Peter Hennessy, *Cabinet* (Blackwell, 1986), p. 26.
39 *Questions of Procedure for Ministers* (Cabinet Office, May 1992).
40 For a character sketch of Trend see Peter Hennessy, *Whitehall* (Secker & Warburg, 1989), pp. 212–19.
41 Burke Trend, 'Machinery under Pressure', *Times Literary Supplement*, 26 September 1986, p. 1076.
42 *Questions of Procedure for Ministers*, 1992 edn.
43 Twentieth Century British History Seminar, Institute of Historical Research, 20 October 1993.
44 *Questions of Procedure for Ministers*, 1992 edn.
45 The minute was leaked in November 1978 in the *New Statesman*, which had already begun the practice of publishing information on the existence and scope of as many Cabinet committees as possible. See Bruce Page, 'The Secret Constitution', *New Statesman*, 21 July 1978.
46 James Callaghan, 'Disclosure of Cabinet Committees', February 1978.
47 The Attlee version appears in PRO CAB 66/67, 'Miscellaneous Questions of Procedure', note by the Prime Minister, 8 August 1945; Wilson's, when it appears at the PRO, will be 'Questions of Procedure for Ministers: Note by the Prime Minister', 5 April 1966.
48 Callaghan, 'Disclosure of Cabinet Committees'.
49 *Questions of Procedure for Ministers*, 1992 edn.
50 Callaghan, 'Disclosure of Cabinet Committees'.
51 Wakeham, 'Cabinet Government'.
52 Charles Reiss, 'Major Wins First Round: Four Right Wingers Outgunned in Vital Cabinet Europe Vote', *Evening Standard*, 29 March 1994.
53 Peter Riddell, 'Oh, for a Modest Speech', *The Times*, 29 August 1994.
54 Peter Hennessy, 'We Need a New Think-Tank Stocked with Free Spirits', *Guardian*, 9 August 1994.
55 *Ministerial Committees of the Cabinet: Membership and Terms of Reference* (Cabinet Office, May 1992); private information.
56 Hunt, 'Cabinet Strategy and Management'.
57 Lord Hailsham, 'The Future of Cabinet Government', the Granada Guildhall Lecture 1987.
58 Walter Bagehot, *Physics and Politics: Or Thoughts on the Application of the Principles of 'Natural Selection' and 'Inheritance' to Political Society*, 2nd edn (Kegan Paul, 1873), p. 27.
59 Twentieth Century British History Seminar, Institute for Historical Research, 20 October 1993.
60 Ibid.
61 Mancur Olson, *The Rise and Decline of Nations: Economic Growth, Stagflation and Rigidities* (Yale University Press, 1982), p. 78.
62 Quoted in Hennessy, *Cabinet*, p. 181.
63 For Lord Lawson on 'departmental deformation' and 'creeping

bilateralism' see his *The View from No. 11: Memoirs of a Tory Radical* (Bantam, 1992), ch. 11, pp. 121–9, and 'Cabinet Government in the Thatcher Years'.

64 Bagehot, *Physics and Politics*, p. 164.

65 Ibid., p. 63.

66 Ibid.

67 Ibid., p. 62.

68 Hugo Young, *One of Us* (Macmillan, 1989), pp. 153, 204–5, 517.

69 For surveys of these see Simon James, *British Cabinet Government* (Routledge, 1992), pp. 193–4; R. Phillips, 'The British Inner Cabinet', *London Review of Public Administration*, vol. 10 (1977).

70 See Peter Hennessy, *Never Again: Britain 1945–51* (Cape, 1992), pp. 213, 299, 301, 360, 378; Hennessy, *Whitehall*, pp. 68, 121, 152–4, 173, 176; Edwin Plowden, *An Industrialist in the Treasury: The Postwar Years* (Deutsch, 1989).

71 See G. D. A. MacDougall, 'The Prime Minister's Statistical Section', in D. N. Chester, *Lessons of the British War Economy* (Cambridge University Press, 1951), pp. 58–68.

72 See Tessa Blackstone and William Plowden, *Inside the Think Tank: Advising the Cabinet 1971–1983* (Heinemann, 1988); Peter Hennessy, Susan Morrison and Richard Townsend, *Routine Punctuated by Orgies: The Central Policy Review Staff, 1970–83*, Strathclyde Paper on Government and Politics no. 31 (Department of Politics, University of Strathclyde, 1985); Lord Rothschild, *Meditations of a Broomstick* (Collins, 1977).

73 Harold Wilson, *The Governance of Britain* (Weidenfeld & Nicolson/ Michael Joseph, 1976), pp. 91, 98–9; Bernard Donoughue, *Prime Minister: The Conduct of Policy under Harold Wilson and James Callaghan* (Cape, 1987), pp. 19–25.

74 See John Turner, *Lloyd George's Secretariat* (Cambridge University Press, 1980).

75 Hennessy, *Whitehall*, pp. 592–610.

76 Ibid., pp. 595–6.

77 Lawson, *The View from No. 11*, ch. 11; Twentieth Century British History Seminar, Institute of Historical Research, 9 March 1994.

78 Twentieth Century British History Seminar, Institute of Historical Research, 9 March 1994.

79 Ibid.

80 Ibid.

81 Ibid.

82 Ibid.

83 Ibid.

84 This is what Cabinet Secretary Sir Norman Brook called them when he

wrote a brief for the returning Churchill in the autumn of 1951 warning in vain against the idea: PRO, CAB 21/2804, 'Supervising Ministers', Brook to Churchill, 15 November 1951.

85 Hennessy, *Cabinet*, pp. 48–9.

86 Twentieth Century British History Seminar, Institute of Historical Research, 9 March 1994.

87 Ibid.

88 See Simon James, 'Cabinet Government: A Commentary', *Contemporary Record*, vol. 8, no. 3 (Winter 1994), pp. 500–1.

89 Twentieth Century British History Seminar, Institute of Historical Research, 9 March 1994.

90 Ibid.

91 Ibid.

92 Hugh Dalton, *High Tide and After: Memoirs 1945–60* (Muller, 1961), p. 16.

93 PRO, CAB 21/2804, 'Supervising Ministers'.

94 In a 1932 memorandum on 'The Reorganisation of Government', Attlee had written: 'what is required is a *small* body of ministers without heavy departmental work, each one in general charge of a particular function of state activity. These Ministers must have leisure to think and freedom from the pressure of day-to-day business which will enable them to see things in proportion.' The memo is reproduced as appendix III in Kenneth Harris, *Attlee* (Weidenfeld & Nicolson, 1982).

95 House of Commons Debates, *Official Report*, 6 May 1952, cols 193–4.

96 PRO, CAB 21/2804.

97 Paul McQuail, *Origins of the Department of the Environment* (Department of the Environment, 1994), p. 11.

98 Hennessy, 'We Need a New Think Tank'.

99 Ernest Gellner, *Conditions of Liberty: Civil Society and its Rivals* (Hamish Hamilton, 1994), p. 3.

100 Ibid., p. 193.

101 Bagehot, *Physics and Politics*, p. 161.

102 'Cabinet Committee Business: A Guide for Departments', unpublished (Cabinet Office, February 1995).

103 Ibid., p. 2.

104 ITN, *News at Ten*, 16 June 1995; Patricia Wynn Davies and Michael Sheridan, 'I'm a Coalition Government on my Own, Declares Major', *Independent*, 17 June 1995.

105 Margaret Thatcher, *The Path to Power* (HarperCollins, 1995), p. 165.

106 John Biffen, 'The Revenge of the Unburied Dead', *Observer*, 9 December 1990.

Chapter 5

1 Sidney Low, *The Governance of England* (Fisher Unwin, 1904), p. xxxii.
2 Ben Pimlott (ed.), *The Political Diary of Hugh Dalton, 1918–40, 1945–60* (Cape, 1986), p. 361.
3 Tony Benn, briefing for 'Cabinet and Premiership' course, Department of History, Queen Mary and Westfield College, held at House of Commons, 1 March 1995.
4 Ian Beesley, now a partner with Price Waterhouse, addressing the 'Hidden Wiring' seminar of the MA course in Contemporary British History since 1939, Department of History, Queen Mary and Westfield College, 1 March 1995.
5 Private information.
6 Private information.
7 Private information.
8 Mr Wilson passed this gem on to me in the mid-1980s. He had perfected it as a Young Liberal attacking the grand, if obscure, at Liberal assemblies.
9 Gresham College Seminar, 'In the Steps of Walter Bagehot: A Constitutional Health-Check', 13 March 1995.
10 Walter Bagehot, *The English Constitution* (Fontana, 1963), pp. 195–9.
11 Ibid., p. 195.
12 For the Rayner approach see Peter Hennessy, *Whitehall* (Fontana, 1990), ch. 14, pp. 589–627.
13 Bagehot, *The English Constitution*, p. 196.
14 Lord Radcliffe, *Power and the State*, The Reith Lectures, 1951, no. 1, 'On Plato's Idea of the State', first broadcast on the BBC Home Service, 4 November 1951.
15 See Norman St John-Stevas (ed.), *The Collected Works of Walter Bagehot*, vol. 6 (*The Economist*, 1974), p. 92.
16 'Competitive Tests for the Public Service', an *Economist* article published on 5 April 1862 and reproduced in ibid., pp. 71–5.
17 See Hennessy, *Whitehall*, pp. 36–51.
18 St John-Stevas, *Collected Works of Walter Bagehot*, vol. 6, p. 78.
19 *The Civil Service: Continuity and Change*, Cm 2627 (HMSO, 1994).
20 House of Commons, Treasury and Civil Service Committee, Fifth Report, Session 1993–4, *The Role of the Civil Service*, vol. 1, HC27–1 (HMSO, 1994).
21 *The Civil Service: Continuity and Change*, pp. 1, 8–9.
22 Treasury and Civil Service Committee, *The Role of the Civil Service*, vol. 1, p. v.
23 See Martin Gilbert, 'Horace Wilson: Man of Munich', *History Today*, vol. 32 (October 1982); Hennessy, *Whitehall*, pp. 85–6.

24 See Hugo Young, *One of Us* (Pan, 1993), pp. 445–6.

25 Julia Llewellyn Smith, 'Secret Rebel in a Sober Suit', *The Times*, 6 September 1994.

26 Public Record Office (PRO), PREM 11/4755, 'Secret and Personal', Sir Tim Bligh to Sir Alec Douglas-Home, 19 December 1963. Another official on the early 1960s private office network who knew Bligh well said: 'He became very close to Harold Macmillan and rather grand. By the end he was very uncivilservantish.' (Private information.)

27 Private information.

28 Kate Jenkins, former chief of staff of the Prime Minister's Efficiency Unit, is especially eloquent about this. Conversation with Kate Jenkins, 4 November 1994.

29 Treasury and Civil Service Committee, *The Role of the Civil Service*, Fifth Report, vol. 2, p. 8.

30 Conversation with Lord Bancroft, 9 January 1995.

31 *Improving Management in Government: The Next Steps* (HMSO, 1988).

32 *Competing for Quality: Buying Better Public Services*, Cmnd 1730 (HMSO, 1991).

33 Treasury and Civil Service Committee, *The Role of the Civil Service*, Fifth Report, vol. 2, p. 52.

34 Ibid.

35 Private information.

36 Anthony Trollope, *Phineas Finn*, 'World's Classics' edn (Oxford University Press, 1982), p. 53.

37 Richard Crossman, *The Diaries of a Cabinet Minister*, vol. 1: *Minister of Housing 1964–66*, esp. entries for his first two and a half months in office, pp. 21–108.

38 Anthony Jay and Jonathan Lynn, *Yes, Minister*, Vol I, BBC, 1981.

39 Lord Bancroft, 'The Art of Management: A Retrospect', lecture delivered to the Royal Society of Arts, 30 January 1984.

40 Conversation with Lord Bancroft, 9 January 1995.

41 Ibid.

42 This is another convention enshrined in *Questions of Procedure for Ministers*: see para. 22(v) in the 1992 edn.

43 Conversation with Lord Bancroft, 9 January 1995.

44 Private information.

45 Treasury and Civil Service Committee, *The Role of the Civil Service*, Fifth Report, p. vi.

46 W. E. Gladstone, *Gleanings of Past Years*, vol. 1 (John Murray, 1879), p. 245.

47 See Hennessy, *Whitehall*, pp. 85–6, 238–41.

48 Sir Anthony Parsons was particularly revealing and funny about this when interviewed for BBC Television's *The Thatcher Years*.

49 Giovanni Sartori, *Parties and Party Systems: A Framework for Analysis* (Cambridge University Press, 1976), p. 196.

50 Sir Terry, former Permanent Secretary at the Department of the Environment, was speaking at the Gresham College Seminar on 13 March 1995.

51 *The Civil Service: Continuity and Change*, pp. 35–8.

52 Ibid., pp. 43–4.

53 Private information.

54 Private information; Roy Hattersley, 'Sir Robin Butler is the Real-Life Sir Humphrey', *Mail on Sunday*, 15 January 1995.

55 Hennessy, *Whitehall*, pp. 302–7.

56 Geoffrey Howe, *Conflict of Loyalty* (Macmillan, 1994), p. 345.

57 Private information.

58 Lord Bancroft, interviewed for Brook Productions/Channel 4 Television, *All the Prime Minister's Men*, 10 April 1986.

59 Quoted in Hennessy, *Whitehall*, p. 638.

60 Private information.

61 David Butler, Andrew Adonis and Tony Travers, *Failure in British Government: The Politics of the Poll Tax* (Oxford University Press, 1994), ch. 9, pp. 206–23.

62 Hugh Dalton, *High Tide and After* (Muller, 1961), p. 16; private information.

63 Nigel Lawson, *The View from No. 11: Memoirs of a Tory Radical* (Bantam, 1992), chs 45, 46, pp. 561–85.

64 John Smith, 'The Public Service Ethos', lecture delivered to the Royal Institute of Public Administration, 8 May 1991.

65 Both Sir Peter and Sir Robin were talking on the BBC Radio 4 *Analysis* programme, 'Whitehall Unbound?', first broadcast on 31 May 1990.

66 Lawson, *The View from No. 11*, p. 393.

67 See Hattersley, 'Sir Robin Butler is the Real-Life Sir Humphrey'.

68 See Kirsty Milne, 'The Advice Squad', *New Statesman and Society*, 13 January 1995.

69 Lord Rothschild, 'The Best Laid Plans', the first Israel Sieff Memorial Lecture, 4 May 1976, reproduced in Lord Rothschild, *Meditations of a Broomstick* (Collins, 1977), p. 171.

70 House of Commons Committee of Public Accounts, *The Proper Conduct of Public Business*, Eighth Report, 1993–4, HC154 (HMSO, 1994).

71 *Report on the Organization of the Permanent Civil Service*. The most convenient way of consulting the Northcote–Trevelyan Report is to examine appendix B of the Fulton Report of 1968 in which it is reprinted: *The Civil Service*, vol. 1: *Report of the Committee 1966–68* (HMSO, 1968), pp. 108–31.

72 Treasury and Civil Service Committee, *The Role of the Civil Service*, Interim Report, vol. 2, p. 23.

73 Ibid., p. 25.

74 Ibid., pp. xxxii, xxxiv.

75 *The Civil Service: Taking Forward Continuity and Change*, Cm 2748 (HMSO, 1995), p. 8.

76 Treasury and Civil Service Committee, *The Role of the Civil Service*, Interim Report, vol. 2, p. 25.

77 *The Civil Service: Taking Forward Continuity and Change*, p. 8.

78 Private information.

79 *The Civil Service: Taking Forward Continuity and Change*, pp. 47–53.

80 Treasury and Civil Service Committee, *The Role of the Civil Service*, vol. 1, annex 1, pp. cxxvi–vii.

81 *Questions of Procedure for Ministers* (Cabinet Office, May 1992), para. 55, reads as follows: 'Ministers have a duty to give fair consideration and due weight to informed and impartial advice from civil servants, as well as to other considerations and advice, in reaching policy decisions; a duty to refrain from asking or instructing civil servants to do things which they should not do; a duty to ensure that influence over appointments is not abused for partisan purposes; and a duty to observe the obligations of a good employer with regard to terms and conditions of those who serve them. Civil servants should not be asked to engage in activities likely to call in question their political impartiality, or to give rise to the criticism that people paid from public funds are being used for Party political purposes.'

82 *The Duties and Responsibilities of Civil Servants in Relation to Ministers: Note by the Head of the Home Civil Service* (Cabinet Office, 1987), distributed under the name of Robert Armstrong.

83 PRO, CAB 21/2804, 'Supervising Ministers', Sir Norman Brook to Sir Edward Bridges, 14 May 1952.

84 For Clive Priestley's original formulation see Peter Hennessy, ' "Harvesting the Cupboards": Why Britain has Produced no Administrative Theory of Ideology in the Twentieth Century', *Transactions of the Royal Historical Society*, 1994, p. 205. See also Jonathan Steinberg, 'Goodbye to "Good Chaps" Government', *Financial Times*, 9 November 1994.

85 *The Reorganisation of Central Government*, Cmnd 4506 (HMSO, 1970).

86 Treasury and Civil Service Committee, *The Role of the Civil Service, Interim Report*, vol. 2, p. lxxvi.

87 *The Civil Service: Taking Forward Continuity and Change*, p. 35.

88 See 'Whitehall: Burns's *Auto-da-Fé*?', *The Economist*, 21 January 1995, pp. 28–9.

89 *Judge Over Your Shoulder. Judicial Review: Balancing the Scales* (Treasury Solicitor's Department/Cabinet Office, 1994), p. 3.

Chapter 6

1 W. E. Gladstone, *Gleanings of Past Years*, vol. 1 (John Murray, 1879), p. 224.

2 Sidney Low, *The Governance of England* (Fisher Unwin, 1904), p. 54.

3 Quoted in the diary of McCallum Scott, MP, entry for 5 March 1917. See Paul Addison, 'The Religion of Winston Churchill', in Michael Bentley (ed.), *Public and Private Doctrine: Essays in British History Presented to Maurice Cowling* (Cambridge University Press, 1993), p. 245.

4 Public Record Office (PRO) CAB 118/32, 'The Application of Democratic Principles of Government: Memorandum by the Deputy Prime Minister', WP (43) 199, 11 May 1943.

5 Earl of Oxford and Asquith, *Fifty Years in Parliament*, vol. 2 (Cassell, 1926), p. 172.

6 House of Commons Debates, *Official Report*, 6 February 1902, cols 550–2.

7 Walter Bagehot, *The English Constitution* (Fontana, 1963), p. 152.

8 Low, *The Governance of England*, p. 55.

9 See my memo to the Treasury and Civil Service Committee, October 1993: Treasury and Civil Service Committee, Session 1993–4, Fifth Report, *The Role of the Civil Service*, vol. 3, HC 27–111, pp. 22–3.

10 'The Parliamentarians', a discussion between Enoch Powell and Robin Day, BBC TV, 4 February 1979, quoted in Rex Collings (ed.), *Reflections of a Statesman: The Writings and Speeches of Enoch Powell* (Bellew, 1991), p. 261.

11 Peter Hennessy and Caroline Anstey, *Jewel in the Constitution? The Queen, Parliament and the Royal Prerogative*, Strathclyde *Analysis* Paper no. 8 (Department of Government, University of Strathclyde, 1992), p. 6; House of Commons Debates, *Official Report*, 4 December 1975, cols 1990–2.

12 Addison, 'The Religion of Winston Churchill', p. 245.

13 John Colville, *The Fringes of Power: Downing Street Diaries 1939–55* (Hodder, 1985), p. 668.

14 Public Record Office (PRO), CAB 21/3739, 'Opening of Parliament and Parliamentary Proceedings, Televising of', July 1953.

15 Quoted in Nora Beloff, *The General Says No: Britain's Exclusion from Europe* (Penguin, 1963), p. 9.

16 PRO, PREM 11/2771, 'Parliament, Procedure'. These exchanges took place in November 1959.

17 S. E. Finer, *Anonymous Empire: A Study of the Lobby in Great Britain* (Pall Mall, 1958).

18 House of Commons, *Official Report*, 13 July 1994, Col. 1020.

19 PRO, CAB 21/4473, 'Select Committee on House of Commons Procedure, 1956–60'.

20 Ibid.; R. A. Butler to M. Reed, 4 December 1958.

21 Ibid.; draft notes for Cabinet for the Lord Privy Seal, May 1956.

22 Anthony Howard, 'We are the Masters Now', in Michael Sissons and Philip French (eds), *Age of Austerity, 1945–1951* (Penguin, 1964), p. 29.

23 PRO, PREM 8/635, 'Parliament, Procedure. Memo Submitted by Sir Gilbert Campion Putting Forward Proposals for Reform of Parliamentary Procedure'. Herbert Morrison's Cabinet paper rubbishing Campion was considered by the Cabinet on 7 March 1946.

24 Ibid.; 'Draft Report of the Sub-Committee on the Recommendations of the Select Committee on Procedure', 13 February 1947.

25 Michael Ryle, 'The Changing Commons', *Parliamentary Affairs*, vol. 47, no. 4 (October 1994), p. 655.

26 House of Commons, *Official Report*, 12 November 1946, col. 44.

27 See my memo to the Treasury and Civil Service Select Committee, cited in note 9 above.

28 Sir John Sainty, 'Managing Parliament: Problems and Perspectives', paper delivered to the Parliaments, Representation and Society Seminar, Institute of Historical Research, 13 October 1992.

29 See Philip Norton, *Dissension in the House of Commons 1945–1979* (Clarendon Press, 1980) and Philip Norton (ed.), *Parliament in the 1980s* (Blackwell, 1985), pp. 222–47.

30 Quoted in John Garrett, *Westminster: Does Parliament Work?* (Gollancz, 1992), p. 16.

31 Peter Riddell, *Honest Opportunism: The Rise of the Career Politician* (Hamish Hamilton, 1993), p. 271.

32 Lord Whitelaw in conversation with Peter Hennessy, 11 January 1995.

33 Lord Healey in conversation with Peter Hennessy for Channel 4 Television/Wide Vision Productions, *What Has Become of Us?*, 29 March 1994.

34 David Judge, *The Parliamentary State* (Sage, 1993), p. 6.

35 Ibid., p. 27.

36 Ibid.

37 Bagehot, *The English Constitution*, pp. 51–4.

38 Ibid., p. 154.

39 Tony Benn, briefing for 'Cabinet and Premiership' course, Department of History, Queen Mary and Westfield College, held at House of Commons, 1 March 1995.

40 *Making the Law: The Report of the Hansard Society Commission on the Legislative Process* (Hansard Society, 1993).

41 Professor Marquand used it in my presence when still a Labour MP in the mid-1970s. He had forgotten it but was happy to have it attributed to him. Conversation with David Marquand, 2 July 1994.

42 PRO, CAB 130/86, Cabinet House of Lords Reform Committee, GEN 432, third meeting, 10 February 1955. Lord Salisbury told the Committee: 'There seemed to him to be several reasons why the vitality of the House was declining. First, the Act of 1948 [*sic*], by reducing the power of the House of Lords, had reduced the enthusiasm, which members could bring to bear on its proceedings; secondly, the economic factor made it increasingly difficult for peers, particularly Labour peers, to attend unless they had particularly good reasons for doing so; thirdly, the Labour peers, most of whom had been created late in life, were growing older and if the present Government were elected for a second term, they might well disappear altogether.'

43 See his *Westminster: Does Parliament Work?*

44 See his *Reinventing Democracy: Labour's Mission for the New Century* (Features Unlimited, 1995).

45 For an eloquent account of the travails of a mid-1990s backbencher see his 'Backbench Influence: A Personal View', *Parliamentary Affairs*, vol. 47, no. 4 (October 1994), pp. 687–704.

46 Quoted in 'Bagehot', 'A Weak Constitution', *The Economist*, 17 December 1994.

47 Ibid.

48 'I had been vaccinated against enthusiasm for legislation on constitutional reform by a salutary experience as Home Secretary when the Labour Government made an attempt to reform the House of Lords': James Callaghan, *Time and Chance* (Collins, 1987), p. 502; 'our attempt to provide devolution for Scotland and Wales proved a disastrous failure, like so many other attempts to reform the British Constitution before it': Denis Healey, *The Time of My Life* (Michael Joseph, 1989), p. 460.

49 House of Commons Debates, *Official Report*, 25 June 1979, col. 36.

50 Norman St John-Stevas, *The Two Cities* (Faber, 1984), pp. 54–7, 104–7.

51 Geoffrey Howe, *Conflict of Loyalty* (Macmillan, 1994), pp. 260–1.

52 Ministry of Reconstruction, *Report of the Machinery of Government Committee*, Cm 9230 (HMSO, 1918).

53 House of Commons Select Committee on Procedure, Second Report: *The Working of the Select Committee System*, HC19 (1989–90), p. 18.

54 Philip Giddings, 'Select Committees and Parliamentary Scrutiny: Plus Ça Change', *Parliamentary Affairs*, vol. 47, no. 4 (October 1984), p. 681.

55 Allen, *Reinventing Democracy*, p. 30.

56 David Butler, Andrew Adonis and Tony Travers, *Failure in British Government: The Politics of the Poll Tax* (Oxford University Press, 1994), pp. 227–33.

57 *Departmental Evidence and Response to Select Committees* (Cabinet Office, 1993), para. 27.

58 Derek Hawes, *Power on the Back Benches? The Growth of Select Committee Influence* (School of Advanced Urban Studies, University of Bristol, 1993).

59 Ibid., pp. 88–92.

60 L. S. Amery, *Thoughts on the Constitution* (Oxford University Press, 1947), p. 12.

61 For the impact of television on the life of the House of Commons in general see Nicholas Jones, *Soundbites and Spin Doctors: How Politicians Manipulate the Media – and Vice Versa* (Cassell, 1995), pp. 13–18.

62 *Departmental Evidence and Response to Select Committees.*

63 *Memorandum of Guidance for Officials Appearing before Select Committees* (Cabinet Office, 1988).

64 *Open Government,* Cm 2290 (HMSO, 1993).

65 *The Role of the Civil Service,* vol. 1, pp. v–vi, xiii–xvi.

66 Peter Jenkins, 'Hopes for the Future Have Begun to Die and With Them Patience', *Guardian,* 26 January 1979, reproduced in Brian Brivati and Richard Cockett (eds), *Anatomy of Decline: The Political Journalism of Peter Jenkins* (Cassell, 1995), pp. 103–7.

67 Letter from Graham Allen MP to Peter Hennessy, 26 October 1994.

Chapter 7

1 Sir Algernon West, *Recollections 1832 to 1886* (Nelson, 1899), pp. 285, 325.

2 Ashley Weinberg, 'Workload, Stress and Family Life in Britain's MPs', research paper, 1993. I am very grateful to Dr Weinberg for sending me a copy of this.

3 Hugh Freeman, 'The Human Brain and Political Behaviour', *British Journal of Psychiatry,* vol. 159 (1991), p. 21.

4 Eric Hobsbawm, *Age of Extremes: The Short Twentieth Century, 1914–1991* (Michael Joseph, 1994), pp. 579–80.

5 John Cole, *As It Seemed to Me: Political Memoirs* (Weidenfeld & Nicolson, 1995), p. 215.

6 Walter Bagehot, *The English Constitution* (Fontana, 1963), p. 61.

7 Harold Wilson, *The Governance of Britain* (Weidenfeld & Nicolson/ Michael Joseph, 1976), p. 27.

8 Anthony Crosland, *The Future of Socialism* (Cape, 1956).

9 Barbara Castle, *The Castle Diaries, 1974–76* (Weidenfeld & Nicolson, 1980), p. 223.

10 Ibid., p. 220.
11 Private information.
12 Private information.
13 John Grigg, *Lloyd George: From Peace to War 1912–1916* (Methuen, 1985), p. 474.
14 Quoted in Peter Clarke, *A Question of Leadership: Gladstone to Thatcher* (Hamish Hamilton, 1991), p. 135.
15 Douglas Jay, *Change and Fortune: A Political Record* (Hutchinson, 1980), p. 132.
16 Lord Donoughue speaking to the 'Hidden Wiring' seminar of the MA course in Contemporary British History since 1939, Queen Mary and Westfield College, 25 January 1995.
17 Jay, *Change and Fortune*, p. 132.
18 Private information.
19 Rhys Williams, 'Birt Warns of Media "Feeding Frenzy" Causing Instability', *Independent*, 4 February 1995.
20 Private information.
21 Lord Donoughue, 'Hidden Wiring' seminar. See also his *Prime Minister: The Conduct of Policy under Harold Wilson and James Callaghan* (Cape, 1987), pp. 1–37, 191–2.
22 Lord Donoughue, 'Hidden Wiring' seminar.
23 Anthony King, ' "Overload": Problems of Governing in the 1970s', *Political Studies*, vol. 22, nos 2–3 (June–September 1975), p. 164.
24 Vernon Bogdanor, answering questions after delivering his paper, 'The Monarchy and the Constitution: A Historical Approach', to the Twentieth Century British History Seminar, Institute of Historical Research, 1 February 1995.
25 Quoted in Aaron L. Friedberg, *The Weary Titan: Britain and the Experience of Relative Decline, 1895–1905* (Princeton University Press, 1988), frontispiece.
26 David Dilks, *The Office of Prime Minister in Twentieth Century Britain* (University of Hull Press, 1993), p. 12. This was a phrase 'of which he was rather fond', Professor Dilks recalled from his time helping Macmillan with his memoirs: letter from Professor David Dilks to Peter Hennessy, 24 January 1995.
27 Private information.
28 Public Record Office (PRO), CAB 118/32, 'The Application of Democratic Principles of Government: Memorandum by the Deputy Prime Minister', WP (43) 199, 17 May 1943.
29 *The Civil Service: Continuity and Change*, Cm 2627 (HMSO, 1994); *The Civil Service: Taking Forward Continuity and Change*, Cm 2748 (HMSO, 1995).
30 The First Earl of Balfour, 'Introduction', in Walter Bagehot, *The English*

Constitution, 'World's Classics' edn (Oxford University Press, 1928), p. xxiv.

31 Ibid.

32 See above, p. 40.

33 Lord Hailsham, 'The Future of Cabinet Government', the Granada Guildhall Lecture 1987, delivered at the Guildhall, City of London, 10 November 1987.

34 PRO, PREM 11/4838, 'The Machinery of Government', Lord President of the Council to the Prime Minister, 23 October 1962.

35 Ibid., Macmillan to Hailsham, 26 October 1962.

36 Ibid., Prime Minister's Personal Minutes, M11–63, Macmillan to Hailsham, 11 January 1963.

37 PRO, CAB 128/36 CC (62) 63, 29 October 1962.

38 See Herbert Morrison, *Government and Parliament: A Survey from the Inside* (Oxford University Press, 1954), pp. 207–20.

39 See Peter Hennessy, *Cabinet* (Blackwell, 1986), pp. 36–48; Peter Hennessy and Andrew Arends, *Mr Attlee's Engine Room: Cabinet Committee Structure and the Labour Government, 1945–51*, Strathclyde Papers on Government and Politics, no. 26 (Department of Government, University of Strathclyde, 1983).

40 See above, p. 108.

41 *The Reorganisation of Central Government*, Cmnd 4506 (HMSO, 1970).

42 PRO, PREM 11/2351, 'The Burden on Ministers', Brook to Macmillan, 20 February 1957.

43 Ibid.

44 Ibid., Attlee to Macmillan, 29 July 1957.

45 PRO, CAB 130/137, GEN 616, 'The Burden on Ministers', first meeting, 31 October 1957.

46 PRO, PREM 11/2351, Davies to Macmillan, 23 July 1957.

47 Ibid.

48 Ibid.

49 Ibid., Bishop to Macmillan, 29 July 1957.

50 PRO, CAB 130/137, GEN 616, first meeting, 31 October 1957.

51 *The Civil Service: Taking Forward Continuity and Change*, p. 35.

52 PRO, CAB 134/1935, 'Study of Future Policy 1960–1970'; FO 371/143702, 'Study of Future Policy 1960–1970'.

53 Colin Brown, 'Major Orders Review of Defence and Foreign Policy', *Independent*, 14 January 1995.

54 Private information.

55 Ibid.

56 Not only have ministers sung the praises of the report on *The Role of the Civil Service*; it won warm acclaim from what the Lord Privy Seal, Lord Cranborne, called 'the inner ring' of ex-Permanent Secretaries and former

senior officials who spoke approvingly of it (especially the proposal for a code of ethics) during the House of Lords debate on the Civil Service sponsored by Lord Allen of Abbeydale on 1 February 1995. See House of Lords, *Official Report*, 1 February 1995, cols 1525–70.

57 For the latest version see *Finding Your Way Round Whitehall and Beyond* (Cabinet Office, 1994), pp. 22–3.

58 Private information.

59 Peter Shore, interviewed for *The Quality of Cabinet Government*, first broadcast on BBC Radio 3, 12 March 1985.

60 Roy Jenkins, 'Castle Battlements', *Observer*, 4 November 1984.

61 He reproduced this test in his *Meditations of a Broomstick* (Collins, 1977), pp. 144–7.

62 David Howell, lead book review in *Political Quarterly*, vol. 58, no. 1 (January–March 1987), p. 102.

63 Norman Dixon, *Our Own Worst Enemy* (Cape, 1987), p. 222.

64 Ibid., p. 213.

65 Freeman, 'The Human Brain and Political Behaviour', p. 30.

66 Michael Foley, *The Rise of the British Presidency* (Manchester University Press, 1993), ch. 5, pp. 120–47.

67 Freeman, 'The Human Brain and Political Behaviour', pp. 30–1.

68 Ibid., p. 31.

69 I am very grateful to Professor Dixon for permission to reproduce these slides, which he demonstrated before the 'Hidden Wiring' seminar of the MA in Contemporary British History since 1939, Department of History, Queen Mary and Westfield College, 22 March 1995.

70 Weinberg, 'Workload, Stress and Family Life in Britain's MPs'.

71 Hugh L'Etang, *The Pathology of Leadership* (Heinemann Medical, 1969).

72 Hugh L'Etang, *Fit to Lead?* (Heinemann Medical, 1980).

73 The latest material on Churchill's post-stroke medication has revealed that he took amphetamines and barbiturates to help him 'get through the night and day': Andrew Pierce, 'Churchill "Took Amphetamines and Barbiturates"', *The Times*, 9 June 1995.

74 Hugh L'Etang, *Ailing Leaders in Power 1914–1994* (Royal Society of Medicine Press, 1995).

75 Ibid., p. 135.

76 Abraham Maslow, *The Hierarchy of Needs* (1943).

77 Peter Riddell, 'Who Will Make the First Team?', *The Times*, 10 April 1995.

78 Colin Brown, 'Sick of "sweet-talking", a Tory MP quits', *Independent*, 24 July 1995.

79 Will Bennett, 'Wilson's Simple Island Burial', *Independent*, 7 June 1995.

80 Private information.

81 Bryan Appleyard, 'Je regrette a thing or two, perhaps', *Independent*, 18 July 1995.

82 Douglas Hurd, *An End to Promises: Sketch of a Government 1970–74* (Collins, 1979), pp. 38–9, 104.

83 Private information.

Chapter 8

1   Max Weber, 'Suffrage and Democracy in Germany', in Peter Lassman and Ronald Speirs (eds), *Weber: Political Writings* (Cambridge University Press, 1994), p. 83.

2   Peter Riddell, 'Needed: A New Mechanism', *The Times*, 27 February 1995.

3   *Standards in Public Life: First Report of the Committee on Standards in Public Life*, vol. 1: *Report*, Cm 2850–1 (HMSO, 1995), p. 16.

4   Lord Nolan, at press conference to launch his report, Westminster Central Hall, 11 May 1995.

5   Private information.

6   Simon Jenkins, 'MPs need Proper Jobs', *The Times*, 17 May 1995.

7   Nicholas Timmins and Patricia Wynn Davies, 'Private Gain, Public Interest', *Independent*, 10 December 1994.

8   Private information.

9   House of Commons, *Official Report*, 25 October 1994, col. 758.

10 'The Great and the Good' was originally a somewhat jesting description for committee folk, coined by Sir Edward Bridges during his period as Head of the Civil Service 1945–56: Lord Bancroft, Gresham College Seminar, 'In the Steps of Walter Bagehot: A Constitutional Health-Check', 13 March 1995.

11 See Peter Hennessy, *The Great and the Good: An Inquiry into the British Establishment* (Policy Studies Institute, 1986); Peter Hennessy, *Whitehall* (Fontana, 1990), ch. 13, pp. 540–86.

12 For a superb account of the Beveridge Committee's genesis and modus operandi see José Harris, *William Beveridge: A Biography* (Oxford University Press, 1977).

13 Peter Hennessy, 'Goodbye to the "Good Chaps" ', *Independent*, 12 May 1995.

14 *Social Insurance and Allied Services: Report by Sir William Beveridge*, Cmd 6406 (HMSO, 1942), p. 6.

15 Harris, *William Beveridge*, pp. 386–7.

16 *Standards in Public Life: First Report*, p. 14. The committee member who suggested this declaration of principles did not cite Beveridge as a precedent but later told a friend that 'I may have had it in my subconscious'. Private information.

17 Sidney Low, *The Governance of England* (Fisher Unwin, 1904), p. 12.

18 George Dangerfield, *The Strange Death of Liberal England* (Paladin, 1983), p. 44.

19 Peter Riddell, 'Hostile Response Reflects Failure of Self-Regulation', *The Times*, 19 May 1995.

20 David Rose, 'Nolan: MPs Must Learn Right from Wrong', *Observer*, 14 May 1995.

21 Private information.

22 House of Commons, *Official Report*, 18 May 1995, cols 481, 488–9.

23 *Standards in Public Life: First Report*, pp. 19–45.

24 See John Campbell, *Edward Heath: A Biography* (Cape, 1993), pp. 239–48, 277–81, 512–17, 538–9.

25 Sir Edward Heath, 'Parliament Must Not Be Run by an Outsider', *Independent*, 20 May 1995.

26 J. Enoch Powell, 'There's No Legislating for Honour', *The Times*, 19 May 1995.

27 See E. C. S. Wade and G. Godfrey Phillips, *Constitutional and Administrative Law*, 9th edn, ed. A. W. Bradley (Longman, 1977), pp. 1141–53; Colin Turpin, *British Government and the Constitution: Texts, Cases and Materials*, 2nd edn (Weidenfeld Paperbacks, 1990), pp. 489, 496.

28 Conversation with Enoch Powell, 22 May 1995.

29 Powell, 'There's No Legislating for Honour'.

30 Walter Bagehot, *Physics and Politics* (1872; Kegan Paul edn, undated), p. 27.

31 Powell, 'There's No Legislating for Honour'.

32 House of Commons, *Official Report*, 18 May 1995, col. 486.

33 Ibid.

34 Garland cartoon, *Daily Telegraph*, 12 May 1995.

35 *Standards in Public Life: First Report*, p. 48.

36 Hennessy, 'Goodbye to the "Good Chaps"'.

37 Zai Bennett, essay for 'Cabinet and Premiership' course, Department of History, Queen Mary and Westfield College, 31 March 1995.

38 *Questions of Procedure for Ministers* (Cabinet Office, May 1992), para. 1.

39 *Standards in Public Life: First Report*, pp. 48–9.

40 Ibid., pp. 49–50.

41 House of Commons, *Official Report*, 18 May 1995, col. 488, David Hunt.

42 Victoria Barrett, essay on *Questions of Procedure for Ministers* for 'Cabinet

and Premiership' course, Department of History, Queen Mary and Westfield College, May 1995.

43 See above, p. 34.

44 Jenkins, 'MPs Need Proper Jobs'.

45 Kenneth Harris, *Attlee* (Weidenfeld & Nicolson, 1982), p. 504.

46 David Hunt, oral evidence to the Nolan Committee, 7 February 1995: *Standards in Public Life: First Report*, vol. 2: *Transcripts of Oral Evidence*, Cm 2850-II (HMSO, 1995), pp. 260–1.

47 House of Commons, *Official Report*, 18 May 1995, col. 488, David Hunt.

48 *Committee on Standards in Public Life: First Report*, pp. 57–8.

49 Ibid., pp. 58–9.

50 Ibid., p. 59.

51 Ibid.

52 Ibid., p. 60.

53 Ibid., p. 59.

54 Ibid., p. 60.

55 Ibid., p. 61.

56 House of Commons, *Official Report*, 18 May 1995, col. 489.

57 House of Commons, Select Committee on Standards in Public Life. Session 1994–5, *First Report*, HC 637 (HMSO, 1995), pp. xxiv–xxxiv.

58 Ibid., p. ii.

59 Private information.

60 Select Committee on Standards in Public Life, *First Report*, vol. 1, p. 16.

61 Quoted in ibid., p. 24.

62 Select Committee on Standards in Public Life, *First Report*, pp. xvi–xvii.

63 House of Commons Debates, *Official Report*, 19 July 1995, cols 1723–31.

64 Peter Riddell, 'Tories Playing into Labour's Hands on Standards in Public Life', *The Times*, 11 July 1995.

65 Private information.

66 *The Government's Response to the First Report from the Committee on Standards in Public Life*, Cm 2931 (HMSO, 1995).

67 Ibid., p. 37.

68 Ibid., p. 32.

69 Ibid.

70 *Open Government: Code of Practice on Access to Government Information* (HMSO, 1994), pp. 5–9.

71 House of Commons Debates, *Official Report*, 18 July 1995, col. 1476.

72 *The Government's Response to the First Report from the Committee on Standards in Public Life*, p. 3.

73 Committee on Standards in Public Life, *First Report*, vol. 1, p. 49.

74 See the timetable proposed by the Chancellor of the Duchy of Lancaster,

Roger Freeman, in the House of Commons on 18 July 1995. House of Commons Debates, *Official Report*, 18 July 1995, cols 1473–4.

75 Ibid., col. 1476.
76 Sir Robin Butler, 'The Themes of Public Service Reform in Britain and Overseas', *Policy Studies*, 16/3, Autumn 1995, p. 12.
77 House of Commons Debates, *Official Report*, 19 July 1995, col. 1694.
78 Private information.
79 Owen Hickey, 'Which Way for Britain?' *The Tablet*, 1 July 1995.
80 R. H. Tawney, *The Acquisitive Society* (Bell, 1921; new edn Wheatsheaf, 1982), p. 9.
81 Conversation with Andrew Adonis, 15 May 1995.
82 Private information.
83 For a fascinating full-length study of the life and thought of Cyril Radcliffe see Edmund Heward, *The Great and the Good: A Life of Lord Radcliffe* (Barry Rose, 1995).
84 Lord Radcliffe, *The Problem of Power* (Collins, 1958), p. 127.

Chapter 9

1 *Report of the Inquiry into the Export of Defence Equipment and Dual-Use Goods to Iraq and Related Prosecutions*, House of Commons 115–4 (HMSO, 1996), paragraph K8.1, p. 1799.
2 House of Lords, *Official Report*, 26 February 1996, col. 1270.
3 Sir Percy was speaking on the BBC Radio 4 *Analysis Special*, 'No End of a Lesson?', 15 February 1996.
4 John Hunt, 'Accountable Government', *The Tablet*, 24 February 1996, p. 251.
5 House of Lords, *Official Report*, 26 February 1996, cols 1243–4.
6 Conversation with Christopher Muttukumaru, Secretary to the Scott Inquiry, 12 March 1996.
7 Mr Riddell was speaking on 'No End of a Lesson?'
8 *Falklands Islands Review: Report of a Committee of Privy Counsellors*, Cmnd 8787 (HMSO, 1983).
9 Sir Frank Cooper in conversation with Peter Hennessy and addressing the 'Hidden Wiring' seminar of the MA in Contemporary British History course, Queen Mary and Westfield College, 13 March 1996.
10 Ibid.
11 See Peter Hennessy, *Whitehall* (Fontana, 1990), pp. 252–66.
12 House of Commons, *Official Report*, 26 February 1996, col. 593.
13 House of Commons Public Service Committee, *Information for the Press*, 7 March 1996.

14 *Report of the Inquiry into the Export of Defence Equipment and Dual-Use Goods to Iraq and Related Prosecutions*, pp. 1799–1806.
15 Ibid., p. 1799.
16 Ibid., p. 1800.
17 Ibid., pp. 1799–1800.
18 Ibid., p. 1801.
19 Conversation with Christopher Muttukumaru.
20 *Report of the Inquiry into the Export of Defence Equipment and Dual-Use Goods to Iraq and Related Prosecutions*, p. 1805.
21 Ibid., pp. 1805–6.
22 Ibid., p. 1806.
23 Hunt, 'Accountable Government'.
24 *Report of the Inquiry into the Export of Defence Equipment and Dual-Use Goods to Iraq and Related Prosecutions*, p. 1806.
25 Ibid.
26 House of Commons, *Official Report*, 26 February 1996, col. 593.
27 Peter Riddell, 'The Etiquette of Office', *The Times*, 19 February 1996.
28 Peter Madgwick and Diana Woodhouse, *The Law and Politics of the Constitution of the United Kingdom* (Harvester Wheatsheaf, 1995), p. 120.
29 Conversation with Christopher Muttukumaru.
30 *Standards in Public Life: First Report of the Committee on Standards in Public Life*, vol 1: *Report*, Cm 2850–1 (HMSO, 1995), p. 49.
31 House of Commons, *Official Report*, 2 November 1995, col. 456.
32 *Report of the Inquiry into the Export of Defence Equipment and Dual-Use Goods to Iraq and Related Prosecutions*, p. 1802.
33 Sir Frank Cooper addressing the 'Hidden Wiring' seminar, 13 March 1996.
34 *Report of the Inquiry into the Export of Defence Equipment and Dual-Use Goods to Iraq and Related Prosecutions*, p. 1802.
35 Ibid.
36 Peter Riddell, 'MPs Have Much to Learn from Nolan and Scott, *The Times*, 21 March 1996.
37 Conversation with Peter Riddell, 15 March 1996.
38 House of Commons, Session 1995–6, Public Service Committee, *Ministerial Accountability and Responsibility*, Minutes of Evidence, 20 March 1996, HC 313–i (HMSO, 1996), p. 21.
39 Ibid.
40 *Standards in Public Life: First Report*, pp. 48–9.
41 We met for this purpose at Queen Mary and Westfield College on 27 March 1996.
42 House of Commons, Public Service Committee, *Ministerial Accountability and Responsibility*, HC 313–i, pp. 22–3.
43 'No End of a Lesson?'

44 The phrase of Sir Percy's is well known inside the intelligence community. Private information.
45 'No End of a Lesson?'
46 Ibid.
47 See Peter Hennessy, *Cabinet* (Blackwell, 1986), pp. 113–20.
48 Geoffrey Howe, 'A Judge's Long Contest with Reality', *The Spectator*, 27 January 1996, and Lord Howe's remarks in the House of Lords debate on the report, House of Lords, *Official Report*, 26 February 1996, cols 1267–9.
49 Ibid., col. 1271.
50 Ibid., col. 1272.
51 HM Treasury, Press Office, 'Scott Clears Waldegrave of Intent to Mislead', Press Notice 26/96, 15 February 1996.
52 There were three of these, all dated 15 February 1996: 'Public Interest Immunity, The Government's Response'; 'The Role of the Attorney-General and Matrix Churchill'.
53 Roy Jenkins, 'A Report Which Teaches Many Uncomfortable Lessons', *Evening Standard*, 16 February 1996.
54 *Report of the Inquiry into the Export of Defence Equipment and Dual-Use Goods to Iraq and Related Prosecutions*, vol. 1, D.3.124, p. 427.
55 An NOP poll conducted for *The Sunday Times*, in the immediate aftermath of the Scott Report's publication, found 64% believing Mr Waldegrave should go, 62% willing a similar fate on Sir Nicholas Lyell and only 17% wanting them to stay in office. Andrew Grice and Michael Prescott, 'Major Cornered as Public Anger Grows over Scott', *The Sunday Times*, 18 February 1996.
56 House of Commons, Public Service Committee, *Ministerial Accountability and Responsibility*, HC 313–i p. 16.
57 House of Lords, *Official Report*, 25 March 1996, col. 1467. I am grateful to Dr David Lowry for bringing this exchange to my attention.
58 House of Lords, *Official Report*, 25 March 1996, col. 1467.
59 *Report of the Inquiry into the Export of Defence Equipment and Dual-Use Goods to Iraq and Related Prosecutions*, vol. 1, D.3.86, p. 408.
60 On the day the Scott Report was published, the Cabinet Office disclosed details of a review of intelligence distribution conducted in the light of the arms to Iraq affair. Cabinet Office Press Release, 'Improvements in Intelligence Handling', 15 February 1996.
61 'No End of a Lesson?'
62 'Scott Leaves "chasm" on Responsibility', *FDA News*, April 1996, pp. 1–2.
63 Hunt, 'Accountable Government'.
64 Private information.
65 Private information.
66 Private information.

Conclusion

1 Tony Benn, briefing for 'Cabinet and Premiership' course, Department of History, Queen Mary and Westfield College, held at House of Commons, 1 March 1995.

2 Quoted in Peter Hennessy and Caroline Anstey, *Jewel in the Constitution? The Queen, Parliament and the Royal Prerogative*, Strathclyde *Analysis* Paper no. 8 (Department of Government, University of Strathclyde, 1992), p. 21. Mr Powell originally delivered his remark in conversation with Tony Benn on the BBC Radio 4 *Analysis* programme broadcast on 6 April 1989.

3 G. D. H. Cole, *A Plan for Britain* (Clarion, 1932), p. 39.

4 R. H. Tawney, *The Attack* (Allen & Unwin, 1953), p. 34, which reproduces his 1917 essay 'A National College of All Souls'.

5 James Lees-Milne, *Caves of Ice* (Faber, 1983), diary entry for 9 January 1946, p. 5. I am grateful to Richard Weight for bringing this to my attention.

6 Blake Morrison, 'Today's Past Master', *Independent on Sunday*, 9 April 1995.

7 Neville Cardus, *Second Innings* (Collins, 1950), p. 240.

8 Angus Calder, *The Myth of the Blitz* (Cape, 1991), pp. 180–208.

9 'England, Whose England?', Special Supplement, *New Statesman and Society*, 24 February 1995.

10 Peter Fraser, *Lord Esher: A Political Biography* (Hart-Davis MacGibbon, 1972), p. 215.

11 This very useful phrase was invented by the anthropologist Clifford Geertz.

12 Attlee delivered this line while addressing the University of Oxford's Law Society in June 1957. See 'Duty of Ruthless Sacking: "Stop Cabinet Talking" ', *The Times*, 15 June 1957. I am very grateful to Stanley Martin (who organized the meeting) for bringing it to my attention. Attlee spoke without notes and, before agreeing to come, had taken a good deal of persuading that he had anything worth saying. Conversation with Stanley Martin, 31 May 1995.

13 Conversation with David Hunt for Channel 4 Television/Wide Screen Productions, *What Has Become of Us?*

14 The phrase comes from Hugh Dalton's memoirs, *High Tide and After* (Muller, 1961).

15 Quoted in Trevor Burridge, *Clement Attlee: A Political Biography* (Cape, 1985), p. 2.

16 Mr Major used this phrase in his address to the 1994 Conservative Party Conference.

17 Patrick Dunleavy and Stuart Weir, 'It's All Over for the Old Constitution', *Independent*, 30 May 1995.

18 Ibid.

19 Ibid.

20 Ibid.

21 Brian MacArthur (ed.), *The Penguin Book of Twentieth Century Speeches* (Viking, 1992), p. 189.

22 George Orwell, *The Lion and the Unicorn: Socialism and the English Genius* (Secker & Warburg, 1941), p.35.

23 'Cabinet Committee Business: A Guide for Departments', unpublished (Cabinet Office, February 1995), p. 2. In the spring of 1996 there were reports that Tony Blair was 'thinking about creating a strategy and legislative priorities committee' consisting of 'superministers' who would chair the most important Cabinet committees if Labour took power. See Peter Riddell, 'How will Blair play it?' *The Times*, 20 May 1996.

24 House of Commons Select Committee on Procedure, Seventh Report, Session 1994–95, *Prime Minister's Questions*, HC 555 (HMSO, 1995), pp. v–xvi. For a succinct and informative account of the history and development of PMQs see Professor Philip Norton's 'Memorandum' to the Procedure Committee in ibid., pp. 1–7.

25 Quoted in Ralf Dahrendorf, *LSE: A History of the London School of Economics and Political Science 1895–1995* (Oxford University Press, 1995), pp. 368–9.

26 Will Hutton, *The State We're In* (Cape, 1995), p. 324.

27 Ibid., p. 287.

28 Nicolson was musing upon the significance of the recently closed Festival of Britain in the 1 November 1951 issue of *The Listener*. I am grateful to Richard Weight for bringing this to my attention. See Richard A. J. Weight, 'Pale Stood Albion: The Promotion of National Culture in Britain 1939–56', unpublished Ph.D thesis, University of London, 1995.

29 Peter Riddell, 'Cabinets, codes and the courts', *The Times*, 13 May 1996.

30 Lord Nolan, 'The Nolan Committee's First Report: One Year On'; paper presented to the Twentieth Century British History Seminar, Institute of Historical Research, 15 May 1996.

31 Peter Hennessy, *Never Again: Britain 1945–52* (Vintage, 1993), p. 196.

32 Peter Hennessy, *Whitehall* (Fontana, 1990), p. 306.

33 Morrison was actually talking about the House of Lords: 'The fact that the House of Lords has many irrational features is not in itself fatal in British eyes, for we have a considerable capacity for making the irrational work; and if a thing works we tend rather to like it, or at any rate to put up with it': Herbert Morrison, *Government and Parliament: A Survey from the Inside* (Oxford University Press, 1995), pp. 368–9.

APPENDICES

Ministerial Committees of the Cabinet and their
Chairmen, July 1995

(committees on which the Deputy Prime Minister sits
are marked with an asterisk)

Committee	Chairman
Ministerial Committee on Economic and Domestic Policy*	Prime Minister
Ministerial Committee on Defence and Overseas Policy*	Prime Minister
Ministerial Committee on Nuclear Defence Policy*	Prime Minister
Ministerial Committee on Northern Ireland*	Prime Minister
Ministerial Committee on the Intelligence Services*	Prime Minister
Ministerial Committee on Competitiveness*	Deputy Prime Minister
Ministerial Committee on the Coordination and Presentation of Government Policy*	Deputy Prime Minister
Ministerial Committee on the Environment*	Deputy Prime Minister
Ministerial Committee on Home and Social Affairs*	Lord President of the Council
Ministerial Committee on Local Government*	Deputy Prime Minister
Ministerial Committee on Public Expenditure*	Chancellor of the Exchequer
Ministerial Committee on The Queen's Speeches and Future Legislation*	Lord President of the Council

Committee	Chairman
Ministerial Committee on Legislation	Lord President of the Council
Ministerial Sub-committee on Health Strategy	Lord President of the Council
Ministerial Sub-committee on European Questions*	Foreign Secretary
Ministerial Sub-committee on Terrorism*	Home Secretary
Ministerial Sub-committee on Drug Misuse	Lord President of the Council
Ministerial Sub-committee on Women's Issues	Lord President of the Council
Ministerial Sub-Committee on London	Environment Secretary

Source: Cabinet Office (18 July 1995)

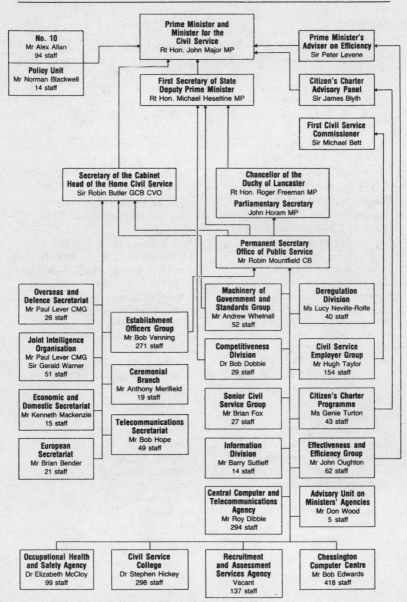

Cabinet Office/Office of Public Service
Source: Cabinet Office.

INDEX

Adeane, Sir Michael, 59, 67–8
Adonis, Andrew, 199
Advisory Committee on Business
    Appointments, 191
Aitken/Ritz affair, 132
Allen, Graham, 151, 160
Amery, Leo, 4–5, 24, 94, 156
Analysis (BBC programme), 57
Armstrong, Sir Robert, later Lord
    Armstrong of Ilminster, 33, 57,
    58, 110–11
Armstrong, Sir William, 128
Ashdown, Paddy, 53
Asquith, H. H., 84, 94, 140, 164
Attlee, Clement Richard, later Lord
    Attlee
    and Cabinet committees, 113, 167
    his Christianity, 190
    in Churchill's War Cabinet, 15–16
    on democratic government, 140,
    146, 165
    after general election of 1950, 51,
    53, 55
    and King George VI, 64, 220,
    234–5, 236
    not Leader of House of Commons,
    87
    and 'overlords', 113, 246
    on the premiership, 74, 97
    his duties as prime minister, 86–7
    his power as prime minister
    constrained, 164

and *QPM*, 30, 190
his sense of tradition, 220, 264

'back to basics' campaign, 106
Bagehot, Walter, 3, 28, 37–9, 41, 163
    and bureaucracy, the Civil Service,
    121–2
    and the Cabinet, 96, 108
    on the executive and the
    legislature, 96
    on 'government by discussion',
    108, 115
    on Peel, 77, 79–80
    on Parliament, 141, 147–8
    on the premiership, 77, 79–81
    and royalty, the monarchy, 46–8,
    50, 51
Baldwin, Stanley, 19
Balfour, A. J., 37, 83–4, 84, 98, 99, 166
Bancroft, Sir Ian, later Lord
    Bancroft, 22, 125, 127, 130
Banks, Tony, 205–6
Barrett, Vicky, 190
Bavin, A. R. W., 55
Baxter, Pamela, 59–60
Beesley, Ian, 120
Benn, Tony, 28, 24, 71–2, 91, 120,
    143, 149, 218, 223
Bennett, Alan, 70
Bennett, Zai, 187
Beveridge Inquiry, 181–2, 258
Bevin, Ernest, 64

Bevins, Tony, 17, 18
Biffen, John, 117
bill of rights, 151
Birt, John, 164
Bishop, Freddie, 170
'Black Wednesday', 165, 176
Blair, Tony, 265
Blake, Lord, 45
Bligh, Sir Tim, 60, 124, 248
Bogdanor, Vernon, 22, 165
Brett, Reginald, 219
Bridges, Sir Edward, 15–16, 64, 99, 258
Britain, the British/English people, 3, 4–5, 39–40, 198–9, 219, 221
Brook, Sir Norman, 54, 55, 111–13, 136, 143, 168
Budgen, Nicholas, 185–6
budget, 58, 89
Butler, R. A., 14, 38, 52, 78, 144–5, 233
Butler, Sir Robin, 24–5
    and the Civil Service, 126, 131, 133, 196–7
    on ministerial accountability, 207
    and the Precedent Book, 41–2
    and *QPM*, 33–6, 131–2
    and the royal prerogatives, 24–5, 57
    mentioned, 17
Butskellism, 70

Cabinet, 92, 94, 95–117, 141, 221–2
    Churchill's War Cabinet, 15–16
    collective responsibility, 28, 94, 97, 99, 101–6, 115
    Michael Heseltine and, 17
    importance of, 95–9, 100, 115–17
    'inner', 108, 109–10, 111, 113–15
    and 'institutional sclerosis', 107–9
    and dissolution of Parliament, 48
    prime minister and, 74, 82–92, 94–117 *passim*, 267
Cabinet committees, ministerial committees, 86, 97, 100, 102–5, 109, 113, 167, 168–9, 267–8

Michael Heseltine and, 17, 18, 19
    and the poll tax, 109, 131
    secrecy concerning, 102, 104–5, 113, 244
Caborn, Richard, 206
Calder, Angus, 219
Callaghan, James, later Lord Callaghan
    and Cabinet committees, 104–5
    on the constitution, 2, 253
    does not emigrate, 163
    learns craft of premiership, 77, 84–5
    on the premiership, 74
    becomes prime minister, 12–13
    mentioned, 65, 152, 162
Campbell-Bannerman, Sir Henry, 141
Campion, Sir Gilbert, 25, 145
Cardus, Sir Neville, 219
Castle, Barbara, 172
Central Economic Planning Staff, 108
Central Policy Review Staff, 108
Chamberlain, Joseph, 165
Chamberlain, Neville, 15–16, 123
Charles, Prince, Prince of Wales, 48
Charteris, Sir Martin, later Lord Charteris, 12, 44, 70
Churchill, Sir Winston
    and deputy premiership, 14–16
    on Parliament, 140, 142–3
    as prime minister and party leader, 49–50
    as prime minister from 1951, 108, 110–11, 111, 113, 167–8, 176
    his stroke, in July 1953, 52, 176, 257
    on tradition, 205
    his War Cabinet, 15–16
    mentioned, 164, 233, 238
Civil Service, 'Whitehall', 120, 121–38
    career public service created in 1870, 122–4

Code, 133–6, 189, 191–3, 194–5,
    196–7
its essence, traditions, purpose,
    124–5, 126–7, 134–6
future of, 132–8, 165–6, 191–3,
    194–5, 196–7
importance of, 121
'market testing', 125–6, 131,
    136–7
'Next Steps' executive agencies,
    125–6, 131, 137, 191–2
Nolan Committee and, 181, 183,
    189, 191–3, 194–5, 196–7
non-political or politicized?, 120,
    123–4, 128–32, 134, 191–3
prime minister and, 87, 88, 126
Scott Report and, 212, 216
new 'senior' civil service, 128–9,
    191–2
*Civil Service: Taking Forward
    Continuity and Change* (1994),
    122–3, 128, 132, 133–4, 170, 191
Clarke, Kenneth, 76
Clarke, Peter, 22
Coates, Simon, 57
Cobbold, Lord, 67–8
Cole, G. D. H., 218
Cole, John, 74, 94, 162
collective responsibility, *see under*
    Cabinet
Committee on Intelligence and
    Security, 215–16
Competing for Quality (1991), 125, 131
Conduct and Procedure for Ministers,
    see under *Questions of Procedure*
constitution, 2, 3–5, 13, 19, 24,
    98–100, 106–7, 218, 219–23
    Bagehot as starting-point, 37–9
    Cabinet as core of, 96, 98–9
    checks and balances, 41, 151
    Civil Service as ballast in, 127
    confidence needed, 41
    conventions, 33, 35–6
    'efficient' and 'dignified' parts
        distinguished, 96

'elective dictatorship' 35
a 'great ghost', unwritten, 28,
    29–30, 33, 183–4, 199, 223
an historical process, 19, 24
mysterious, 29
Nolan Committee's effect on, 180,
    181, 183–4, 198–200, 222–3
politics as the main determinant,
    22, 24
precedent as basis of, 11–12, 41–2,
    219–20
procedure is all, 23, 31, 35
a recent controversy concerning,
    10, 11–14
reform of, 29–30, 40–1, 107, 136,
    151, 152, 180, 181, 183–4,
    198–200, 218, 221–3, 253
see also government
Continuity and Change, see *Civil
    Service: Taking Forward Continuity
    and Change*
Cooper, Sir Frank, 100, 203–4, 209
Cradock, Sir Percy, 202, 212–13
Crick, Bernard, 219
Crosland, Anthony, 163
Crossman, R. H. S., 28, 126–7
crown, *see* monarchy

Dalton, Hugh, 111
Dangerfield, George, 28
Davies, Clement, 169–70
'Deadlock' file (Oct. 1964), 52,
    59–61, 226
Dell, Edmund, 101
Department of the Environment, 113
deputy prime minister, 14–19, 267–8
devolution, 158, 159, 170, 253
Dicey, A. V., 33–4, 141
Dilks, David, 74
Disraeli, Benjamin, 78–9, 80, 84, 143
Dixon, Norman, 173, 174–5
Donoughue, Bernard, later Lord
    Donoughue, 164, 164–5
Douglas-Home, Sir Alec, Lord
    Home, 52, 59, 233

Downing St, No. 10, 75, 238
Dunleavy, Patrick, 220–1
Duties and Responsibilities of Civil Servants in Relation to Ministers (1987), 136

E(LF) Cabinet committee, 131
Economist, The, 91
Eden, Sir Anthony, later Lord Avon, 14, 15, 52, 64–5, 233
'elective dictatorship', 35
Elizabeth II, Queen, 29, 44, 47–8, 49, 65–70, 223, 237
England, Englishmen, *see* Britain
Esher, Viscount, 218
European Union, 4, 91, 105–6, 109, 149, 150, 156, 158, 159, 181
Exchange Rate Mechanism, 109
executive agencies, *see* 'Next Steps' *under* Civil Service

Festival of Britain, 265
First Division Association, 216
First Lord of the Treasury, 75, 87, 238
Foley, Michael, 173
Fox, Sir Marcus, 11
Fraser, Ronald, 51, 226
Freeman, Dr Hugh, 162, 173–4
Freeman, Roger, 17, 195–6, 196

Gaitskell, Hugh 64
Garrett, John, 125–6, 151
GCHQ, 25
Geertz, Clifford, 264
Gellner, Ernest, 115
GEN 616, 169
general elections
    indecisive, 25, 51, 52, 53, 57, 58, 59–63
    1950, 51, 53–7
    1959, 60, 75
    1964, 52, 53, 59–60, 124
    March 1974, 52
    October 1974, 163

1983, 52
1987, 52
1992, 25, 52, 53, 63
George V, King, 46–7
George VI, King, 14, 15, 16, 47, 49, 64, 120, 234–5, 236
Gibbs, Norman, 55
Giddings, Philip, 154
Gladstone, W. E.
    and the Cabinet, 83, 95–6
    on the constitution, 23, 127
    on Parliament, 140
    on the premiership, 79, 81–2
    mentioned, 69, 78, 122, 162
'golden triangle', 52–3, 55, 58, 63, 86
'good chap' theory, *see under* government, central
government, central, 22, 23, 101, 162
    must be carried on, 12, 57, 59, 60–1
    if defeated in Commons, 53–6
    by discussion, 108, 115
    distrusted, 40–1
    'good chap' theory, 53, 61, 136, 187
    open, 30–1, 102, 105, 158, 195–6
    relations between executive and legislature, 12, 35, 96, 127, 142, 146, 153, 157
    see also Cabinet; Civil Service; constitution; ministers; monarchy; Parliament; prime minister
government, local, 170, 181
'Great and Good' inquiries, 181, 258
Griffith, John, 2, 223
Grimond, Jo, 60

Hailsham, Lord, 23, 35, 48, 98, 166
Haldane Report (1918), 81, 154
Hankey, Lord, 99–100
Harris, Sir Charles, 55
Harris, Kenneth, 48
Hawes, Derek, 156–7
Hawke, Bob, 65, 237
Healey, Denis, 146–7, 152, 253

Heath, Sir Edward
  and 'overload', procedural reform,
    81, 108, 111, 137, 168, 169
  and Mrs Thatcher, 74
  mentioned, 52, 184
Heiser, Sir Terry, 128, 130
Henderson, Sir Nicholas, 77
Hennessy, Peter, 3, 24–5, 30, 34–5,
    41–2, 57, 188, 210, 215
Heseltine, Michael, 14, 16–19, 75, 227
Heseltine, Sir William, 48
Hickey, Owen, 197–8
Hobsbawm, Eric, 162
Hogg, Sarah, 31
Home, Earl of (Sir Alec
    Douglas-Home), 52, 59, 233
honours lists, 65
House of Commons, 35, 94, 140,
    141, 142, 148–9
  Leader no longer the Prime
    Minister, 87
  ministers accountable to, 99–100
  Nolan Committee and, 184–6,
    193–4, 197–8
  Prime Minister supported by, 11,
    12, 83, 85
  Prime Minister's Questions, 89,
    164, 222
  shortcomings of, 146–7, 149–51,
    184–6, 193–4, 197–8.
  see also Select Committees; *also*
    Parliament
House of Lords, 89, 146, 151, 253,
    265
Howe, Earl, 215
Howe, Sir Geoffrey, later Lord
    Howe, 14, 129, 154, 202, 213–14
Howell, David, 173
Hunt, David, 11, 186, 192–3
Hunt, Sir John, later Lord Hunt of
    Tanworth, 12, 92, 100–101, 103,
    106–7, 202, 207, 216
Hurd, Douglas, 49, 66, 95–6, 106,
    177
Hutton, Will, 222

Ingham, Sir Bernard, 129
'institutional sclerosis', 107–9
International Monetary Fund, 101
Iraq, arms for, 34, 155, 205–6, 213, 215

James, Sir Robert Rhodes, 49
Jay, Douglas, 164
Jenkins, Lord, of Putney, 215
Jenkins, Kate, 233
Jenkins, Roy, Lord Jenkins of
    Hillhead, 57, 172, 202
Jenkins, Simon, 10, 13–14, 180
Jennings, Sir Ivor, 98–9
Joint Intelligence Committee, 213
Judge, David, 147

Keir, Sir David, 23
Kemp, Sir Peter, 131
Keynes, John Maynard, 74
King, Anthony, 75–6, 77, 86, 90, 165
King, Tom, 215–16
Kinnock, Neil, 53, 131

Labour governments
  1945, 15, 145–6
  1950, 51, 53–7
  1964, 28, 53
  1974, 163
Lamont, Norman, 31
Lang, Ian, 204
Lascelles, Sir Alan, 54, 56–7, 58, 64,
    234–5, 235
Laughrin, David, 171–2
Lawson, Nigel, Lord Lawson, 65,
    96–7, 108, 109–10, 131
L'Etang, Dr Hugh, 175–6
Le Jeune, Martin, 32
Le May, G. H. L., 33
'leadership stretch', 173
Levene, Sir Peter, 125
Lloyd George, David, 74, 99, 109
Low, Sir Sidney, 53, 83, 120, 140,
    141
Lowe, Robert, 122
Lyell, Sir Nicholas, 203, 214–15

McCall, William, 129
Maclennan, Robert, 10, 197
Macmillan, Harold
  on Bagehot, 38
  and ministerial 'overload', 78, 165, 166–7, 168, 169–70
  becomes prime minister, 52, 233
  as prime minister, 78, 143, 151, 166–7, 168
  and his successor, 52, 233
  mentioned, 75
McQuail, Paul, 113
Macrae, Norman, 238
Major, John
  and Cabinet government, 105–6, 116
  his conservatism on constitutional matters, 151–2
  and general election of 1992, 57, 62–3
  and leadership election of 1995, 11, 12, 13
  on the monarchy, 46
  establishes Nolan Committee, 181
  and open government, 31, 102, 105
  and *QPM*, 30, 31, 36, 105
  unpopular in the polls, 40, 231
  workload, 91, 92, 164, 165, 176
  mentioned, 204, 220, 241
market testing, *see under* Civil Service
Marquand, David, 150
Marten, Sir Henry, 47–8
Maslow, Abraham, 176
Matrix Churchill case, 155, 212–13
Mellor, David, 75
ministerial committees, *see* Cabinet committees
ministers, 17–18, 94, 97, 99–100, 140
  accountable to Parliament, 34–5, 99–100, 111, 112, 135, 136, 187, 202, 204–12
  appointed and dismissed by prime minister, 84, 86, 196
  business appointments after leaving office, 190–1
  and civil servants, 135, 136, 250

effectiveness and efficiency, workload, 137, 167–77
guidelines for, *see Questions of Procedure for Ministers*
Nolan Committee and, 181, 183, 184, 186–91, 195–6
need not have a seat in Parliament, 140, 146
supervising, 'overlords', 108, 110–11, 111–13, 246
see also Cabinet; prime minister
Mitchell, Austin, 146, 151
Mitchell, Sir Derek, 59–60, 67, 226
monarchy, the crown, the sovereign, 23, 29, 41, 44, 45–72
  Bagehot's trio of rights, 47, 48–9, 63–9
  future of, 70–2
  and dissolution of Parliament, 25, 48, 49, 53, 54–8, 84, 234–5
  not party-political, 50
  political functions, reserve powers, 50–63
  and prime minister, 10, 11, 13, 15, 25, 48, 51–70, 84, 86, 88, 236
  a disguised republic?, 48, 63
  royal prerogatives, 15, 25, 48, 53
  see also Elizabeth II; Royal Family
Morley, John, 82–3, 90
Morrison, Herbert, 15, 145, 223, 265
Mottram, Richard, 124
Mountbatten, Lord, 67–8
MPs, *see* members *under* Parliament

Napier, Sir Albert, 99
National Audit Office, 158
National Health Service, 64, 181
New Statesman, 244
Newton, Tony, 18, 71–2
'Next Steps' executive agencies, *see under* Civil Service
Nicolson, Harold, 222
Nolan Committee on Standards of Conduct in Public Life, 32, 37, 143, 180, 181–200, 222, 223

established, terms of reference, 143, 181, 183
recommendations, 180, 181–200, 210
government's response to, 184, 189, 190, 191, 192–3, 194–7
Parliament's response to, 183, 184–6, 193–4, 197
see also under Civil Service; constitution; House of Commons; ministers; Parliament; prime minister; *Questions of Procedure*
Northcote–Trevelyan Report, 123, 132–3
nuclear weapons, 65, 87, 90

Oakeshott, Michael, 222
Olson, Mancur, 107
opinion polls, 40, 220, 234
'opposition of events', 165
Osmotherly Rules, 158
'overload', stress, 78, 79–81, 91–2, 108, 162, 163, 165–77, 212, 214
'overlords', supervising ministers, 108, 110–11, 111–13, 245–6
Parliament, 136, 140, 141–60
dissolution of, 25, 48, 49, 53, 54–8, 84, 88, 234–5
faith in, declining, 220–1
importance of, 141–2, 143, 149, 159–60
members of, 143, 150, 162, 175, 181, 183, 184–6, 193–4, 197–8; *see also* House of Commons
ministers accountable to, 34–5, 99–100, 111, 112, 135, 136, 187, 202, 204–12
Nolan Committee and, 181, 183, 184–6, 193–4, 197–8
relations between legislature and executive, 12, 35, 96, 127, 142, 146, 153, 157
representative, not democratic, 147
and Scott Report, 215–16
televised, 141, 142–3, 157

workload, excessive and increasing, 162, 167, 175
see also House of Commons; House of Lords
Parliamentary Commissioner for Standards, 184, 193
party leader(s)
election of, 52
prime minister as, 10, 12–13, 49–50, 51–2, 58
Peel, Sir Robert, 77, 78, 79, 80, 82, 83, 91
Pickthorn, Sir Kenneth, 23, 35
Pimlott, Ben, 95
pit closures, 106
Pitblado, Sir David, 110–11
politics, 22, 24, 28, 180
polarization, 70, 128
stressful, 173
see also under Civil Service *and under* monarchy
poll tax, 109, 130–1, 155
postwar consensus, 70, 95, 204
Powell, Sir Charles, 123–4, 129
Powell, Enoch, 10, 11, 13, 14, 82, 141–2, 184–5, 218
Precedent Book, 41–2, 51
Priestley, Clive, 136
prime minister, 12, 14, 30, 33, 74, 75–92, 98–9, 107, 126
advised by the sovereign, 63–9, 236
appointed by the sovereign, 10, 11–13, 15, 25, 48, 51–63 *passim*
and the Cabinet, 74, 82–92, 94–117 *passim*, 267
and the Civil Service, 87, 88, 126
functions and powers of, 75–7, 79–91, 163–4
House of Commons, Questions in, 89, 164, 222
House of Commons no longer led by, 87
House of Commons' support needed, 11, 12, 83, 85

prime minister – *cont'd.*
ministers appointed by, 84, 86, 196
Nolan Committee and, 186,
187–8, 190, 196
origin of the office, 14, 77–9, 82,
99, 238
and dissolution of Parliament, 49,
53, 54–8, 84, 88
and party leadership, 10, 11–13,
49–50, 51–2, 58
and select committees, 216
workload, excessive, 78, 79–81,
91–2, 173, 176
Prime Minister's Efficiency Unit, 109
Prime Minister's Policy Unit, 108–9
proportional representation, 61–2
'public interest', 209
Public Record Office, 24, 25, 144

quangos, 156, 183
Questions of Procedure for Ministers
(QPM), 28, 30–7, 102–5, 186–91,
195–6
Attlee and, 30, 190
and Cabinet committees, 102–5
and Civil Service, 135, 136, 250
and collective responsibility, 102–5
a constitutional convention, or
discretionary?, 32–7, 190
declassified, published, 30–2, 190
importance of, 37, 190
John Major and, 30, 31, 36, 105
new draft by author, 210–12
Nolan Committee and, 32, 37, 184,
186–91, 195–6
non-party, 32
to be retitled *Conduct and Procedure*
for Ministers, 188, 195
Scott Report and, 202, 204, 204–5
207–10
Mrs Thatcher and, 30, 36
Harold Wilson and, 28, 34, 104
Quist-Johansen, Julie, 236

Radcliffe, Lord, 121, 199
Radice, Giles, 210

Redwood, John, 11
regius professorships, 88
Reorganisation of Central Government,
The (1970), 81, 137, 168
Rhodesia, 65, 67–8
Rickett, Denis, 54
Riddell, Peter, 18–19, 46, 146, 180,
194, 203, 207–8, 209–10, 223
Rifkind, Malcolm, 76
Role of the Civil Service, The (1994),
122–3, 256–7
Rosebery, 5th Earl of, 83, 84, 85
Rothschild, Victor, 132, 173
Royal Family, 45, 46–8, 62, 70; *see*
also monarchy
Russell, Lord John, 101

St John-Stevas, Norman, later Lord
St John of Fawsley, 153
Salisbury, 3rd Marquess of, 83–4
Salisbury, 5th Marquess of, 151, 253
Sanders, Matt, 33
Sartori, Giovanni, 128
Schama, Simon, 219
Schuster, Sir Claud, 95
Scott, McCallum, 142
Scott, Sir Richard, Scott Report, 34,
202–16
key findings on 'ministerial
accountability', 204–7
perhaps his most important
paragraph, 206
most specific recommendations,
207–10
response to, 212–16
Seaton, Jean, 41
Second World War, *see* Churchill's
War Cabinet *under* Cabinet
Select Committees (of House of
Commons), 35, 104, 145–6, 150,
152–9, 175, 216
Environment, 155, 156
National Expenditure, 145–6
Procedure, 144–5, 154, 222
Public Accounts, 132, 145, 154

Public Service, 204, 207, 210, 215, 216
Standards in Public Life, 184, 193
Trade and Industry (TISC), 206
Treasury and Civil Service, 35–6, 122–3, 125, 132, 133–8, 159, 171, 191
Seymour-Ure, Colin, 100
Shore, Peter, 172
Shultz, George, 214
Simon, Lord, 55
Smith, John, 131
sovereign, *see* monarchy
Statistical Section, 108
Stowe, Sir Kenneth, 12–13, 60–1
Stuart, James, 144
subsidiarity, 149, 151, 158
Suez, 64–5

'Talking about the Office', 102
Tanner, Professor J. R., 46
Tawney, R. H., 2, 198, 218
Thatcher, Margaret
 her fall, 13, 49, 85–6, 116–17
 as prime minister, 30, 36, 65, 66, 74, 76, 94, 96 ('conviction government'), 109, 109–10, 123–4, 128, 129, 153, 163, 177, 216, 237
 mentioned, 33
Thorneycroft, Peter, 163
TINA, 108
Tonypandy, Lord, 177
Trend, Sir Burke, later Lord Trend, 32, 102–3
Trinity College, Cambridge, 88
Turner, Graham, 66

Victoria, Queen, 69

Wakeham, John, later Lord Wakeham, 97–8, 105

Waldegrave, William, 19, 124, 203, 214–15
Walden, George, 176
Wales, Prince of, 48
Walpole, Sir Robert, 82, 99, 238
Weber, Max, 180
Weinberger, Ashley, 162, 175
Weir, Stuart, 220–1
West, Sir Algernon, 162
Westland crisis, 75, 95–6, 129, 216
Wheare, Sir Kenneth, 39, 47
Wheeler-Bennett, Sir John, 14–15, 47
Whitehall, *see* Civil Service
Whitehall and Industry Group, 171–2
Whitelaw, William, later Lord Whitelaw, 14, 109–10, 146–7
Wilson, Des, 121
Wilson, Sir Harold, later Lord Wilson
 on Bagehot, 38
 'burned out', 177
 wins general election of 1964, 53
 wins general election of Oct. 1974, 163
 honours lists, 65
 inner cabinets, 111
 on the premiership, 77, 84
 Prime Minister's Policy Unit, 109
 and *QPM*, 28, 34
 resignation in March 1976, 12–13
 and Rhodesia, 67–8
Wilson, Sir Horace, 123
Worsthorne, Sir Peregrine, 45

Yes, Minister, 127
Young, G. M., 74
Young, John, 4

Ziegler, Philip, 5, 42, 44, 233